T0243424

More
Richly
in
Earth

More
Richly
in
Earth

A Poet's Search for
Mary MacLeod

Marilyn Bowering

McGill-Queen's University Press
Montreal & Kingston • London • Chicago

ISBN 978-0-2280-2112-4 (cloth)
ISBN 978-0-2280-2167-4 (ePDF)
ISBN 978-0-2280-2168-1 (ePUB)

Legal deposit second quarter 2024
Bibliothèque nationale du Québec

Printed in Canada on acid-free paper that is 100% ancient forest free
(100% post-consumer recycled), processed chlorine free

Funded by the Government of Canada   Financé par le gouvernement du Canada   Canada   Canada Council for the Arts   Conseil des arts du Canada

We acknowledge the support of the Canada Council for the Arts.
Nous remercions le Conseil des arts du Canada de son soutien.

McGill-Queen's University Press in Montreal is on land which long
served as a site of meeting and exchange amongst Indigenous Peoples,
including the Haudenosaunee and Anishinabeg nations. In Kingston it
is situated on the territory of the Haudenosaunee and Anishinaabek. We
acknowledge and thank the diverse Indigenous Peoples whose footsteps
have marked these territories on which peoples of the world now gather.

Library and Archives Canada Cataloguing in Publication

Title: More richly in earth : a poet's search for Mary MacLeod / Marilyn
    Bowering.
Names: Bowering, Marilyn, author.
Description: Includes bibliographical references.
Identifiers: Canadiana (print) 2023058683X | Canadiana (ebook)
    20230586910 | ISBN 9780228021124 (cloth) | ISBN 9780228021674 (ePDF) |
    ISBN 9780228021681 (ePUB)
Subjects: LCSH: Bowering, Marilyn—Travel—Scotland—Hebrides. | LCSH:
    Màiri nighean Alasdair Ruaidh, approximately 1615-approximately
    1707—Homes and haunts. | LCSH: Poets, Scottish—17th century—Biog-
    raphy. | LCSH: Hebrides (Scotland)—Description and travel. | LCGFT:
    Biographies.
Classification: LCC PS8553.O9 Z46 2024 | DDC C811/.54—dc23

A mystery abides. We move from silence into silence, and there is a brief stir between, every person's attempt to make a meaning of life and time. Death is certain; it may be that the dust of good men and women lies more richly in the earth than that of the unjust; between the silences they may be touched, however briefly, with the music of the spheres.

– George MacKay Brown

Contents

Preface

Is mór an ionndrainn tha bhuainn
Air a dùnadh 'san uaigh,
Ar cùinneadh 's ar buaidh,
Ar cùram 's ar n-uaill,
Is ar sùgradh gun ghruaim:
Is fada air chuimhe na fhuair mi féin deth.

Much we long for what we lack, for what is closed within
the grave, our treasure and triumph, our care and our
boast, our glee without gloom. What I myself have
received thereof I shall remember long.

– Mary MacLeod, "Marbhrann" / "Dirge"

O glory, and light of other poets! May the long zeal avail me,
and the great love, that
made me search thy volume.

– Dante, *The Divine Comedy: Inferno*

(Simple)

your heart is an island of stones
and one bone missing

this bone is courage, whole bone

and this is self-heal
(a turfy simple
of fame and wonder)

and this, sleepwell
(or mirror and water): these

for reason's guide
when you faint among stones and ghosts
– Tighnacraig

More
Richly
in
Earth

I

A Traveller's Tale

1.

From the deck of the MacBrayne ferry that will carry us from the Isle of Skye to the Outer Hebrides, the shores of Uig harbour, under a low dark sky, are bright with bands of orange and yellow seaweed. The little town straggles up a bench that rises from the harbour's foot as if seeking light. The weather remains grim, rain hurtling in serried sheets from the southwest. My small lime-coloured umbrella shelters in my backpack while I struggle with the snaps of a new tarpaulin-like poncho I bought on the way to the ferry. Within minutes, though, as we head into the waters of the North Sea Minch, the jade green sea-cliffs of the harbour's south curve sharpen in clearing light, and the three Italian couples who had boarded on motorcycles tie their wet black gear to the ship's stern rail, where it flaps and snaps in the wind like the tethered crows of a vermin line.

This westward crossing takes an hour and a half, about the same as passage across the strait between Vancouver Island, where I live, and the mainland of British Columbia. Here, the journey is to the outer extent of settlement and the empty reach of the Atlantic – not a route threading islands almost within spitting distance, as at home. El, with his binoculars, points out islets too small and storm-scraped for year-round habitation, used for grazing sheep, and then – inferring themselves into the view – the mussel-backed and misty lumps of the islands Lewis, Harris, and Berneray. I try, like him, to make out others – North and South Uist and the triangles of Barra, he says – but I'm too cold to look for long and all I want is a cup of coffee and to listen to the Gaelic-speakers gathered within sound of the BBC's Gaelic television channel in the lounge. To the conversation of people going home.

2.

1978

We live in Tighnacraig, the gardener's cottage, on the Borland estate in Glen Lochay. Each morning I write poetry and reviews at my desk in a tiny attic room with skylight views of Sròn a' Chlachain on the south side of the glen and Creag na Caillich on the north. The cottage is unheated. I'm wrapped in blankets with a hot-water bottle and the dog at my feet, wearing a beaver-lamb (sheared sheepskin) coat lent to me by El's mother. In the afternoons, I walk up the glen past the red and black bulls Rob pastures in one of the fields, to say hello to Zian, Rob and Betty's horse, at Daldravaig, or in the opposite direction into the village to buy meat and vegetables; or I leave the cottage by the back door and start climbing until I reach the cairn at the top and gaze over Loch Tay and the blue-cast mountains beyond. Once, on a walk up a shoulder of Creag na Caillich to visit the old shielings, El and I lay in the heather and made love. When we looked up, a herd of red deer had stopped above us, respectfully it seemed, to watch.

In these hills and glens, ancient peoples and their battles and ghosts and purposes can feel nearby. In the evenings, our walk takes us to a path that cuts from the road to a small stone bridge over a stream where we swear we feel the presence of a Highland soldier. Other walks have brought us to standing stones and stone circles in farmers' fields, and I have wondered if they were raised there to mirror galaxies. Poetry, not belief, is the filter through which I absorb this world. A ghillie one glen over tells us a story of a time he was caught by darkness in a pass still far from home when out tracking poachers. He lay down in the heather with his plaid over his head against the midges and slept until he was awakened by shouts and the noise of horses and clashing swords. Later, he found battle artifacts in the peat. He is a storyteller, a violin-maker, and his own cobbler. I listen, sip whisky, and watch the shadows and smoke of his turf fire reconfigure the cottage walls.

Celia, my friend who works in the woollen shop in the Old Mill in the village, has a key to the grill that guards the eight healing stones used by the eighth-century monk St Fillan to cure bodily afflictions. Each stone represents a different part of the body. They rest on a bed of river wrack which their traditional keepers renew on Christmas Eve. People write to the mill with requests for St Fillan's intervention and Celia does her best to help them. If they enclose an object or scrap of cloth and let her know in which part of the body they are suffering, she will touch it to the correct stone, ask for St Fillan's blessing, and return it to them. I write Great-Aunt Daisy in a nursing home in England and tell her this. She sends me a handkerchief in hopes of help for her chronic pain. In the mill, I follow Celia from the desk where she keeps the key. We circuit past displays and bins of merino and cashmere sweaters and scarves, tweed hats and walking-sticks, until we reach the grill-covered niche in the wall. She opens it and tells me I can stay with the stones as long as I want and gives me the key to lock up when I am finished with Aunt Daisy's request. There is nothing secret about the relics; the niche is labelled. I go often to visit them and talk to Celia between her customers, but there is never anyone else in the mill who shows an interest in them.

At Croftmoraig circle, hens scratch between the boulders, slabs, and standing stones. The first time I visit, a few cows roam the frosted field blowing grey silky breath into the air. At home, I make a paper model of the circle's rings and fasten them together so I can turn each ring separately. Along with quail's feathers, a puff of sheep's wool, and postcards sent by friends, I tack the model to the wall above my writing desk.

When he was my grad school tutor, the poet Robin Skelton taught me Irish and Welsh metres. I've studied the work of his friends who draw from Celtic sources – and met some of them. Poets such as Robert Graves, Seamus Heaney, John Montague, and the Blake scholar and Neo-Platonist writer Kathleen Raine. In this landscape and with such furnishings in my mind, I feel I have found my niche. Since I am in love with El, in this place that meshes with my nature and feeds my curiosity and my poetry, I have never been happier.

3.

The bus to Leverburgh, via the west coast of the Island of Harris, doesn't leave the Tarbert ferry dock for two hours. Rather than wait, we walk south out of the town and plan to flag the bus down when it turns up. From a headland, I look across to Skye and down on near green islets blotted with shadow as rain clouds sweep through and then the sun kindles the details of their folds. The hills ahead are rocky and bare except for pockets of pale winter-worn grass and patches of springy heather coming into flower. Already my pack is too heavy and after a while, sympathizing with my back pain but not my packing skills, El switches his lighter load for mine, and we walk on.

I'm only here because of a mix-up. I will be teaching at Moniack Mhor, the Scottish Creative Centre near Inverness, but next summer, not this one as I'd thought when I'd booked the flights. El has persuaded me that I need a break anyway; and it gives him a chance to show me a part of Scotland that he loves but I have never seen. It has been too long since we travelled together with no work or other obligations, and I am tired and disengaged from writing, work which I have always loved.

When we're at home, and I'm not preparing lectures or marking for my classes at the University, I sit in the glider swing my late father built and watch the birds that live in the forest around us – the sparrows, nut hatches, and flickers close by, the ravens and eagles in the immensely tall Douglas firs; and the quails that scurry in family queues over granite outcrops under the noses of our cats. When a horse and rider pass the foot of our driveway, I know they are headed for the Galloping Goose, a railway line converted to a trail at the end of our dead-end street. On a day of high wind, the sky above the bay, which the trail skirts, is a sheet of paper scribbled with blue that the clouds repeatedly erase. Often, El brings me tea so I can stay where I am, swinging back and forth, keeping track.

The Leverburgh bus halts for us. We remain aboard long enough to pass from the barren east coast of the island to the low-lying grassy plain – the machair – and the sandy beaches of the west coast. About a kilometre after we get off, we come in range of a prehistoric standing stone, the MacLeod stone / Clach Mhic Leòid, which dominates a hill of grassland overlooking the sea. The fast-changing, wind-driven weather is exhilarating. The sands shift colour from white to yellow to pink; clouds press shades of darkening green onto the near hills, and grey and black and blue onto those more distant. Frilled green water surges and breaks on shore, the fluctuating light flattening then unveiling its shallows.

We're not far from the day's destination of Scarista when we arrive at Clach Steineagaidh, the last stone standing in a five-thousand-year-old Neolithic complex that included a stone circle forty metres across. Its orientation is towards the island of Taransay, as is the MacLeod stone we passed, so that the three sites appear to be connected, once used possibly as solar markers. A nearby field wall is made of stones with a more recent history: these are from crofts destroyed in the nineteenth-century Clearances. I can't help but think that some of those evicted from their homes on Harris will have ended up – as many did from throughout the Highlands and Islands – in forced immigration to my homeland, Canada.

At Sandview House, our B&B, I remember this when, leafing through a magazine, I find the verses of the Canadian Boat Song, written in Upper Canada in 1829, when the Clearances were well underway. It is a song I haven't thought of since I sang it in school:

Mountains divide us, and a waste of seas;
yet still the blood is strong;
the heart is Highland
and we in dreams behold the Hebrides.
Deep the longing that has seized me,
Song nor fiddle lifts it off,
In my ear the ocean sounding
Sets me roving from the glen,
And sea-voices ever call me:
Come, o love to thy homeland.

Nostalgia, the emotion of exile, makes me uneasy, caught as it is between here and there; but the "waste of seas" is a perfect metaphor for loss of place in the world. I shut the magazine and glance out the window

at a sky of black cloud lit in a band along the horizon. Higher up, the
black is punched through by holes of fire.

4.

My paternal grandfather came from generations of Newfoundland
fishermen and boat-builders who had settled in that British colony early
in the nineteenth century from Somerset, England. My grandmother's
family were Newfoundlanders, too, but of longer standing: both her
parents were Mercers, one branch, from Jersey, having set up fishing
camps before the colony's official sixteenth-century founding, and the
other having arrived by 1705 from Hampshire. For Canada, this is early
immigration. My maternal grandfather was a Barnardo's orphan, sent
from London to work on an Ontario farm in the first decade of the
twentieth century. My mother's mother was descended from United
Empire Loyalists of Dutch extraction who sought refuge in Canada after
the American War of Independence. It is a mixed English and European
heritage, with northwest German roots. It is certainly not Scottish. My
mother, who had olive skin and black hair, was often mistaken for
French. We have First Nations relatives. I have never tested my DNA.
Why would I? I think I know who I am.

The string of fire along the horizon has just about disappeared.

I am looking out the closed Velux window in the B&B bedroom at a
sweep of hill, and birds swooping after midges. The room is stuffy. El
wants me to hurry so we don't miss breakfast and can get an early start,
but I'm trying to remember the dream I had of a gathering of poets at
the standing stone. The poets were reading to a large audience which
had come to hear them. All went well until a woman poet, one I know
slightly, wrote a line of one of her poems on cardboard and held it up
for the audience to see. A word in it is an obscenity which gives such
offence that the audience leaves in an uproar. I'm not bothered by the
word, nor are any of the other poets, but I wonder why the woman
chose that poem to share? I sit with the poets and talk to them. They
ask about my work, but instead of telling them my story as I mean to,
I repeat a joke I'd heard on the bus to the airport.

A polar bear goes into a bar. "What would you like?" the barman asks. "Umm, ahhhh ..." the bear says. The bartender waits. The bear hems and haws, unable to make up its mind, until finally the bartender asks, "Why the big pause?" At which the bear lifts its "paws" and says, "I was born like this."

I believe I know what this is about, and I don't like it. It's about what I'm not writing and about losing my way. When I say all this to El he says, "Don't worry. It's not a very good joke."

5.
1978

We travel up the west coast of Scotland in our British-racing-green MGB in tandem with our friends Sam and Carolyn in Sam's father's grey electrical engineering van. Near Sand, Aultbea, we stop to gaze at Gruinard Island a kilometre offshore. It is a small, bare, low island about two kilometres long and one across. In 1942, during WWII, the British government tested the use of anthrax spores – deadly when inhaled – on Gruinard Island as a potential biological warfare weapon. The test, too dangerous to carry out in England, was fine, apparently, for rural Scotland. The aerosol-delivered spores killed a flock of sheep, and the contaminated island remains uninhabitable. El says that infected animals washed ashore and there were deaths in local flocks. No one knows the effect of the spores on seabirds or marine animals. Since there are no visible warning signs, he and his friends used to swim in the beautiful bay before they knew of the quarantine.

I watch Carolyn in her yellow slicker and green wellies negotiate her way down the rocks towards some caves, one of which, a sign tells us, was a meeting ground of the evangelical Free Church of Scotland after its 1843 break with the established Church of Scotland. I like caves and when I lived on a Greek Island five years previously, used to sit in one from which the seventh-century-BC poet Archilochus watched dolphins and wrote verses: "Don't any of you be surprised in future if land beasts change places with dolphins and go to live in their salty pastures, and get to like the sounding waves of the sea more than the land." I had watched the dolphins, too, only mine chased the local ferry into the bay. Just as I'm about to follow my friend, a ewe leads a blood-stained newborn from a cave entrance and up the slope onto the winter-bleached grass in front of me. I back off to give the ewe and lamb space, and watch a seal pop up in the waters close to shore.

A few minutes later, I peer into a cave which is now a sheep-shelter but in 1885 was lived in by an old woman and a girl who had done their best to make it a home. They had closed off part of the entrance with cloth and turf and left an opening for the smoke from their fire to escape. In the aftermath of the Clearances, when tenants were evicted by anglicized Scottish landlords from homes they and their forebears had occupied for generations, many people scrabbled out a living however they could. In 1885, too, the Métis leader Louis Riel, who is buried at St Boniface, Manitoba, where I was born, was hanged for rebellion against the Canadian authorities who had seized Métis and Cree land for settlement by some of those same displaced Scots. It is a painful thought. Ironic doesn't cover it.

While the others continue to explore, I sit on the rocks, take out my notebook, and imagine a voice for the young girl who lived here.

As always, a paperback sticks out of Carolyn's anorak pocket. Today it is Neil Gunn's 1941 novel *The Silver Darlings*. As soon as we are back in our vehicles, she will resume reading.

When I first came to Scotland, I knew little of its literature, but under Carolyn's guidance I am discovering its novelists; and since I have begun publishing poetry in Scottish magazines, I've encountered Scotland's older poets – Robert Garioch, Norman McCaig, Hamish Henderson, William Montgomery, Ian Crichton Smith, George McKay Brown, and Sorley MacLean – at parties, readings and celebrations. As much as I admire their work, it bothers me that I haven't met or heard of equivalent women poets. I've been through this at home and worked through the dismissal of women poets as "not very good" to discover an important modernist poetry lineage.

I put the notebook away. The long waves of the North Minch, caught by Gruinard Bay, curl and break; clouds stack the snow-talced mountains to the north, and we return to the cars.

From Sand, the single-track road skirts the sea-lochs Little Loch Broom and Loch Broom through winter-hued hillsides and fields: beige snow lies on sepia grasses and bracken in sheltered patches, and the grey stumps of clear-cut trees look like rocks. Only in the busyness of trawlers working their way down the sea-lochs, and in the swollen, green tips of clumps of ash and birch trees along the rivers, is there a hint of spring.

6.

After we drop our backpacks at Sorrel House B&B, we continue to the post office in the village of Leverburgh, where El mails cards and buys socks and I find a heavy black Harris Tweed sweater woven by the post-mistress's husband. I bury my nose in its odour of lanolin and promise to pick it up the next day on our way to the ferry. At the pier café we lunch on parsnip soup and bread, and watch cars line up for the ferry to North Uist; and then we head out on a shore track that will take us to Rodel / Roghadal at the island's south tip. A pair of golden eagles soars, and glides on thermals in the watercolour-blue sky. A couple strolling towards us stops to watch them too. It isn't long after we say goodbye to them that El says, "When we round the next curve, we'll come to the place where I met a man building his garden four years ago." We round the curve: the garden is flourishing, rockery on rockery, and the man is in it. "I met you four years ago," El reminds him. "I'm waiting for the water man," the man says after he explains that he is building a waterfall. "He should have been here last month, but he had to go down south because his mother was ill, in fact she died, and now he's staying for the wedding." I want to ask whose wedding it is but feel I should already know. He seizes one of the stones he is laying to secure the cladding of the water feature wall. "I collected these from the shore and from dismantled dykes," he says and returns to his back-breaking work.

Most places we come to are as El has talked and written about and photographed years earlier. The houses, the people in the yards, the plants in windows, the subjects and rhythms of conversations remain as they were. I live in the country and know how little changes year to year. A new planting, necessary repairs, a health concern that alters schedules, a visitor's arrival, or a child's return from distant schooling can be transformative, but little shows to the outside world and certainly not to strangers. Even so, there is a feeling of time suspended and of rules that are different from those I am used to. The feeling isn't rational, but I have met it before, once when climbing Doon Hill (the fairy hill) near Aberfoyle where the path rose through bands of trees that corresponded to letters of the Celtic alphabet: oak, holly, rowan … and at the top, pine. Up there, a wind roared and swirled just beyond the trees and nearly plucked my twelve-year-old daughter from the edge. I grabbed her arm and hauled her back. Later, we spoke of our time there as a story we'd constructed together and recalled that it had begun near the bottom of the path with the appearance of dozens of tiny golden frogs on the roadway. The feeling, with its invitation to suspend judgment, is like the stirrings of a poem, but it is different, too, with an accompanying impression of having unwittingly trespassed into someone else's territory.

El has told me of another dwelling, a loving conglomeration of stones and glass and fancy, near the end of the Harris track. He'd had a conversation he'd liked with its owner on a previous trip, and by now I expect to see the man when we reach it. He isn't there, though. A little disappointedly, I examine the elaborate stonework and the planters in the yard, all of which are inset with shells and beach glass. I am turning away when a car drives up and El speaks to the driver, a woman. A man jumps from the passenger side and comes over to me: "Are you enjoying your holiday?"

"Yes, it's my first time here but El has been here before. He said he'd met you."

"Did he now?" The man pauses and looks over his shoulder at El then turns back to me. "Are you interested in the Gaelic? "

"I can't speak it, but I've heard Sorley MacLean read in Gaelic and in English in Edinburgh."

"Oh, yes, he could read, but where did he get that voice? They don't talk like that on Raasay."

El joins us and says they'd discussed Sorley MacLean's poetry the last time he was here. The man looks doubtful, but offers, "They were all clever, it was a very academic family, but Sorley turned against the Kirk, you know – it didn't think he should write such things ..."

We think our own thoughts about what "such things" could be.

"Well," he says a few moments later – his wife is waiting beside the car – "let me put you on the right way to the Roghadal footpath."

7.
1978

The MGB and van play tag on the single-track north from Ullapool where we have spent the night. El likes this kind of driving with its brief, rhythmical pauses at lay-bys to let oncoming traffic – what little there is of it – go by. We are in an informal race with our friends to a planned lunch stop at the Point of Stoer. We've not long left the Falls of Kirkaig behind, where I made us halt for a look, when I notice a "Bookstore" sign at the side of the road with an arrow pointing up a gravel driveway. "Wait, go back!" I say. El pulls over a little grumpily, but after a brief consultation with our friends, we proceed up the hill. Our hopes aren't high: I imagine we'll find something along the lines of the tiny plywood book shacks – sheds stuffed with musty paperbacks – I've come across down farm roads off the highway between Quesnel and Prince George in British Columbia; but we park near a shut-up-tight large new prefab building below an older house.

Carolyn and I walk up the incline and knock at the house door. The woman who answers looks surprised to see us. "We'd like to look at the books," Carolyn says. Without speaking, the woman fetches keys, and we follow her back down the hill to where El and Sam wait by the cars.

It is evident, the moment we are inside, that the store is stocked by knowledgeable hands and with so much care that I find myself asking the proprietress if it is all right to browse. Before too long, as El reassures her that we sincerely love books, it is all right to ask questions and she directs me to the Scottish poetry section.

I have not yet seen a book or map or any of the small collection of handcrafted items in the store that I wouldn't love to own; but now, confronting shelves of poetry, I am overwhelmed. There are hand-sewn pamphlets, broadsides, and hardbacks of an astonishing range of Scottish poetry of all types, a far better collection than I have seen in Edinburgh bookshops. We are there for over an hour, and in the end, I must choose between the two books I want most: a volume by the eighteenth-century poet Duncan Ban MacIntyre, who wrote not far from where I'm living in Perthshire, and the seventeenth-century poems of Mary MacLeod of the Hebrides. Both interest me, but there is no question of being able to afford them both. In the end, I select the Duncan Ban MacIntyre. Yet, in Scourie that evening as I look out the window of the hotel at a small flock of Jacob sheep – Carolyn is somewhere reading – I find I can't settle, can't write or read as I'd planned to, and can't get Mary MacLeod off my mind: so I give up trying and join Sam and El in the bar. They drink beer, as always; and I discover I like green Chartreuse.

8.

The path is hilly, turfy, and green above sea-fingers reaching into the land below. Sheep meander then quick-step away when I come too close. I find a knoll on which to sit and gaze down at a white-washed house, smoke slithering from its chimney under the press of wind, on the shore of a peaceful perfect bay. In front of the house is a narrow beach with a boat upturned on the sand, and then the silvery sea and islands and the ghosting coastline of Skye. Eventually, the track tips steeply down to Rodel, a few scattered houses, a hotel at the jetty, and St Clement's – an early-sixteenth-century church El has said I will like – showing its squat frame and square tower on a rise.

After a look at the little harbour, and tea and scones at the hotel, we walk up to the church. Wild fuchsia surfs the drystone dykes of enclosures in the churchyard and in sections overwhelms the graves, but the emerald grass is sheep-cropped and there are views up a glen and into the hills, as well as over the sea.

The interior of the church is dim, lit by low windows that shed soft light on grey stone walls and flagging. The only furnishings are three tombs set into the walls. On an information board I read that the church was likely built by Alexander MacLeod / Alasdair Crotach. His tomb was completed in 1528 and he was buried there between 1545 and 1547. I puzzle through the tomb's medieval iconography, liking best a galley (*birlinn*) under sail and the dogs in a hunting scene that "represents the world of living mortals." Carved gravestone slabs lean against the wall of the north transept, and in the south transept a stone MacLeod knight in armour "sleeps" below a window. Pale sunlight splashes in and washes his features. I walk back and forth for an hour, returning often to the south transept and the view out its window to the sea. El suggests I am lingering because I don't want to face the walk back to the B&B, but before I go, I climb a series of ladders into the tower, and then come back down to wander in and out of the church and through the churchyard until El finally pulls me away.

Sometime after dinner when I'm trawling through bookshelves at Sorrel Cottage, I pick up Finlay J. MacDonald's memoir of growing up on South Harris, *The Corncrake and the Lysander*. In it, he writes of visiting St Clement's church as a boy, and that "Mary MacLeod of the seventeenth century, whose songs live on as memorials more lasting than stone," is buried there. I tell this to El and recall how I'd tried over the years, in pre-internet days, to find out more about her, intrigued that she had made a space for herself as a poet in a time when few women could. I had asked my central Scotland writer friends about her, but none had heard of her, and I had never happened across her work again.

In the morning, I wake with awareness that I have been dreaming about Tighnacraig where we lived so long ago. I sit up and glance at El asleep beside me and turn to look out the window; but the window isn't there. I face round to where the door should be, but it isn't there either. I wait for the strangeness to pass, but it doesn't. My sense of physical space is at odds with the room, its actual windows and doors in places they have no right to be. I try, but can't remember anything of how I came to be wherever it is I am. After a few minutes of worry that I might have had a stroke, I get up and find my notebook and read what I've written of the days and weeks of travel right up to the time I went to bed. Even with that, my sensations have me elsewhere. Eventually, I explore the room and find the bathroom and get dressed. When El is awake, we take out the map, but nothing I find on paper tells me how to solve this puzzle.

Each step I take on the way to the Leverburgh pier is a wade through thickened air. In an effort to be normal while we wait for the ferry that crosses the Sound of Harris, I volunteer to buy coffee from a van selling snacks. Several workmen lounge inside it out of the rain. When I go to pay and don't know what to do with the money in my hand, they grow watchful. "It must be the medication," the van owner says after a pause. All of us laugh as he helps me count out the coins.

From our view at the stern, we watch the Island of Harris diminish. Big puffs of cumulous clouds loll among its hills, but the skies directly overhead are blue and sunny. We point out Harris landmarks to each other, and my feeling of being out of sync and behind a glass wall vanishes. On board with us are people we've been seeing on and off over the last few days: French girls from the B&B, a family on a cycling holiday, and two French boys who have been hitchhiking. It is good to feel more down to earth and to greet familiar faces. The boat slaloms through a dense scattering of islands and islets into the Sound, its progress south and then west. Seals and seabirds contemplate us from skerries a safe distance across the space of silvery waters.

We land at the south end of the island of Berneray, which is joined by a causeway to North Uist. At the bus shelter there we join the two French boys to wait for the bus south to Lochmaddy on North Uist. It takes a while to come, and when it does, the driver tells us he is still on the outward part of his route – he's here to let off, not pick up, passengers – but he'll be back at the ferry slip after dropping his remaining passengers on the island. "You can come for the tour if you want," he says. "I won't charge you." The French boys choose to stay where they are, but we get onboard.

The bus hustles along a narrow road into a landscape of low hills, rough green fields, and stones. The island is small, scoured, and windblown. A seaweed-strewn eastern shoreline unwinds as we travel. Everyone except us disembarks at a crossroads, and then we continue north.

There are a few houses and crofts but no sign of anything like a town. "I love it, we've got to come back!" I tell El.

"Didn't Prince Charles have a croft here?" he says vaguely.

At the end of the line, a bus stop within sight of the sea and not far from some ruins, the driver turns his vehicle around and shuts off the engine. He moves past us to the back and switches on a radio. "I'll be ten minutes," he says above the music and takes his lunch from a knapsack. "You can get off and look around, if you like."

Once I am outside, the exhilaration I've felt since arriving on the island softens to happiness. The air is rich with the scent of the sea. Keeping an eye on the bus, I walk about twenty metres, then alter course through a field towards the water while El follows a track to the ruins. Part way across the field I stop and soak in the peace; but worried about how much time I've got left to explore, I move on up the side of a hill that rises from behind the bus shelter. At the top, I slowly turn all the way round to take in the shapes of rock above the beach, the gables and rectangles and thatches of the ruins, the blowing grasses, a few sheep, and the small undulations of the inland hills. The sound of bees fills my ears. I feel at home, and when El joins me, I tell him so. If I could, I say, I'd sit down and go no further. But it is only a sandwich or two the driver has to eat, and he starts the engine, and we have to leave.

We reach Lochmaddy, check into our B&B, and head out for a walk. A path leads over a narrow sea-inlet via a suspension bridge with sea wrack draping its cables: the tidal strip is opulent with seaweed and redolent with the sex-tang of shellfish. Then it's across a field to a thatched rock hut – like a scaled-down blackhouse – on the shore. Inside, a small rectangle of light on a dark inner wall mirrors the outside seascape by way of the lenses of a camera obscura. I get El to walk on the beach so I can see him enter its frame. The reflected seascape on the wall is lively and shimmering, a ghosting watercolour. Again on the path, and a moment before we decide to turn back, three dark sleek otters run up the side of the bluff opposite. Just as they dash into dense bushes, a large bird of prey swings by and dives for a closer look.

Over dinner I tell El I've started scrawling lines of poetry – nothing much yet, only a few fragments – but I hope there might be more, and I'd like to follow the notion that has taken hold since Harris: to see what

I can find out about Mary MacLeod. "If I lived here," I write in my note-book, with noteworthy lack of modesty, "the songs would form in the spray and in the mouths of birds …" Not that I know the language of birds or a word of Mary's language, Scottish Gaelic.

II

The Language of Birds

A red dog lays
its head in your lap,
and lambs howl under the wind.

A thin blade from the rubble of the stone-age
twists in a hunter's hand a hill away.

The wind turns northeast
and the western ocean swells and murmurs
with winter birds.

The dog stricken with its chain,
strains towards moonrise.

– Tighnacraig

9.

When I make the usual computer searches for the outlines of Mary MacLeod's story, I find there is little agreement about it, not even to the chronology of her life. Anthologists and collectors in the nineteenth century, drawing on oral accounts, have her born in the sixteenth century and living beyond the age of one hundred in the seventeenth century. One says that Mary MacLeod was born in Rodel (or Roudel, Rodil, Roghadal, or Roudal as it is also spelled), Harris, in 1569 and was buried there at the age of 105; another that she lived 103 years from 1590 to 1693. Even in the twentieth century, the *Encyclopedia Britannica* gave variations of these dates.

Yet other scholarship, from 1934 onwards, estimates her dates as c. 1615–c. 1707, although a birthdate of c. 1625 "might be an equally good guess." Mary was born, it seems, not in the sixteenth century at all, but in the seventeenth, and she was dead of old age in the first decade of the eighteenth.

Rodel, Harris, is most often claimed to be Mary's place of birth, but there are traditions that have her born on the Isle of Skye, on the Isle of Pabbay, on the island of Berneray, or at Nisisidh on Harris, past which former settlement I had walked on the road south from Scarista. She may have died at Dunvegan, Skye, or on Pabbay or Berneray, but wherever she died, most writers are firm in their assertion that Mary was buried in the south transept of St Clement's / Tùr Chliamain in Rodel, where I had lingered.

With that exception, it begins to feel as if I am carrying water or sand as each fact I come across slips through my fingers. I become more curious – and cautious – about the reality of what is remembered and what is forgotten. Some of Mary's songs were still recalled in the 1950s when they were recorded by field workers from the University of Edinburgh and added to a collection begun in the 1930s. Farmworkers, travellers, crofters – men and women – kept this oral culture alive, but there is no way to know, or recover, what or how much is missing.

Unlike more general recollections, poetry and song are constructed with rhyme, rhythm, repetition, and other devices to make a unique combination of sound, sense, and imagery. Once learned, their unfolding can be retained for a lifetime: but there must be a need and opportunity for their memorization to begin with.

Skipping and ball-bouncing songs, chants, and games were part of my girlhood; I knew dozens; they functioned as social passwords. I memorized Bible verses, too, because this was my family culture, reciting them to my mother in the kitchen on Saturday evenings to be ready for Sunday School in the morning, while my father polished the family's Sunday shoes. As I write, I recall a sequence of kitchens (we moved house nine times before I finished school) with different configurations and colour schemes, but in each my father is seated on a kitchen chair, bending to reach the shoes on newspaper on the floor, and my mother is at the table, sleeves rolled or pushed up, a small emerald and diamond ring on her left hand as she leans over the Bible, her stockinged feet tucked beneath her as she checks my recitation against the text.

Poems and songs are time capsules that preserve the mental patterns and bodily senses of their originators. George Faludy, the Hungarian poet, whom I met when he collaborated with Robin Skelton on an English translation of his poems (a project into which Robin brought many of his poet friends) in the early 1980s, told how fellow prisoners learned the poems he composed when he was imprisoned in Hungary's Stalinist concentration camp from 1950 to 1953. Released prisoners would visit Faludy's wife and dictate the poems to her so that whatever happened to him, his poems would survive.

The poems were witnesses to what was done in secret. They were not easy to destroy.

Which does not mean they are exactly literal. They convey material and mental reality, but they come soaked in individual perception and emotion, whether withheld or explicit. How they sit within a reader's frame of reference is beyond their control.

10.

A nineteenth-century collection containing Mary MacLeod's work, which I look at initially because it promises familiar ground, is the Reverend Alexander Maclean Sinclair's *The Gaelic Bards from 1411 to 1715*, published in Charlottetown, PEI, in 1890; it gives Mary's birthplace as "Roudal" and her dates as 1590 to 1693. I am curious about what lies within this Canadian connection.

Alexander's parents were immigrants from Scotland. His grandfather, John MacLean (Iain MacGillEathain), b. Tiree 1787, had immigrated to Nova Scotia in 1819. He had been bard to the Lord of Coll and brought important Gaelic manuscripts to Canada with him.

One of these manuscripts was given to John MacLean by the daughter of its collector, Dr Hector Maclean. This material reached back four generations, through Dr Maclean's mother, to Sir Norman MacLeod, Mary MacLeod's patron, to whom much of her poetry was dedicated – that is, to Mary's lifetime. In 1869, Alexander Maclean Sinclair himself journeyed to Scotland where "he met his grandfather's relatives and wrote down from their dictation in Gaelic, a considerable amount of genealogical and literary information" to add to his store. This argues for a reliable transmission of information, but modern text-based scholarship shows that reliability may not be what it first appears.

Major Gaelic-speaking immigrations reached Canada from the 1770s through the 1920s. In the first half of the nineteenth century alone, 30,000–50,000 Highlanders emigrated to Cape Breton, which became the most populated Gaelic region outside Scotland. The pressure on land was so great that some of these immigrants left for Newfoundland, where they settled in the Codroy valley in the southwest and maintained a Gaelic-speaking character there until the 1960s.

At the time of Confederation in 1867, Gaelic was Canada's third language after English and French. In 1890, the year of publication in Canada of *The Gaelic Bards 1411–1715*, a British Columbia senator tabled a motion to make Gaelic an official language for official proceedings in Canada's Houses of Parliament. He cited ten Scottish and eight Irish senators as well as thirty-two members of the House of Commons who spoke either Scottish or Irish Gaelic.

Dr Hector Maclean's manuscripts, "on which Maclean Sinclair worked assiduously," were not atypical. Much information – songs, stories, and other materials and traditions – was brought by these thousands of Scottish immigrants. Back home, the links of transmission were broken through conflict, disease, famine, and the commercially driven break-up (the Clearances) of a once-settled way of life in the Highlands and Islands, which devastated and scattered the remaining populations. Recovery of this cultural property is an ongoing project. Songs and stories, traditional dances and styles of music have been repatriated to contemporary Scotland from PEI, Cape Breton, mainland Nova Scotia, and elsewhere, their provenance recorded up to and subsequent from the date of immigration. Traditions of step-dance, the

Highland violin, oral poetry, and stories based on the supernatural or humour, all of which tended to exist within small community and family circles and be kept outside official education, government, and church control, remained remarkably intact in Canadian Gaelic communities, nearly to the present day. How "lost" some of these materials were was brought home to me when El told me that when he grew up in Scotland, step-dancing was assumed to be an Irish custom. Its forgotten Scottish origins are much older than the "Scottish" Victorian-established traditions of Highland Dancing and Scottish Country Dancing, which are accepted as cultural norms.

Oral culture is a living entity with multiple variations, but a fading oral culture faces a problem. To preserve it is to remove some of its organic matter, not so much through alteration of forms – these are inherently protective; their time-capsule nature remains effective – but through well-meaning adjustment of content – a more subtle form of erasure. The alternative, though, is to watch the culture irreversibly disappear as need and opportunity for transmission fade away.

The Reverend Maclean Sinclair, the Canadian Gaelic scholar of impeccable antecedents, was also a well-meaning Victorian. Like other anthologizers of his era, he "improved" on the work he published, altering some Gaelic oral materials to make them morally and aesthetically acceptable to his views and times. Once the oral sources and their variations died out, as they did, there remained only the anthologizer's choices to represent what had been in the living community storehouse. Maclean Sinclair and other collectors did a tremendous service in their work of preservation, but they also left weighty thumbprints on the older materials they worked from.

Modern scholars, in recognition of these limitations, consult the notes and journals these collectors left behind to try and see past them to the originals; but any written record is only as valid as the skill of its recorder, and every recorder and every translator can't help but communicate a degree of their own desires, hopes, views, and aims.

This is not news, but I am not glad to be thinking of it as I try to make my way through the contradictions of what is written about Mary MacLeod. I am glad, though, to find that in another way, I am on familiar ground. Poetry demands an ability to hold on to contraries. A poem retains an objective intelligence in its structure, but it is also in the nature of a poem to assert the complexity and ambiguity of language and poetic and rhetorical devices as they conjure shared human experience. To enter a poem is to accompany the perceptions of another as if they are our own, and to remember simultaneously that they are different from ours. Poetry, even the most discursive such as a list of names in the Iliad or a Biblical genealogy, communicates in shades and pictures and sounds; it reveals its face and figure slowly, gradually emerging from its background; and there is also its inbuilt singing which we may be lucky enough to hear.

11.

Early every morning, my grandfather lit the fire in the kitchen stove. He put the kettle on for tea, made porridge, and sang hymns in full voice until everyone was awake. While I sat with him and he told stories, he carved miniature wooden boats, which we later sailed across the surface of a water-filled galvanized steel laundry tub. The house held few books. The ones I recall were *Pilgrim's Progress*, several translations of the Bible (the King James and Scofield's along with various concordances), and the terrifying *Foxe's Book of Martyrs*. Stories, at least my grandfather's stories, were true. In my grandfather's opinion, fiction equalled lies. When he told me that his companion had drowned beside him after their dory overturned in Conception Bay, and how he had begged him to hold on "but he couldn't," I knew it was so.

He had little formal education. He could not abide lying, swearing, or breaking the Sabbath. He was agile and double-jointed. I watched him run along the rafters of a house he was building and, at my urging, do handstands on them. He did all his figuring in his head. As well as houses, he had built iceboats, dories, large fishing boats, and even schooners, along with his brothers. He drew complex figurative or geometrical patterns on brown paper that my grandmother followed for her hooked rug patterns. He believed that keeping the rules as he knew them – including no dancing, no drinking, no card-playing or movie-going – played an important part in the salvation of the soul. Yet once, after supper, something brought him to his feet, and he danced a jig like the Irish did in Newfoundland.

In later years I learned that he had seen angels in the apple trees, the same trees I climbed in the orchard in my grandparents' yard; and he had danced before the Lord in front of the altar in the Methodist church. For the psalm says: "Let them praise his name in the dance: let them sing praises unto him with the timbrel and harp" (Psalm 149.3).

The enemy of creativity is fixed belief; but an equal enemy is fixed unbelief. The art of creativity, of poetry, of life itself I believe, is a negotiation with these contraries. Within this negotiation, slivers of magic may work their way through the impossible to the surface.

Hannah Arendt refers to "the precise generality of the literary art." The world of "the singing poem ... is not ... a means to an end ... The poem places a dark, silent margin around its object, a horizon that turns us back to the specificity of its words – of its own words, for its own sake. Yet its removal of itself and its object from the in-between is only provisional."

Mary MacLeod's story rests in the in-between of memory and the recording of oral culture: what exists beside it, along with it, what we do not see because we have never suspected its existence, is in there too.

It can only ever be provisional to examine what is written about the life and work of Mary MacLeod for what it has to say about her, and more provisional for me than for some since I am a stranger to her world; and yet, I have decided that what I lack matters less, at least for now, than that I am a poet drawn by what feels like a recognizable poetic process and poet. It is also abundantly clear that I am going to need help.

12.

I leaf through a copy of *Gaelic Songs of Mary Macleod*, edited by J. Carmichael Watson – the book I did not buy long ago, and which I have now found through the internet. Watson has gathered and assessed the information about Mary available up to the time of the book's publication in 1934. He includes and translates only the poems he can reasonably attribute to her. There are other poems, but these are in dispute. From what I can find, subsequent approaches to Mary and her work have been based on Watson's foundation.

Watson, I discover, is almost an old friend: he carried on his grandfather Alexander Carmichael's work on *Carmina Gadelica*, a collection of oral Scottish Gaelic Hymns and Incantations, continuing from where Alexander stopped after publishing two volumes in 1900 (he died in 1912). Watson completed two further volumes in the early 1940s. A final two volumes were finished by others. These six volumes have been in my library since just before I met El at a poet friend's house in 1977. El's knowledge of the collection made me take a second look at him after I had unfairly dismissed him as a jock. Robin Skelton had introduced me to the *Carmina Gadelica* as a resource for anyone interested in Celtic ceremonies and folk practices. He found inspiration there for the healing spells he had begun to write. He did not suggest it was authoritative or sacred, although the Iona Community, in which El and I were to spend an uncomfortable weekend (we found it cult-like) when we visited Iona and its Abbey in 1978, drew heavily on the *Carmina* to build its version of a Celtic service. As I read through Watson's introduction, I note his warning that "seekers of Celtic Mysticism will not find it here [in Mary MacLeod], or in any other Gaelic poet."

With the help of Watson and others, I learn that Mary is commonly believed to be descended from Uilleam Cléireach, the fifth MacLeod chief of Harris and Dunvegan (from about 1390 until his death in 1405), through her father. Watson adds that there is no proof of this. Mary's mother was (perhaps) of the MacDonalds of Morar (Clanranald), which is not far from Mallaig where we still take the ferry to Skye. Her brother, Neil, almost certainly lived on Pabbay in the Sound of Harris, a short distance from Berneray (and was MacLeod's factor for St Kilda, the westernmost archipelago in the United Kingdom). A sister appears to have lived for a period in Benbecula (an island close between North and South Uist), where Mary's mother's family had land. There is no mention of Mary having married.

Likely of low economic status but of high caste, Mary is thought to have joined the MacLeod chief's household at Dunvegan, Skye, as a "nurse" to the chief's children. She began writing "somewhat advanced in life" and grew to occupy a position "of privilege and prestige little if at all inferior to that enjoyed in a great household by a trained bard in the preceding period" – that is, before the decay of the traditional bard's role under the impact of anglicization. For reasons much speculated about, but all associated with her writing, Mary was expelled from her home and position and sent into exile, possibly more than once, by one or more of the MacLeod chiefs whom she offended. When she was brought home, it may have been by a different chief than whichever one had sent her away.

As notorious as her exile(s) and the reasons for it (or them) is Mary's treatment after her death. Watson tells, "She directed that she should be placed face downward in her grave – '*beul nam breug a chur foidhpe* [The mouth of lies to be put under her].'" She did so to repudiate her own work; or it was imposed on her as a punishment for writing songs in a style reserved for men. Face-down burial, it is said, was "usually reserved for those accused of witchcraft."

13.

Opinions about Mary's worth as a poet are as divergent as the accounts of her life. They range from John Mackenzie in 1841, who calls her "the most original of all our poets … There is no straining to produce effect … Her versification runs like a mountain stream over a smooth bed of polished granite," and George Henderson's belief that "[h]er Gaelic poems are unsurpassed poetic classics; on reading them one involuntarily remembers she was contemporary with Shakespeare and Milton," to the more modern assessment of Derick Thomson, who says her strength, *par excellence*, is music and rhythm, but who also compares her to her contemporary Iain Lom and finds that she is "lacking his range and subtlety as well as his power." Overall, Thomson finds "much repetition from poem to poem of basic ideas and phrases … one can scarcely escape the conclusion that this poet's reputation has been greatly inflated. She wears the narrow strait-jacket of the bardic panegyrist without his learning, his occasional wit, and his metrical virtuosity, bringing to her work, however, the positive virtues of musical phrasing, not infrequent verbal felicities, and occasional images of some vividness." Sharron Gunn defines Thomson's "narrow strait-jacket" as "meeting the expectations of a Gaelic-speaking audience," something male professional poets apparently did with learning, wit, and metrical virtuosity – and Mary did not.

Thomson dislikes Mary's use of repeated ideas and phrases. But repetition can be an important poetic and song-writing technique, an aid to memory, affirming and culturally orienting – as in classical Greek poetry. Sometimes it carries the power of incantation. Could Thomson have missed something?

The great Gaelic poet Sorley Maclean, whose haunting readings I recall each time I visit Skye and look across to the island of Raasay where he was born, grouped Mary with other seventeenth-century Gaelic poets of "clan-and-chief" style. Despite the acknowledged "freshness and beauty and evocative power ... rhythm and phrase" of their work, he finds in these poets "a narrowness and lack of wide human significance."

"Lack of wide human significance" is even more dismaying than Thomson's faint praise. It houses Mary within a strait-jacket from which few would bother to unbind her. MacLean does note exceptions: "those great but brief moments when Mary MacLeod forgets her Normans and Rodericks of Dunvegan of whom there appear to be many, and we see herself in her loneliness, her memories of a great MacCrimmon [piper] and perhaps her love for Norman of Berneray, who was something more to her than all the rest of the MacLeods were." I sympathize with MacLean's impatience with MacLeod naming: sorting through the Normans, Rodericks, and Johns (Iains) of several centuries to find which chief or chief's relative in this numerous and branching family is being referred to can be a challenge. Although what he is really complaining of, I think, is Mary's focus on these figures at the expense of a kind of poetry she might have composed. Gunn remarks that these figures "were the movie stars of their day and people were intensely interested in following their activities." That is, with different content, Mary's work "might not have been so well-remembered in the Highlands."

MacLean's words conjure a Mary too curbed to give her talent room, but elsewhere he pays tribute to the "moment" where her originality breaks through. He believes the talent is there, but alongside the Gaelic anonyms of the period in which there is "a rich texture of imagery," poetry of Mary's style can seem thin-blooded.

Sorley MacLean's most important poems are impelled by a distressing failure in love and by his experiences of war; these are soul wounds. Both changed him personally and as a poet. The brokenness of his certainties reformed as a deepened humanity in poetry that retained roots in tradition but spoke with the transparency of confession. It seems as if this integration is what he wished for Mary, and it is easy to understand why. When we respond to poetry, it is often because the authenticity of the poet mirrors a sense of our own – however hidden – authentic being. MacLean's poetry resonated in a time that called for brokenness to be acknowledged. His cultural inheritance gave him means to quantify the loss. The Gaelic anonyms of Mary's period did so as well, and with beauty and pathos; but they had no need (as MacLean did) to navigate their emotional identification through place. Place was inherent in the mode of expression, as it was in Mary's poetry; but she worked with an additional responsibility towards the survival of the internal codes of her culture. Or so it seems to me.

The persona of clan-and-chief poetry did not appeal to MacLean; he did not find himself mirrored there. I can't help but believe, however, as I look again through what is said about Mary's work, that it might help to read her poetry for what it is, rather than searching for an aesthetic it did not seek to follow. That is, to take her seriously and at her word.

14.

I turn to Carmichael Watson's *Gaelic Songs* for guidance as to how to proceed. Not only does he counsel against a search for Celtic Mysticism, but he tells us to "remember that her [Mary MacLeod's] songs were meant not to be printed but to be sung. We are to approach her with the ear and the heart," he writes, "and not attempt to judge her poetry as if it were meant to appeal to the intellect."

It is Saturday night. I have finally finished marking for the fiction and poetry classes I teach. My desk is piled with books and papers, to-do lists, applications for funds for programs I run, and drafts of poems I have begun to write in response to my engagement with Mary Mac-Leod. I can hear the *Hockey Night in Canada* commentary through the two closed doors and the hallway between where El watches the game on television and where I gaze out my study window through the dark trees to a few lights showing from houses in the hills across the waters of the Sooke Basin.

I look back and forth from one of Mary's poems in Gaelic to its English translation, trying to understand its shape. Watson gives notes on the forms she uses. It is a simple enough matter to identify rhymes, various sonic devices, and repetition, count lines and syllables, and develop a feeling for a song's music from its appearance on the page. Some of the forms are similar to Irish metres I have worked through with Robin, although Watson does not try to replicate the Scottish Gaelic shape in English: for the most part, his are prose versions.

On an impulse, I shuffle through the papers on my desk and find the torn-off corner of an envelope with a name and phone number on it. El had passed it on to me weeks before from a Scottish acquaintance of his who knew I was searching for local Gaelic speakers. I dial the number. Before the woman who answers can do more than confirm her name, I launch into an account of my "relationship" with the seventeenth-century bard Mary MacLeod, my need for someone to translate her work, and my willingness to pay. About half-way through I realize that the woman I am speaking to – with no idea of who I am or any context for what I ask, and likely no interest in poetry or bards – must think I am mad. I finish and take a breath, prepared to apologize and for her to hang up. Instead, she says, "I didn't know anyone else had a copy of the poems." There is a pause.

"Do you sing?" she says.

"Yes," I say.

"I'll translate one poem for you, but if you come to the Gaelic choir, I'll do them all. Which poem do you want first?"

At the Wednesday practice of the Victoria Gaelic Choir in a shoe-box-plain community church auditorium on a dark fall night, I sit between Sharron Gunn, my contact – she is short, auburn-haired, and attractively energetic – and Beth, a small, helpful Celtic harpist, and try to hear the words they sing. I listen hard when Anne, from South Uist, demonstrates correct pronunciation. But the Gaelic bounces off my untutored ears and I have little sense of where we are in the sheet music, even though normally I sight-read well. I studied piano for ten years and played in a brass band for six; recently, I have been taking voice lessons: I thought I was up to this, but after half an hour of my bleated notes and growing confusion, it is clear I am not. It does not matter, though, for the sounds made by the thirty-or-so-voice a capella choir fill a well inside me. For much of the practice I am near tears. Whatever the type or tempo or rhythm of the singing, it takes me to a land on "the tip of my tongue;" and with each new song I feel I am continuing a long-planned journey with fellow passengers.

Afterwards, when a group of the women singers invite me to go along to their regular after-practice drink at the Legion, I realize I had already met several of them. I had recognized a few of the men at the practice: they were colleagues of El's from a Scottish cultural group he belongs to. These women, though, are from disparate backgrounds and contexts: one is a friend of a friend, met at a dinner party, whom I remember liking because she had brought her huskies with her and took me outside to her van to meet them; another talked with me at a garden party where she sat against a background of roses and looked like one of the gypsies I used to see in El Parque de Maria Louisa near where I lived in Seville, Spain. She tells me now that as well as singing and studying in Gaelic, she dances flamenco. The choir director, whom I'd met at fundraisers for a literacy society she administered, had transmitted encouragement and support in the green room when I had waited to go on stage to read: that energy has become focused on these singers – for singing, it occurs to me, is a kind of literacy, too.

And of course, there is Sharron who is responsible for my being there. As well as a translator, she is a Gaelic teacher, historical consultant, and author. We talk through my poetry-interpretation questions, find friends and acquaintances in common, and she gives me the basics of the mythic and historical background to Mary's poems. Women bards, she tells me, were referenced in Celtic writings in the eighth century; they were known, even though by Mary's time, formal bardic function was denied to them. Several other women wrote as bards in Mary's period and were also treated badly.

No one can stay late; all of us have work and other obligations to return to, and I have an hour's drive home. Before I go, though, Barbara, a piper, tells me there are pipers' stories about Mary MacLeod, and strong opinions for and against the wisdom of performing any music associated with her. Some pipers speak of a haunting. I have much to think about and I welcome the time to absorb it on the drive, but most of all I have a sense of others whose perception of Mary, like mine, is not static or solely academic, but alive.

That night, and many nights afterwards in the weeks I sing with the choir, I wake in the dark with the choir's singing in my ears and fall asleep again as the songs continue.

15.

In the house we lived in with my grandparents, I spent most of my time with my grandmother. While the others were at work and my brother in school, my grandmother and I tidied the house, kept the fire going, cooked and baked, beat carpets hung from a tree, fed laundry through the mangle and hung it on the line. The grocery store was a half-mile walk up a gravel road and near the church. Sometimes, we went on bus trips into town to buy her new spectacles from Woolworths or a print dress or cotton stockings from Eaton's. We patronized Eaton's because Timothy Eaton refused to sell cigarettes, and because my greatest pleasure was to run the length of a tunnel that connected the two Eaton's buildings underground. When she needed to rest in the afternoons, I played in the yard or the neighbouring orchard or in the farm fields and woods across the road. She had raised a large family of boys. It did not occur to either of us to worry about where I went. The long strand of this time – it lasted two years – with little interference from my parents or grandfather gave me a love of discoveries made in solitude and of companionship with her. She recited poetry and told me of the fairies back home in Newfoundland until my grandfather forbade her to speak of them again.

16.

Aonghas Dubh, "Black Angus," is an old acquaintance. When I lived in Edinburgh, and afterwards on return visits to Scotland, I often heard him read his work in Gaelic and in English at literary events. As he puts it, when I contact him by email, it has been "many turnings of the tide" since we were in touch. Despite this, he is encouraging and generous with his thoughts about Mary. "What makes her particularly interesting," he writes, "is that she lived during a time of transition: She was born less than a decade before the passing of the Statutes of Iona, which, among other provisions, required that Highland chiefs sent their heirs to Lowland, Protestant, English-speaking schools. Among other effects of the policy was the total elimination of the professional Gaelic bard." Aonghas associates her exile (or exiles) and treatment at burial with her expressed "disapproval of the indifference to tradition of the later chiefs of her clan – who had obviously had that alienating Lowland education."

It is not that I haven't come across elements of these ideas before, but that they strike me, in Aonghas's phrasing, as speaking to conditions now. His own poetry bridges the ancient and contemporary worlds; his negotiation of that span, in two languages, engenders grief and joy and power; his awareness of the losses of identity that bridging requires is apparent in his monologue "I'm on a train again," where he writes, "And there are hidden islands of us in the cities, holding on to who we think we are, or trying to create ourselves anew ..."

"Transition," in Mary's time, would be short form these days for the impact of colonization; of erasure of language and culture and rootedness in land and community; of species endangerment, and pollution brought by industrial and agricultural practices that permanently alter the character and use and consumption of the natural world. The story of the overwhelming of indigenous nations by an expanding dominant culture is a familiar one and is ongoing in its global economic form. With this kind of impact comes a shift from the role of the arts as crucial memory- and essence-keeping, to entertainment: the accessible pool widens and shallows, even as deeper pools dry up or lose relevance. Is it any wonder that much poetry consists of grief songs? Or of brokenness? Or of a call to arms? I am a member of PEN International, a world-wide association of writers: I am sure Mary's case could have found a slot in its files of advocacy for writers in exile.

Yet, I don't believe it is a political retreat to sing as well of love and resilience: but it is obvious that such singing is a spring song in a dark and shortening season. It is not the only one there ever was, but this is our season, and we are responsible for it and for altering the human climate to bring it about.

That season mirrors my own, my age, the dimming of the voice of poetry: to sleep, to sleep, there is nothing we can do but forget.

But Aonghas, in a reply to me, says, "I hope these fragmentary thoughts are of some use. Any specific questions, I'm happy to have a go at finding answers. I like the thought that Màiri might have some kind of twenty-first-century rebirth in the far West."

III

Kennings

Tha mise air leaghadh le bròn
O'n là dh'eug thu 's nach beò
Mu m'fhiùran faidhidneach còir
Uasal aighearach òg
As uaisle shuidheadh mu bhòrd:
Mo chreach t'fhaighinn gun treoir éirigh.

Since that thou art dead and livest not, I am melted
with grief for my kindly patient youth, noble, merry,
and young, that sat the stateliest around a board; alas,
to find thee without strength to rise.

– Mary MacLeod, "Marbhrann do Fhear na Comraich" / "Dirge for the Lord
of Applecross"

17.

El and I first drove to Applecross (Abercrossan) village, on the west coast
of Scotland, over the Bealach na Bà, known in English as the Pass of the
Cattle, through ice and snow and fog in our MGB, in 1978. We turned
onto the single-track for no other reason than inquisitiveness about
what we would find at the end of the only road shown on the map to
cross the triangular bulk of Applecross peninsula. I am not sure we
would have attempted the pass, which lies along an old drove road, if
we had known it offered driving "opportunities" like you find nowhere
else in the country, even when the weather is good. Within a distance

of four miles, the road twisted and turned to a height of over two thousand feet. Near the summit, the hairpin bends, with a one-in-four rise, were simply terrifying. Our task, using snow-and-fog-obscured vision, was to find the road and stay on it without plummeting over the edge. Fortunately, the Michelin tires answered whenever we began a skid and we met no one else travelling in either direction. Bealach na Bà, we later learned, should have been closed.

The views are magnificent from the top of the pass westward over the inner sound of the Minch to the Isle of Skye, north to the mountains towards Loch Torridon, and south even as far as Ben Nevis, and I have seen them since, but not on that day with an outlook limited to an arm's length away from me. The icy descent was as thrilling as the climb, since El dared not touch the brakes all the way to the bottom.

In the pub, we spoke with locals who told us of the decline of the village since they'd lost access by ferry to the mainland, and of crofters having to leave to make a living elsewhere even while holidaymakers were buying up cottages for summer-only use at prices no locals could afford to pay. The tale was grim, and it was impossible to miss the weight of pride and despair carried by those we met that day, most of them Gaelic speakers, some of them elderly.

It was too cold to look around for long, and we needed to drive back over the pass before dark. We saw little of the village surroundings other than a plain and stony beach facing a stippled grey sea closed in by weather. A strip of joined houses along the shoreline was in the midst of change: some houses with nets and tools out front and smoke coming from chimneys; others abandoned and in disrepair.

It must have been in the pub that I picked up a pamphlet that told part of the Applecross story. Of St Maelrubha from Ireland, who founded a church at Apor-Crossan in 673; of its importance – sheltered from Atlantic gales by the "wings" of Skye and by the curve of its own small bay – to sea travellers; of its fertile valley and wooded hillsides. Apart from a period under the Vikings in the ninth century and during clan feuds in the sixteenth, the church offered sanctuary within a six-mile radius, to "all fugitives from justice or persecution." There is even a tradition, which I come upon later, that the body-snatcher Hare, of Burke and Hare infamy (Burke was hanged in 1829), lived peacefully under a new name among the several thousand inhabitants of the peninsula, after the Edinburgh trial in which he gave evidence.

For over a thousand years, Applecross was a hub on the sea-road network connecting Ireland, the islands of the Hebrides, and the Scottish mainland. Isolation was a matter of opinion to people who made a living from the land and from the sea and who had commercial and political intercourse with the rest of the world. Even decades after anglicization effaced much Gaelic culture elsewhere in Scotland, the people of Applecross remained relatively unaffected and independent. But things changed: access by land remained limited and access by sea fell to a single ferry route and then to nothing. For the few left in the village, Applecross was a shadow of its former reality.

It had stopped snowing and the fog had lifted enough by the time we drove out over the pass that we could stop and take photographs. One of these became the cover of my 1980 book of poetry, *Sleeping with Lambs*. Each time I looked at it, I felt returned to a wildness that gave me heart, and to a fortune that allowed me to hold a thread of continuity for a moment, just before it broke.

By the time we returned to Applecross in a cold week in the early 1980s, every window displayed a "Holiday Let" sign and there was no evidence of life in the cottages at all. But change continued, and when we came back again in mid-September 1991 down a viable road along the coast from the north, you could stay in the village at a B&B, if you wanted, and the pub was full of English voices. El and I and our daughter pitched our tent in the only available space, high up and exposed on west-facing bluffs. We cooked supper on a small Gaz stove and watched the sun set dark and red in a yellow sky that turned smoke-coloured over Raasay and Skye. The wind came up after midnight. For the rest of the night, El and I took turns checking the tent moorings. By morning, although most of the ropes had held, wind and driving rain had flattened the flexible hoops of the tent frame so that there was scarcely room for us inside, and we, and everything else swathed in the collapsed tent fabric, were wet. My daughter and I handed out belongings to El, who ran back and forth in the gale, stowing them in the car.

I was last out of the tent, my weight scarcely enough to hold it to the ground. We wrestled the tent into a heap and hurled it into the boot.

Rain spilled from our clothing and hair: it was far too late to think of keeping any part of ourselves dry, and so we danced and laughed and shouted into the weather pelting at us from the Hebrides.

Down below, in the village, the inn was just opening: the holiday cottages were becalmed, their blinds drawn. No one would have noticed if we had boiled into the sky from our clifftop campsite, drafted by the wind along with other debris, into the clouds.

From Applecross, after we had dried out and breakfasted, we drove the improved Pass of the Cattle once more. Rain slammed the flanks of the car with heavy fists; the roadside shoulder sagged, flesh-soft and slippery. In the game I played with our daughter as El drove, she was the girl and I the younger brother. We had babies to care for – Jennie, the teddy, and Sarah, the crying doll – because our parents had died this morning and left us alone with the sleeping bags, a broken tent, the kettle, and a single-burner stove and three cups.

18.

I choose "Marbhrann do Fhear na Comraich" / "Dirge for the Lord of Applecross" to begin with, not only because of my associations to Applecross, but because it is the earliest work ascribed to Mary that includes what Watson calls "a certain date." I am looking, literally, for a starting point. I have not been a reader of Mary's poetry for long, and my reasons for being one are complicated. The work attracts me at the same time as its unfamiliar traditions push me away. However, I like a challenge and despite Sorley MacLean's (and others') reservations about the quality of Mary's work and her creative decisions, I am going to put one reading foot in front of the other and see what I find.

Not everyone believes this poem is by Mary or even that the Lord of Applecross, Roderick, who died 6 July 1646, the man the poem is meant to memorialize, is the Roderick found in it. Watson and others, though, have stood by the composition even while noting its anomalies. Watson implies that there could be reasons for apparent slips in factual accuracy within the verses and refers to a possible figurative use of language. This aligns with my impression that the poem possesses a consistent logic, but that its real nature escapes me. The poem affects me viscerally, but I don't see why it should.

Some of what follows I find immediately; other thoughts take me longer to pull together as I distil what I learn about Mary and her world and try to bridge the gap between what I expect from a poem and what I find here.

John MacInnes says that in its seventeenth-century vernacular, strophic ideation – a development that freed bardic poetry from the fixed metres and heightened language of classical verse – the compositional style that Mary practises, is panegyric (praise) poetry, and it is done, nearly exclusively, from within the outlook of the clan. A poetry of praise reaffirms the values of the community, and it employs "inherited rhetoric," so that what is praised supports the social construct of the system to which the poet belongs. Praise of great deeds, alliances, ancestry, land, personal beauty, and generosity are some structural elements of the societal system and therefore values to be affirmed by the poetry. We should expect to find these features present throughout the work of any seventeenth-century panegyric Gaelic bard, Mary included.

In the "Applecross" poem, Roderick is lauded for his kindness, nobility, cheerfulness, youth, strength, physical perfection, ancestry, honesty, thoughtful speech, fighting courage, leadership, and scholarship. Some of these qualities are mentioned more than once, war-fitness second only to youth.

The death of a leader provokes a crisis for those left behind, especially when it occurs at a critical moment for the clan. A bard's heroic elegy helps bring everyone together and carries them through the process of grieving while acknowledging the difficulties posed by the death's unfortunate timing.

It says, to the heart of individuals, that grief is worth bearing because it is witness to the significance of the people and their leader, and to their existence as a unity. Its solution is not grief counselling, but catharsis. This intensity is conveyed through metaphors. These are not newly minted figures as are found in contemporary poetry, but traditional metaphors (in the spirit of Homer's "wine-dark sea") that carry narrative and historical association, and in skilled hands weave multiple meanings and further associations from within the culture into a commentary on the significance of the loss now.

Mary (if she is the author) begins with death twice over in a figure of un-structuring – a dissolving of the shape of "how things are" that continues throughout the poem: "Since thou art dead and livest not, I am melted with grief …" I am not sure I can explain why, but this is exactly how grief feels: the words "dead" and "livest not" should mean the same, but they do not. "Dead" is a fact, it is an end; "livest not" is a removal from life ongoing and implies a continuing, active absence. Combined with the "melting" (*luighe/leaghadh*) – which Sharron Gunn explains is meant literally, as when the feeling is of having received news so devastating it seems "the bones no longer support a bereaved person" – it signals the precise emotional tone and colour of all that follows. I am told by Aonghas that a similar emotional assignment is given at the beginning of many Gaelic poems, and when I leaf through Watson's collection of Mary's poetry, I see it in the openings of each of them.

Now that we have the measure of grief, its stream accompanies each commonplace of praise and provides context for the great, traditional metaphors of loss the poem goes on to employ. Roderick is embodied as a "scion of the apple-tree of virtues," a metaphor invoked in the first verse with a word (*fiùran*) which suggests a young man who is a branch of a mighty tree, and which aligns him with Celtic mythic origins. Further on, he is a tree that "hath fallen headlong" and so removed its protection from those it has been sheltering: this, too, is a link to the mythic past, and evokes the Gaelic sacred wood and sacred trees. It is also, along with the "bee" verse that comes at the end of the poem, a kenning.

A kenning is more than the type of two-word phrase that describes an object through metaphors, as it is often explained to beginning students of Anglo-Saxon or Norse poetry. It is an accumulation of a way of seeing unique to a people, which is connected to a literal object or to layers of objects.

Each part of these metaphors is cultural, sacred, and natural, and is felt in the body. The absence of the great tree threatens the sacred wood and all it represents; those once shielded by the leader's physical and cultural presence are left exposed to elements that threaten their way of life and their literal survival. (It has affinities to the clear-cutting of first-growth forest where I live: its loss impacts a variety of species as well as the centrifugal force of indigenous belief, practice, and sustenance; and it negatively affects all life on the planet through climate change and other consequences of its absence.)

The power of the bee kenning is increased by its presence as climax and closure. In familiar dramatic story pattern, once the climax occurs, things will never be the same again. This song for the young Lord of Applecross is an emotional one of grief and finality. Before the bee kenning, we have already felt, as listeners, singers, or readers, the overall injury and exposure resulting from Roderick's death, and now, at the last moment of a chance for farewell as people gather around the body – a literal closure as well as the closure of the song – we find the community unified by its nature as "bees" but also confused and helpless in the face of the "plundering" that robs the hive of its nourishment and sweetness: the ability of the hive to survive is in doubt. "When the folk gathered, there they suffered a bitter / parting, as bees in a bank cry loudly when their honey / hath been taken from them; as they surrounded the / captain of the heroic host, mournful and wretched was / their burden."

Through the crying of the bees – a sound we instantly re-create for ourselves when we read of it – we are drawn into the expression of sorrow as the bees/people surround the dead "captain of the heroic host." If there is any comfort to be found in the verse, it lies with the awareness that the soul may take the form of a bee. An ordinary, cyclical continuance is at work, even in such distress; and it may relate to a regenerative immortality inherent in the natural world and its mythic origins.

Once, as a young poet, I was counselled by an older, celebrated poet, a socialist and modernist, not to conflate literal and material with spiritual and emblematic: it was all right to associate these, but they should remain distinct for the reader. This was good advice for modern verse, but only because much contemporary poetry has severed itself, or been forced to sever itself, from its broader roots. Another way to put the difference between poems like Mary's and contemporary work may be to think about trust. Mary's verse relies on it: the hearers, singers, and readers bring not only personal associations to their reception of the work, but a collective foundation of knowledge, pattern, commonality of land and language, and concept of origin as they engage. With her rhythms, narrative, and metaphors, the poet touches and summons the foundation at a hundred points. No wonder, for readers like me, the work can seem enclosed. Almost, it is like lacking the body and nerve ends with which to understand it.

John MacInnes has famously termed representation of the texture that poets such as Mary could rely on "a code." There is the emotional code, carried by metaphors and kennings, which I have attempted to describe. The code also exists as a stream of Gaelic nationalism or the concept of Gaelic nationhood. In the panegyric poem – in Mary's poetry – we gaze through Gaelic eyes and with an imperative of a Gaelic continuity. How this imperative played out historically became the account of clan warfare, each clan intent on an idea of a continuity that might be differently sourced and executed. These struggles were – if I read MacInnes correctly – even in the well-known clashes between Campbells and MacDonalds over choices of alliances (and land), at least in their beginnings, based on differing interpretations of where Gaelic nationalism or nationhood might lie. They were much less driven by outside politics than may be supposed. To understand Gaelic shifts in allegiances, engagement, and disengagement during the Wars of the Three Kingdoms, this should be remembered.

And so, as I try to approach the Applecross poem through Mary's eyes, I must also read with her clan's choices in mind and be grateful that when it came to the MacLeods of Berneray and Norman MacLeod, Mary's patron, their allegiances were remarkably consistent.

19.

As much as "Dirge for the Lord of Applecross" incorporates panegyric requirements and references, it is also a narrative pool. Praise brings with it not only a pattern of intensity, but a journey best understood as a gathering – a seeking outward, bringing back, and directing towards a centre – in much the way I saw collies move out and away from the shepherd into valleys and gullies of the hills above Glen Lochay to return sheep to the flock, and the flock to Daldravaig at the bottom of the glen. In this movement, the pattern of watercourses running from the hills and the animals' descent becomes one. Praise also happens in the moment: this stream is time, and it cannot be separated from the consequences of the death of the leader and its significance to the clan right there and then.

Roderick's father, Alexander, whom the poem calls "the loud-shouting hero of tough stern wounding swordblades," and who had made his name in clan wars with the Glengarry MacDonalds and the MacLeods of Lewis, outlived his son's death of July 1646 by four years. Alexander had acquired Applecross from his father around 1582 and passed it to Roderick at some time following Roderick's birth in 1592. Roderick, therefore, was about fifty-four years of age when he died from a malady the poem tells us left him "without strength to rise."

The song indicates that a death in battle would have suited Roderick better; and he would have acquitted himself well in combat if he had kept his strength – the construction of the verses finding a way to praise Roderick's prowess in war (a key heroic virtue) by placing it in an unfulfilled future. More comfortably, the poem lauds other traditional assets – Roderick's sureness with horses, his leadership of others, his scholarship and physical beauty. His "youth" is referred to in more than a quarter of the poem's stanzas, although if they are truly about this Roderick, as has been questioned, he was unlikely to have been, at time of death, the winsome, firm-fleshed youth the poem describes. However, youth in the sense of its strength and energy is what is expected of a leader, and we may be presumed to absorb the ambiguity of age along with the complex relationship between traditional metaphors and a narrative time that can have an allegorical presence in a panegyric composition. The battles Roderick has not lived to fight co-exist with the qualities of "youth" in a condition of a future that remains unmet (unopened) and where he will always be on the brink of its promise.

What, then, keeping in mind the potential for a stream of Gaelic nationalism, was the immediate context of Roderick's death and why might its timing have left his clan particularly bereft? What was that immediate future?

20.

The war of Charles I, backed by English and Scottish Royalists against English Parliamentarians and Scottish Covenanters, had reached a critical point following the significant defeat at Philiphaugh near Selkirk (September 1645) of Charles's Scottish forces led by James Graham, 1st Marquis of Montrose. In its aftermath, Montrose began to gather a new army and make fresh alliances with northern clans. Through the spring of 1646 he believed he would be able to build a force sufficient to secure victory for Charles, despite his being repeatedly frustrated in his strategy by vague and unfulfilled promises from allies such as his former enemy, George Gordon, Earl of Huntly, who supported the King's cause but was less than eager to help Montrose, himself.

The Mackenzies, led by George Mackenzie, 2nd Earl of Seaforth (related to Alexander, Roderick's father, through their fathers who were brothers), prevaricated. In 1645, the earl had fought with the Covenanting army against Montrose at the Battle of Auldearn (which Montrose won with the help of other clans including the MacDonalds). But in April of 1646, Seaforth publically joined Montrose's side at the siege of Inverness. Hoping to build on this, Montrose drew up a Board of Confederation with Seaforth and other northern chiefs. The confederation did not hold, and Seaforth withdrew and pursued his own interests. Montrose still believed he had a viable plan, but before he could act on it, Charles, writing at the end of May 1646, ordered Montrose to disband his forces. The King had decided to throw in his lot with the Scottish Covenanting army, believing he could make common cause with them against his English enemies through a compromise of religious aims. The gamble failed and the Covenanters imprisoned the King.

We do not know exactly when the poem for Roderick was written, only that it was after Roderick's death on 6 July 1646. On 7 July, the terms of Charles's surrender were published at Dundee. On 16 July, Charles wrote to Montrose telling him he could no longer offer him support of any kind, effectively removing all possibility of action on his behalf. In September, Montrose evaded the Covenanting searchers and escaped by sea to Bergen, Norway.

In exile, Montrose and other Royalists made plans to return Charles I to the throne, but just a few years later, in 1649, the English Parliamentarians beheaded the King. At this point, Seaforth permanently joined in attempts to make Charles II, the dead King's son, the new King. At the time of Roderick's death, this final Mackenzie adjustment lay at the end of a twisting path; but in the summer of 1646 all possibilities were in play and Seaforth and the Mackenzies were crucial to immediate Royalist hopes. It is one of the many strangenesses of these conflicts that the Mackenzies, who were fundamentally Royalists, with a Royalist past, frequently fought on the Covenanting side.

If, before his death, Roderick was looked forward to as a leader of hosts in battle, then the battles were those of these ongoing Wars of the Three Kingdoms. If Mary were the poem's author, then the only side he could be on, given the sentiments in the poem and the beliefs of Mary and her patron, was Royalist. One verse in the poem has caused particular trouble for those trying to settle the question of the poem's subject and attribution. In it, the poet's grief is pointed at an irony: instead of "thy company" gathered in Roderick's chamber "in readiness for the joy of thy wedding, / with the daughter of Clan Donald's earl seeking after / thee, as were due," the company has assembled to view Roderick "bestowed in the satin shroud beneath thy shirt," i.e., at his wake. The problem is that the fifty-four-year-old Roderick was already married. His wife was Fionnghal, daughter of Murdock Mackenzie of Redcastle. How could there be an anticipated wedding with a "daughter of Clan Donald's earl?"

Watson suggests the marriage may be figurative. He does not explain, but a marriage is an alliance, and naming of allies is to be expected in this type of poem. For those in the know, the poem could be alerting its hearers to a realignment of allegiances. It is also possible that alterations in the text have occurred over time, although the insertion of an impossible marriage would be such a flaw that one would expect those who transmitted the song to have corrected it. A further possibility lies within Gaelic secular marriage customs, which lasted into the seventeenth century, long after these were successfully suppressed by the church elsewhere. Serial marriages were a means of forging important

connections between families, but as circumstances changed, old part-
ners might be put aside in favour of new ones bringing fresh political,
social, or other advantages with them.

Norman of Berneray's aunt Margaret, sister to his father Sir Rory
MacLeod of Dunvegan, the 15th chief on whose plank floors Mary Mac-
Leod danced as a girl, was one of Ranald MacDonald of Benbecula's
wives. One account says that by the time of his death in 1636 he had
fathered ten sons with five wives, three of whom he had put away.
Margaret died while still married to Ranald. Whatever was thought by
the Berneray MacLeods about Ranald and his multiple relationships,
the purpose of serial marriage was familiar to them. A reference to one
would not have seemed out of order within the "Dirge for the Lord of
Applecross" poem.

The only title of earl connected with clan Donald that I find at first
is the earl of Ross. Its final clan Donald holder was John of Islay (John
MacDonald), last Lord of the Isles. He forfeited the title in 1476, from
where it passed to the Stuart line. The ultimate holder of that title was
Charles Stuart, who was given the title in 1600. He held it until he became king in 1625, after which the title reverted to the Crown. It was
Charles I's Royalist cause that was in peril in 1646. The marriage verse
in "Dirge for the Lord of Applecross" might be code – or more than
that – for a Royalist/Macdonald "marriage" that would support Macdonald claims. Tellingly, in the spring of 1646, a few months before
Roderick's death, Royalists under Alasdair MacColla, acting at the in-
stigation of the Irish earl of Antrim whose objective was to recover
clan Donald South land from the pro-government clan Campbell, defeated Campbell forces at the Battle of Lagganmore. This more recent
news, and the possibilities it opened, may also be a reference within
the projected "wedding" between Roderick and "the daughter of Clan
Donald's earl."

At the least, the poem's texture and content add evidentiary weight
to the hearer's experience of grief, and record its impact for posterity.

Another marriage, a real one, has a part to play in this poem. This is
the marriage between Norman of Berneray, Mary MacLeod's patron,
and his wife Margaret. She was a Mackenzie, related through her grand-

father, Kenneth, first Lord of Kintail, to Roderick. Roderick's grandfather was Kenneth's brother, Colin. Roderick's father, Alexander, born out of wedlock, was not what we could call Margaret's father's full cousin: but he was openly acknowledged, honoured for his fighting abilities, and given a great deal of property (including Applecross) by his father. It is more than likely that Roderick and Margaret were in contact.

In 1646, the year Roderick died, Margaret gave birth to a son, John (Iain), to whom Mary was close throughout her life. Nothing more is known of Margaret after John's (Iain's) birth, including when she died, or if the poem intended any connection between these events. Norman eventually remarried, some sources citing him as a widower until 1666.

Watson has noticed another family connection. This was between Roderick's mother and William Dubh MacLeod of Harris and Dunvegan, to whom Norman MacLeod was related. Although William had lived two hundred years before the poem was written, his inclusion in the ancestry of both families helps strengthen the appropriateness of a MacLeod interest in Roderick's death. Taken together with the closer relationship between Roderick and Norman's wife, Margaret, it makes a case for Norman's poet, Mary, to have been the author of this work as tradition has said she was. It would make sense, too, of the poet's expression of feeling.

"The Dirge" is said to be an outlier, too early for Mary to be its author given the probable dates of her other surviving work. Mary is thought to have begun composing "later" in life, well into middle age. When Roderick died, she was a young woman about thirty years old. However, given the political upheaval and dangers to the MacLeod Royalists between the execution of King Charles I in 1649 and the Restoration of the monarchy in 1660, it should not be surprising if Mary's activities in this period – if she were privately composing – were not publicized. The MacLeods were anathema to Cromwell's commonwealth. Norman and his brother, Roderick of Talisker, led the clan in support of King Charles II at the battle of Worcester in 1651. The MacLeods were shattered, and Norman was imprisoned. After his escape from the Tower of London, he spent years travelling back and forth between the Hebrides and the continent, raising money and troops, and taking part in skirmishes.

Cromwell is said to have sent a ship to watch for Norman in case he returned from France, and to have had troops encamped upon "the mountain overlooking the house." When the announcement of the Restoration was made in early 1660, Norman was in Denmark on a mission for Charles II.

Before leaving the Applecross poem, I want to mention a verse that has stayed with me as I have tried to work through the poem's puzzles.

O it is that I am sad and sorrowful, the tinge of weeping
on my cheek! Sore is the bitter pang that I have
suffered; comely rider of swift steeds, prime leader
over a host, alas that thou hast forsaken me in the time
of my need!

A conventional reading would take this as a professional stance of grief, but I hear the poet speaking. She has felt the bitter pang; she has been forsaken, and she is in need. She is speaking to and from her times to anyone who has been bereft.

21.

I climb on a wooden kitchen chair and put my face to the window. The glass is cold against my nose. At first, I see only black, but as I continue to look, the outlines of the fruit trees become visible against the sky. My grandmother is indoors with me. She comes and goes, to and from the woodbox, adjusting the fire in the stove, and then she puts water on to boil.

My parents and grandfather are outside. While I watch for them, the apple, cherry, and plum trees reveal grey lace drapery and spiders' webs. A cool low sunlight pearls through these veils from a bleaching sky. Even the grass is without colour. A world in a threadbare dressing gown in early spring.

I have been told that tent caterpillars eat the trees' leaves. I know that caterpillars make cocoons, which is what is in the trees, and what is in the glass jar I have been keeping on the kitchen windowsill; but what I see through the window is a muzzy, silken fabric wrapped around the trees' limbs, and it is beautiful. I hold my breath in case a wind comes and blows it away.

My grandmother sits across from me with a cup of milky tea. We wait. The house is quiet. Through the window, we watch my grand-father and father, and after them, my mother, appear from around the corner of the house. The men carry kettles of smoke. They stand at the bottom of the trees and swing them back and forth, adding cut branches to the coals while my mother flaps a burlap sack to waft the smoke up and over and between the branches. In a little while, the air is so thick with smoke that the trees have vanished again. Then my parents and grandfather are gone, too – to another part of the orchard, my grandmother tells me.

She clears away her cup and saucer and the teapot and wipes down the table. Her long grey hair is plaited and wrapped into a bun. She ad-justs a hairpin. She wears her habitual print dress with lisle stockings, and with slippers indoors, and black shoes and hat and gloves and handbag with a black or navy coat when we walk to the store or take the bus downtown.

I look at my jar: nothing moves in there. I have waited such a long time for the caterpillars to emerge changed.

Outside, sunlight yellows the stricken trees and in the dissipating smoke; it soils rather than brightens the cocoon-heaped branches.

I go to the cellar and fetch a bowl of last year's apples from one of the bins. My grandmother peels and slices and I make bracelets and necklets with the peel. I lick a finger and draw it through a scatter of cinnamon and sugar on the counter. She measures flour and lard into a bowl. When the pastry is rolled out and ready, I prick the top shell with a fork.

I don't remember the others coming in or noticing the trees again or wondering what happened to their lacery of cocoons. When I thought to look for my jar, it was gone. A bonfire flared in the yard, and everything was burning.

22.

El and I had left Tighnacraig in 1978, before we were ready. We wanted to stay and establish a permanent home in this place where we felt we belonged. After we went, I charted my way in poetry with the intensity of a bereavement. In it were the hills, the lambs, the Iron Age sites, even the dog we took back with us to a suburbia in which she had to be kept indoors much of the time. Once, I came home from a day of work to find she had taken the treasures on my desk – the stones, bones, pieces of wood and pottery, and books that I had brought with me from Glen Lochay. They lay together, well-chewed, in a heap on the floor over which she stood guard.

Two separate periods of my life – the first when I was a young woman finding her way in writing and publishing with no notion of limits, and this late stage where I am the product of how I have spent the time since – have seamed together in this walk on Harris and in the figure of Mary MacLeod. A friend observes that it sounds as if I had slipped into a state of fugue – which would explain the amnesia I experienced, although nothing like it had happened to me before. If it is "fugue" – a dissociative disorder – why now, like this? Or, perhaps, as another friend, a poet, put it more simply, "You've been grabbed by the throat by a seventeenth-century bard!" Either way, or in some other that hasn't yet occurred to me, my hope of understanding will be through poetry.

Mary – Màiri – belongs to the Gaelic world: I should be talking to Gaelic poets. And so, I make plans to return to Scotland to do so.

IV

O'erswept by a Deluge

Of eight stones
the largest is for weeping,
the heaviest, the heart,
a wearystone, the back,

two socket stones
for grinding corn.

Of three more,
the head stone
binds an oath,
the footstone
finds cattle,

and the last
is the teaching stone,

the voice
of the ash tree,
the winter flood-spate.

Its keeper is *deòradh*,
the exile, the wanderer.

She sleeps on river wrack,
she swears a blind oath.
She sings from a psalter

of eight hard stones
in the tones
of a warm west wind.

– Sleat, Isle of Skye

23.

In Edinburgh, I visit the National Library, read through more of Mary's
critics, spend time in the Map Library with the geology and geography
of the Hebrides as it was recorded in earlier centuries, and then arrange
to meet Aonghas MacNeacail and his wife, the actress and writer Gerda
Stevenson, for lunch. The black beard and head of bushy black hair that
gave Aonghas his nickname (Aonghas Dubh – Black Aonghas) have
turned white since we last met, but he is the same: serious and approachable, generous, and lighthearted and knowledgeable. We have
had enough correspondence ahead of time that once we have found a
table in Henderson's Salad Bar (where the procedures – a general mil-
ling about to select, order, and pay for food – have always mystified me)
away from the crowds, I don't need to explain further about what I
would like to know, or the difficulties involved in an exploration of
Màiri nighean Alasdair Ruaidh (Mary MacLeod).

Aonghas's view is that Mary was exiled because her verses were critical of the MacLeod chief at Dunvegan. Exactly when this was, and
which chief was involved, is unresolved. He reminds me that "Mary was
born less than a decade after the passing of the Statutes of Iona [1609]
which, among other provisions, required that Highland chiefs sent their
heirs to Lowland, Protestant, English-speaking schools. Among other
effects of the policy was the total elimination of the professional Gaelic
bard." The purpose of the Statutes was to break the linguistic, cultural,
and religious connections between the chiefs and their people, a process
that will be familiar to any colonized indigenous population. In con-
sequence, poets with standing but without formal professional training,
"court-poets" who incorporated the vernacular into their verses and
were not limited to the strict syllabic structures of professionally trained
bàrds, carried out important poetic functions for those clans whose

chiefs still wanted to preserve at least some Gaelic traditions. Over time, though, as the English-educated heirs succeeded to their responsibilities as heads of clans, they felt their authority over the clan and their status with the colonizing government undermined by those who still spoke the language and advocated Gaelic values. Mary, one of these vernacular bards, was very unusual, Aonghas says. "She belonged to the aristocracy of the clan but [because she was a woman] she had no [recorded] formal education. She must have had a tutor because of her awareness of the rhythms, the forms of poetry, the sophistication of language."

The poem that got Mary into trouble and resulted in her exile, according to Aonghas, was "An Talla am bu ghnàth le MacLeòid" / "MacLeod's Wonted Hall," generally dated to 1661 or later because in it, Norman, Mary's patron, is called "Sir" Norman. (In 1661, Charles II had knighted Norman as reward for his services towards the restoration of the monarchy.) It is a wrenching, moving poem, one of her best-known, formed as a lament for Norman although when she composed it, Norman was alive. Watson passes on the tale that the song was written at Norman's request when he was suffering an illness, so he could hear what Mary would make for him if he were to die. The song describes how things were in the hall – presumably Norman's mansion house on Berneray – when Norman was present, and then how things feel without him there. In essence, the song explains, all that gave life its vividness and pleasure has gone with him, leaving Mary feeling "strange and forlorn to be anigh it."

I believe that the depth in the poem comes not so much from Mary imagining Norman's future loss, but from the grief and uncertainty already suffered during the near-decade of Norman's absences from Berneray in the Royalist cause. Cromwell's ships patrolled the seas on the lookout for him; his activities had to be carried out in secret. Berneray, to all effect, was under siege, the hall, its activities, and those people in and around it, or strongly associated with it, silenced.

Aonghas views the poem through a different lens. The song laments the changes that have taken place "in the hall / where MacLeod [the chief] was wont to be." Mary's usage of the title "MacLeod," given only to the overall chief of the MacLeods who lived at Dunvegan, is not a mistaken or sly or text-corrupted reference to Sir Norman of Berneray as some have suggested, but a deliberate assignment of blame. The alterations and losses that have occurred, which Aonghas says refer to the destruction of traditional practices, are equivalent to the MacLeod chief's dwelling itself, where people used to gather for music and wine and tale-telling, having been "o'erswept" by a "deluge."

By contrast, Mary goes on in the poem to celebrate the Gaelic virtues embodied in the person and the hospitality and practices of her patron, Sir Norman MacLeod of Berneray. Figuratively, the loss is Gaelic culture, and the poem is a critique of the overall chief of the MacLeods' facilitation of its destruction. The poem "is beautifully constrained, uses no abusive language, but it says a great deal between the lines." Worryingly for the chief, too, was that Mary's views were expressed in songs which were popular: they quickly went round the islands; once on their way in the mouths of the people, there was no stopping them. Not only was the chief at fault in the song and exposed to general censure, but his relative of lesser status, Sir Norman, was held up as an exemplar.

As soon as we have finished eating, we push aside the plates, I open my book of Mary's poetry, and soon, with the clatter of the restaurant in the background, and the greetings of Gerda's theatre friends and El's Henderson's pals – old family and school friends – I am listening to Aonghas read in Gaelic and then talk through translations of some of the poems, getting rid of their archaic language, so that their power in English is vividly present. People stop to listen, caught for a few moments by the resonances of the Gaelic in Aonghas's recitative voice, and then by our discussion. The feeling around the impromptu reading is welcoming; something has come full circle.

Just before we part, I ask Aonghas if he knows anything more about the story of Mary's last request than what he has already told me – that the "face-down" burial she is said to have asked for was a Norse practice performed on witches. He shakes his head: "No."

No one I have asked has been able to say more than that this story is "what is said." Close to 4,000 accused witches were put on trial in Scotland between the sixteenth and eighteenth centuries, four to five times the number of cases in nearby European countries. Up to two-thirds of them were executed. What surely must have been understood in all its terrifying implications in Mary's time has become a dim and troubling echo.

Back at Sam and Carolyn's house where we are staying, I turn Aonghas's words over in my mind and consider how Mary's poem, seen in their light, would have been received. The poet describes the hall where the chief should be and finds it "without shelter or guard." All that had once made it "blithe and festive" – full of "young men and maidens" and "where the clangour of the drinking-horns was loud" – has been consigned to a past preserved only in the poet's memory. In the figurative absence of the chief, everything that the hall represented has been effaced. It is as clear a picture as possible of a chief's negligence.

The poet turns to recollection of how things were when Sir Norman traversed "the peaked hills" with his gun, or aimed at the target with "thy tough, ruddy bow of good hue," wearing a headdress, "a crest from the wings of the eagle," and later, at home, was available to all who needed him while the harper played, and "the chessmen would rattle," and the epic "of the Fiann, and of the white-flanked antlered band," was chronicled. Mary's verbal re-creation of MacLeod's "Wonted Hall" as it was becomes the solution to her state of "lacking melody" and the aching dislocation and alienation that have prompted the verses. The poem's path returns her – literally, with mention of the epic tale of the Fiann – to the voices of her bardic home. The hero who guides the way is Sir Norman.

I am beginning to think that Aonghas is right. In this poem, Mary stepped over a line.

But when? Watson's story of Norman's illness could push the poem's composition from 1661 (Norman's knighthood) closer to his death in 1705 at age ninety-one if the illness were a lingering or last one. Or it could have been an illness at any time. We do not know; but *when* matters to the unravelling of Mary's story. I return to the poem's emotional foundations, laid down in its beginning verses, to explore their initial metaphor. Loss and change are experienced as a "deluge."

Once known as "The Deluge," the Old Testament story of Noah and the Flood is embedded in Gaelic origin stories. It could be that Mary wanted a world-punishing Flood for resonance, and yet her metaphor leans on feelings of personal misfortune, which seem to be literal as well as analogous to cultural loss. What else could be in the mix?

There are three MacLeod halls eligible to be the one Mary meant as "where MacLeod [the chief] was wont to be." These were at Dunvegan on Skye, on Berneray, and on the island of Pabbay. Dunvegan Castle is built on elevated rock some fifty feet (15 m) above the sea. It is factually unlikely ever to have been "o'erswept"; but the islands of Berneray and Pabbay are low-lying: their shorelines have frequently been altered by storms. In the great Hebridean sandstorm of 1697, they were profoundly affected.

Pabbay was separated from Berneray to the south by a channel so narrow that "a wife could throw her washboard across the channel between them," but during the storm, low-lying land on either side of the original channel was "swept away." The widened and dangerously sandbarred channel is now more than three kilometres wide. MacLeod's Pabbay Castle, once with good harbour access, became stranded inland over time as a result of sea and sandstorms, but the catastrophic scale of the 1697 event brought about its final abandonment.

If the 1697 sandstorm may be associated to Mary's metaphor, it would bring the poem into the chieftainship of Roderick (Ruairidh Òg), who was chief from 1693 to 1699. According to Aonghas, this Roderick was notorious for his rejection of Gaelic customs and values and for his strong desire to be as English as possible. Nicolson reports that "[t]he bards have nothing to record in praise of this chief. To them he was *crìonach gun duilleach* ('a barren tree without fruit or foliage.') The traditions of his race and its culture were alike insipid and uninspiring to him, for his artificial mind assiduously aped the manners of the South."

It would be no joke if Mary had offended him.

24.

The Red River meanders over an enormous, flat, ancient lakebed and when there is heavy rain and snowmelt, the river rises, and the ancient lake begins to refill. This is a natural and predictable phenomenon, but knowing so brought no comfort to those whose houses were flooded that spring, just as it brought none to my parents. In 1950, when eight of the city of Winnipeg's dikes failed and the region returned to its nature, our house on the banks of the Seine River, a tributary of the Red River, filled with water. When the waters retreated, the first floor was covered in mud, a replication of the process that began with the laying down of sediment when the glacier that created the ancient lakebed and lake first began to withdraw. I have a photograph of the house, taken from the sandbags that failed to protect it, showing the reflections of trees in the water, and the storage shed on slightly higher ground in which my mother had sheltered her most precious belongings. The shed was flooded, too, and when my father returned to start the clean-up, he had to burn all that remained to my mother of her mother – a chest of documents, photographs, keepsakes – along with my mother's wedding dress. My mother was disconsolate: she had nothing to pass on of the world and people who had made her.

I was just a year old, but I remember – it does not feel as if I was told this – standing on the kitchen table watching out the window as our neighbours paddled a canoe past the back steps; and I remember my parents roping the refrigerator to the first-floor landing. In the last of these remembrances, I am looking from my mother's lap through a dark windshield as we embark on the dangerous crossing of the last bridge open over the Red River. The truck's headlights shine on water, silky surging water, and nothing else. Of all that followed, including our evacuation by train west to Vancouver Island to stay with my grandparents, I have no recollection. I am told that not long afterwards, my grandparents came to Winnipeg and helped my parents build their own house – the flooded one was rented – and that my grandmother looked after me most days while my parents and grandfather (and my mother's father, too) were building. I did not know I had already met my grandparents when we moved west three years later to live with them. Only the flood, in a few images vivid with strangeness, stuck.

The immense stretch of water, which floated the shacks and sheds and chicken and pig pens of the riverbank yards, held echoes of my familiar world yet was so altered from what I knew that I did not feel like myself: all sense of what small identity I had disappeared in the transformation. When I gazed into the narrow streams of light on water from the truck, I was gazing at a lake first formed more than ten thousand years ago. It isn't surprising that the flood with its images and symbols and connections has appeared and reappeared in my writing from my first pamphlet, *The Liberation of Newfoundland* (1973), to the present. This isn't to compare Mary's possible use of a great sandstorm as "the deluge" to anything of mine, but to point out that metaphors are constructed from the sticks and blood and bone of a poet's mind; they are organic, made of materials to hand, and Mary's use of this metaphor may have incorporated a striking contemporary event. She placed herself in the poem "anigh" or "coming near" the o'erswept dwelling, a witness to a disaster. Those who held the literal event in memory would recognize the scale of the figurative catastrophe she intended to convey.

V

A Picturesque Figure

Dressed in tartan tonnag fastened with silver brooch, and carrying
a silver-headed cane and snuff-horn, she was a picturesque figure to whom
it was natural to break with some of the older metrical conventions.

– George Henderson

25.

I have walked the path to Ken Latta's croft near the point of Sleat, on
Skye, many times since the first midnight, moonless trek with El in 1977.
We'd arrived on the last ferry to Armadale from Mallaig, viewed a piece
of property overlooking the Sound of Sleat that El's mother and stepfather intended to buy, and then gone into the pub at the Ardvasar
Hotel. Before I met them that night, I'd heard stories of Calum "the
bus" keeping tourist cars in their place on (or off) the single-track road,
and of Seòras "the post" who delivered mail down the miles-long footpath to Ken's croft several times a week. Lord MacDonald worked behind the bar that night. El, a frequent visitor and a friend of Ken's, was
liked. When we came in, the conversation switched from Gaelic to English to include us.

After leaving the pub, we parked at the Aird layby and started out in
the dark to walk to Ken's. We had no flashlight. I saw only dim shapes of
low hills and then the shocking bulk of cows. A few feet from the threading track, a bull supervised us from the bank above. The trail ran along

steep sides of turf, then dropped into hollows where we sloshed through
mud, our squishy footsteps intruding on a silence otherwise emphasized
by the breathing of cattle, and by water riddling through peat. At one
point, I sat down and refused to go on, convinced we were lost and there
was no cottage, and that I might as well sleep on the ground. When we
finally arrived at Ken's, El found the key and opened the door while I
watched lines of white-water break onto the rocks near the pier. I slept
on a bench in the kitchen, and El on the porch; and in the morning Ken
turned up with tea and eggs and bread. Since the breakdown of his small
boat, *Wallower*, he had carried all his groceries in on his back.

When the tide allowed, we climbed an islet patrolled by seabirds pro-
tecting their nests. The islands of Eigg and Rum gently notched the distance, watery and yellow and pink, so transparent and dream-formed
that if I hadn't been told what they were, I'd have thought I was making
them up. Sleat was a speaking landscape – this is obvious to any who
go there – with much to say through its history of settlement and absence, trauma, and beauty, but it was different from Glen Lochay where
I had made a home. Both localities shared with the forested landscape
and pristine shores of Vancouver Island, where I had spent my childhood, a sense of their being an active space in which an ancient world
was on watch, where the relationship between humans and the rest of
the living world still thrived; and, on the other hand, where if its power
were not respected, it could be further broken.

On another visit to Ken, we slept in a big open room at the Armadale
Yacht Club where Ken was the Commodore. We were on hand for the
Tobermory yacht race prizegiving. Lady and Lord MacDonald – he
more remote than when he had been behind the bar – arrived to present
the trophy. Later, while El visited with Ken, I drove to Breakish to meet
the publisher J.C.R. (Jim) Green, of Aquila Press. I'd published poems
in the magazine *Prospice*, which he co-edited. Jim played recordings of
Alan Stivell and Boys of the Lough and other contemporary Scottish
musicians I had not heard before. We planned a volume of my selected
poetry, to be edited by Martin Booth whom I knew through publishing
in his Sceptre Press chapbooks. Martin completed the manuscript, but
by then Jim was ill, and far too quickly, he died. Martin is dead now,

too, as is Ken, and there are times when I revisit Skye that it can feel, if I allow it – so rarely are there references to those I once knew – that I, too, am a ghost.

Over and over, on our return trips, El and I walked the track, gradually widened to accommodate local vehicles, towards Ken's cottage through the grey, silver, fizzy and exhilarating light of Sleat. A library of voices was stored in its empty spaces and ruins, a background to our own conversations, a sense I had tried to convey in poems that were three-quarters of the way towards song. This time, though, I am not in Sleat to revisit old haunts, but to meet one of several Gaelic poets to whom I have introductions from Aonghas MacNeacail.

26.

In the mirror of the B&B in Ardvasar where I sit, back to the window, at the dresser I am using as a desk, and sort out notes for my meeting with the writer Angus Peter Campbell (Aonghas Phàdraig Caimbeul), clouds pillow in grey and white bands. Behind them, the mountains of the mainland bulk dark blue; and between that shore and the island runs the textured hide of the sea.

The mirror reflects, as well, the bright flowers of the neighbourhood gardens bordering lanes and new houses, many of them owned by English retirees like those who run the B&B. Since I first came here in the 1970s, the overall number of Gaelic speakers in Scotland has dropped by about thirty thousand. The "deluge" continues its sweeping-away work even now.

I walk the few blocks to the small red corrugated-roofed former post office which Aonghas Phàdraig and his wife use as a studio. I am a few minutes early and so I wait beside a telephone box from which I can see the main road. I am not at all certain what to expect from the conversation. By email the writer has said, "I know nothing about Màiri nighean Alasdair Ruaidh" and "I know even less, generally, about Gaelic poetry," but he is willing to meet, and as a major Gaelic author, poet, and broadcaster living in what was part of Mary's landscape on Skye, he will – if he wishes – be able to help me understand more about the context within which Mary's work and life should be seen.

I certainly need help, and if not here, on Skye, I do not know where I shall find it. In Edinburgh and Glasgow, I have asked mainstream Central Scotland poets I know if they are familiar with Mary MacLeod. None have heard of her; but they haven't heard of any Gaelic writers, ancient or modern, except for the late Sorley MacLean and Aonghas MacNeacail. It is not that they wouldn't be interested, but ... nothing has come their way, and will I tell them if I turn up anything interesting? An author I worked with at a writing centre told me he didn't know why Gaelic-language signs and Gaelic classes were supported by the Scottish government; both he, and a teacher of classics at one of Edinburgh's "best" schools, told me Gaelic was never spoken outside a tiny part of the country, it wasn't relevant, and it had never produced any significant literature; although, as I know, up until about 1400, Gaelic was the language spoken in Scotland, including Strathclyde and the Lothians where these conversations took place. In fact, Gaelic was the original tongue of the Kingdom of the Scots and was spoken by half the population of Scotland at the time of the 1603 Union of the Crowns.

I have reached this point in my thoughts when Aonghas Phàdraig drives up in an older car, jumps out and says apologetically, "Something fell off the bottom and I had to take it to the garage – they immediately put it on the hoist. They'd fixed it earlier, but at the first bump, it fell off." Years of having driven cars for which I'd paid five hundred dollars or less, and which were always breaking down, make me empathetic. One of these vehicles, a 1964 Chevy Biscayne, I traded back and forth with a friend depending on which one of us was in and which one of us was out of the country. It was stolen when I was teaching in Vancouver but conveniently turned up a year later, just after I returned from living in Scotland. When my friend and I put the car to rest at last, it was only because of mice nesting in the upholstery and running along the dash once the engine warmed up the interior.

As he goes to unlock the studio door, Aonghas Phàdraig, who is middle-aged, slim, and full of nervous energy, calls out Gaelic greetings to passers-by. Once we are inside, he sits me down amidst his wife's canvases, then steps into an alcove to put the kettle on for coffee. "What is your story?" he asks me from around the corner where I can't see him. "Who are you, what are you doing, what is your connection to all this?"

I tell him about my history in Scotland and coming across Mary MacLeod's work, and then say that when I woke up this morning and was trying to decide what I would talk to him about, I found myself thinking about marginalization: how a poet's achievements can be pushed aside for spurious reasons. Mary's ambition, "eccentric" appearance, and liking for whisky and snuff are often mentioned when assigning her to the fringes. "I don't think Mary MacLeod has received the attention she deserves, she has been undeservedly dismissed," I say. "Once you get past the surface of her as a 'court' poet, there is a great deal of feeling in the poems, much emotion and engagement with contemporary life. I don't understand the neglect."

"I agree," Aonghas Phàdraig says unexpectedly. Given his reluctance to meet, I had been prepared for a brisk dismissal. He pops into view, hands me a cup, and sits down opposite. "I have been guilty of that. I thought of her just as a figure in textbooks, but when I got out the poems and re-read them and paid attention, I was astonished. They are so deep, and deeply full of the culture." He has put his finger on it. She has been in plain sight, but little "seen."

Neglect of Gaelic culture isn't only consignable to the past, he tells me. Norman Campbell (Tormod Caimbeul), a poet born in 1942, wrote a great novel in the 1970s, one not as great in the 1990s, and has more recently written what Aonghas Phàdraig believes may be the greatest work in Gaelic ever. "It is Joycean stream of consciousness, completely rich in language; coming from a pre-television time and steeped in the Bible and songs, and it is full of the *joie de vivre* of language.

"These great sections in the old poems and stories – a long piece about a sword, for example," he continues, "they are digressions from the narrative, but completely riveting and what you remember when you think of the epics. These places where the language contains the *joie de vivre* are the essential places, not the narrative as we tend to think now, but those places where the rhythm of the voices and the stories and the waves of meaning run deep. Mary MacLeod's poems are full of this *joie de vivre* – her rhythms, the sounds, the cadences, the life in them …" and he reads aloud from the first poem in Watson's *Gaelic Songs*, "Pòsadh MhicLeoid" / "The Wedding of MacLeod." He knows its attribution to Mary is disputed but is not concerned: the poem shows the kind of language he means. "It places, it says, 'this is who you are, and this is who you belong to, you are one of the great, look at all the people who went there, everybody was there, and you were there' – and there's a sting, obviously to come, which comes quickly.

"It was music to my ears to hear you speak of marginalization," Aonghas Phàdraig says a little later, after we have finished looking at Mary's poem "Do Mhac Dhomhnaill" / "To MacDonald," written for Sir Donald MacDonald of Sleat – the part of Skye where we are, and which I know best.

"But where did all this come from in Mary?" I ask, meaning her remarkably developed skill and talent and learning. The reality of what she wrote – and which we have been discussing as Aonghas Phàdraig translates – is impossible to harmonize with the oft-accepted view of her as an amateur, a kind of female poetry-jackdaw.

His eyes – which often glance away when speaking, in a manner I'm told I do myself – fix on mine. "Let me tell you a story," he says. "I was at an event in Edinburgh with [a certain lauded Central Scotland poet] there. She listens to me read and then asks me, 'Where did you come from?' As if I had sprung from nowhere. I said nothing for a moment and then I said, 'I have been there all along.'"

Then he tells of a recent book about Flora MacDonald (1722–1790), the Jacobite heroine famous for the help she gave to Bonnie Prince Charlie. Flora was known to be well-educated, but the book says she couldn't have been educated at the island of Benbecula as it is known she was by people in the Hebrides, because there was *nothing there*; and so, she must have gone to Edinburgh.

"This is pernicious thinking," he says, and instances, also, the Lewis chessmen, now finally returned (at least in part) to the island of Lewis from Edinburgh. (Some of the chessmen remain in museums in London and Edinburgh.) "The latest thinking says that they may not have been made by the Norse after all, but possibly by the Isle of Man – it is all just theory: it seems impossible for them to admit that they were made on Lewis, which was part of the same Bishopric at the time.

"Dunvegan, where Mary likely went when she was twelve or thirteen, would have been like a university: that's where she would have learned. And she was respected for it." Mary's male relatives, such as Norman of Berneray, were sent to Glasgow University (founded 1451, the fourth oldest university in the "English"-speaking world). "That education wasn't available to her, as a woman, but she was far from uneducated."

At the court of MacLeod of Dunvegan there was poetry, tale-telling, harp and pipe playing; dancing, feasts, chess, draughts, cards, and wine-drinking; and outdoor sports and hunting with weaponry – bows and swords and guns – made in the armoury. Boat-building and seamanship were a large part of this world, too, vital for the making (and breaking) of political and trading alliances. Visitors came to Dunvegan from France and Ireland and England, as well as from the Isle of Man and all over Scotland, bringing news and conversation with them. And there were hereditary physicians with knowledge of botany and medicinal herbs, as well as hereditary trained bards; and there were colleges of music. The last MacLeod chief to live there in full Gaelic style "with bards, pipers and genealogists" was Iain Breac, who succeeded in 1665 and died in 1693, which would be about fourteen years before Mary died. This is not the picture of the Gaelic world generally held by outsiders.

"The pibroch, for which the MacCrimmon pipers [whom Mary refers to in her poems] were famous," Aonghas Phàdraig continues, "developed in a period of about one hundred years, in the same time as Mary. It is said that when someone went to see one of them, and he was away, his wife played the pibroch the visitor wanted to hear; and it is said that all three wives of the [three] MacCrimmon pipers could do the same. They lived that music; they were just as much geniuses as the men. People knew this at the time, but it is now forgotten. Mary somehow managed to stand out and be acknowledged and recognized for her work – and then when that changed, when she was separated from that culture of music, meaning, poetry – it was devastating to her. She is not, during her exile [in the songs she wrote because of it], longing for the past, it is the pain of separation from something living.

"What we can do about the marginalization you mentioned, the lack of care for this deep language, this *joie de vivre* of language, is to talk to each other, be with each other, encourage each other."

Just before I leave, Aonghas Phàdraig describes being with Sorley MacLean and his wife in the car, not long before Sorley's death, returning from Sligachan (on Skye), where they'd gone for a photo, to Braes where Sorley lived at the time. "He would fall asleep against my shoulder – he was on medication – and then wake up and immediately start talking; and was immediately into the stories. He'd fall asleep, wake up; it never shut off, that telling."

27.

I take my time returning to the B&B thinking of the nature of the on-going "telling" we are born into, and which may only surface later in life. My father, in the weeks before he died, would, like Sorley in the car, suddenly wake, talking from the midst of a story. The last one I remember is of an island in a lake near the Manitoba-Ontario border where he camped with four of his brothers in the 1920s, no food with them but some fruit and a few tins and the fish they caught: and the stars overhead, and the Northern Lights. "Who is going to carry on my work?" he asked, but I knew from his closed eyes and the way he spoke, it wasn't a question for me, but part of his travelling an interior space. He had always done this in some way, but in this period he spent more and more time there. He was not a poet – he was a carpenter, careful with his craft whether he built a house, a piece of furniture, or a toy for a child. He read a great deal and took his religious faith seriously. Even his daily exercises, stretching and breathing before he prayed each morning, a regime begun during rehabilitation after a serious accident when the scaffolding he worked on broke, never struck me as routine. He would rise, make coffee for my mother, and then enter what can only be described as a moving meditation or a re-entering of a stream that he knew was always there. He believed the Bible literally, every word; and yet, unlike many who do, there was no censure or unkindness in him. In his nature, despite his loyalty to the hellfire and damnation of evangelical fundamentalism, he was accepting and non-judgmental. Getting there, of course, was a process, one my brother and I helped with by presenting him with near-insurmountable challenges. Once, after I announced while still a student that I was living with a boyfriend and had no intention of getting married to him, he did not speak to me for months: but in the end, through far more sorrowful crises, what won out over dogma was his love.

"What are you thinking of, Dad?" I'd asked him a few days after my mother's funeral when I feared for his will to live.

"The only way to assess a thing is to step outside the theories in which you exist," he said. "As you construct something according to a theory, you affect the result. So that you cannot assess the results."

"What do you mean?" I had never heard him speak like this before. His tools, as I knew them, were the hammer and saw and level – all certainties – not metaphysical speculations.

"The world is made of mixes – it is difficult to separate from the mix. The material is all mixed in with the spirit."

It was a peculiar interval. Several times my father saw and spoke to my mother as if she were present. Once, he said, she was with a little boy who walked with her around the dining room table.

"What did they look like, Dad?"

"It is sort of like early lore when they stamped expressions on people's faces. They were stamped on the face in days of yore."

When he couldn't remember that my mother was dead, I told him, "We saw Mum in her coffin, we went to her funeral, there was a graveside service and we said goodbye."

"Yes, we did," he said, "but it's hard to say goodbye when you're saying goodbye to yourself."

28.

In the evening, I walk the path over the hills to what used to be Ken's croft. I am sure that each person I meet along the way would agree that the landscape is beautiful. We pass through it and are refreshed by it; but we – most who come this way – do not know its names and stories

or what happened to the people who once lived here. Aonghas Phàdraig
had told me a story of a time when a rider rode a horse all the way from
South Uist (where he was born) to St Kilda – that is, northwest – on
land now separated into many islands, including Berneray and Pabbay.
When the woman rider returned, her apron was full of hazelnuts. In
that time, there were trees and nuts and berries and apples where none
grow now: the coastline has been completely altered by rising seas. As
well, the trees of Uist were destroyed by Norse over-use, and later, much
of the land was denuded by sheep brought in by landlords who cleared
the land of its people in order to profit from livestock. I understand
that whenever Aonghas Phàdraig speaks of those things, these matters
form part of the underlay of what he says, whether I'm aware of it or
not; and that there is inherent conflict between a culture's need to preserve its truth and the wish to educate others to what is right in front
of their eyes, what "has always been there."

   In North America, as the poet Robert Bringhurst writes, "poets and
writers … had a long-standing habit of ignoring Native American oral
literature and at the same time blindly romanticizing whatever little
they knew of indigenous tradition … The implicit assumption of colonization and missionization is that invaders and aboriginals are, metaphorically speaking, separate species … A lot of teachers have hopped
aboard that train and have taught that American life, American art and
American literature do not have or need indigenous foundations."

   It wasn't any different in Scotland.

   In Aonghas Phàdraig Caimbeul's book, *An t-Eilean / Taking a Line
for a Walk through the Island of Skye*, there are two texts, one in Gaelic,
the other in English, and they are somewhat different in their perspec-
tives of the same experience. A hand-drawn map of Sleat is mentioned
in the English text, but in the Gaelic version it is depicted and includes
notes – in Gaelic. I puzzle out a few of the map's designations: points,
promontories, bays, woods, hollows, burns, etc. It is only when Sharron
Gunn translates several of the annotations for me that I begin to sense
the scale of what I have missed on my visits to Sleat.

   One note tells of Capasdal farm near the Aird (the start of the walk
to the Point), at the end of the road from Ardvasar, which I have passed
by many times on my treks to Ken's cottage. Donald Angie MacLean,

who drew the map, writes (in Gunn's translation): "However it got the name, it gave rise to an amazing history from the days of Sir James Mac-Donald. It seems that this man, the Lord of Capasdal, was killed at the Battle of Rory's Field (Killiecrankie, 1689). On the evening that James was killed, the cattle gave blood in their milk."

29.

I open my copy of the *Gaelic Songs of Mary Macleod* and take a deep breath before diving once more into the complexity of Scottish history and its interlacing with the poet's life.

Mary's poem to Sir Donald MacDonald of Sleat (c. 1665–1718) – one of the poems I discussed with Aonghas Phàdraig Caimbeul – was written sometime after 1695 when Donald's father, the 11th chief of Sleat, died and Donald succeeded him to the title as the 12th chief. That much is certain, or as certain as can be with a poem about which there is little agreement about its text or purpose or timing. Mary was older than Donald by half a century. When she died aged about ninety-two, c. 1707, he was only forty-two. Yet, the tone of the poem is personal, hinting at secrets in the metaphors of its opening verses and in an extended call to battle. MacDonald is the leader Mary has been hoping for as she lists potential enrollment in a MacDonald-led clan rising.

Six years before he became chief, when he was in his mid-twenties, Donald MacDonald fought for the then recently deposed Stuart James VII & II against his replacement, the Protestant William of Orange, at the battle of Killiecrankie or Rory's Field in which the Lord of Capasdal lost his life. On that July day of 1689, taking over from his father, also called Donald MacDonald, who had fallen ill, he led his clan to victory alongside other Scottish clans in a Jacobite army outnumbered two to one by the Williamites. It was a great, but pyrrhic, triumph.

Many Sleat MacDonalds, including five of their principal officers, died along with the Lord of Capasdal. Considering the scale of the losses, it might be more of a wonder that all the Sleat cattle did not have "blood in their milk" that day. More than a third of the Highland Army overall, along with their leader Viscount (Bonnie) Dundee, perished. Dundee's loss was disastrous since he was the only leader who might have kept the army together. Despite the Highlanders' sacrifices in that and other clashes, it was not long before James VII & II's forces were defeated. After the Battle of the Boyne in Ireland in July 1690, James fled to France, never to return. By then, the Sleat MacDonalds, and many others, were paying for their part in the opposition to King William.

Donald's father refused to make peace with William when given the opportunity. His estates were put under penalty of forfeiture and the King sent two frigates that bombarded the MacDonald chief's residence at Armadale (Skye), intending to force submission. In the end, a Williamite party landed near where the ferry from Mallaig docks today and were scattered and killed – reportedly having sexually assaulted village women – hung on tripods made of oars, and buried. One group of these men was interred a little northeast of Capasdal at the top of Dùn Flò.

By the end of 1691, as William continued his campaign of suppression throughout the Highlands, the elder Donald had accepted King William's offer of amnesty. The MacDonalds of Glencoe, whose chief missed the 1 January 1692 amnesty deadline through delay and misdirection, were massacred, most of them while still in their beds, by the King's clan Campbell troops billeted with them. Escaping MacDonalds were hunted through the snow-bound mountains where the young, weak, and old died of the cold. To this day, Glencoe remains a haunted landscape and a horrifying example of violation of clan hospitality.

All through the 1690s, Jacobites were imprisoned, murdered, and executed. In 1696 a Jacobite plot to murder King William was uncovered. At least nine Jacobites were subsequently executed for their part in the plot and a planned invasion of England. Many others were arrested and died in prison. It was not a period in which advocacy for their cause could safely be expressed. Most chiefs – most people! – trod carefully.

But Mary's "To MacDonald" is not a careful poem.

We cannot know how much contact or friendship there was between Sir Donald MacDonald and Mary, but his father's sister Catherine was Sir Norman of Berneray's second wife. Another sister, Florence, was married to Iain Breac, Mary's MacLeod chief at Dunvegan. The MacLeod establishments at Berneray and Dunvegan (Skye) are both known as Mary's homes. With each presided over by an aunt of Donald MacDonald and the clans linked through a depth of other alliances, it is fair to assume they knew each other well.

At Dunvegan, Iain Breac kept court in full Gaelic style with bards, harpers, pipers, and genealogists, but after he died in 1693 when Mary was about seventy-eight years old, he was succeeded by his anti-Gaelic, pro-English son Roderick (Ruairidh Òg), who dispensed with Gaelic traditions "to make room for grooms, gamekeepers, dogs and the various etceteras of a fashionable English establishment." Roderick "dismissed Blind Rory (Ruairidh Dall) Morrison, a poet and harper who wrote two poems which were highly critical of him. [Roderick] did not maintain poets nor was he generous or hospitable with his clansmen and tenants. He wasted money on fine English and French clothes and other luxuries and left the estate in debt." Whatever recognition Mary may have been given during the chieftainship of Iain Breac, it would not be maintained during the rule of Roderick.

Two years after Roderick became MacLeod chief, Donald MacDonald of Sleat succeeded (in 1695) to his title and became Sir Donald MacDonald, the title given him in Mary's poem. The new Sir Donald continued under the cloud of potential forfeiture after his father's death. If he stepped out of line again by supporting the enemies of King William, his money and property – the entirety of his inheritance – would be taken by the Crown, and he could expect severe punishment.

In 1699 when Mary was around eighty-four years of age, Roderick died. His brother, Norman, became chief and once again Dunvegan was hospitable to Gaelic mores. That this new MacLeod chief looked favourably on Sir Norman of Berneray, Mary's patron, who had never wavered as a supporter of Gaelic culture or the Jacobite cause, is shown by his appointment, in 1700, of Norman's son John (Iain), a lawyer, as his factor. Likely, this chief looked favourably on Mary, too, but the need to tread carefully around King William and his wife, Queen Mary, remained.

Complicating these allegiances was that although William and Mary were Protestants, they were also Stuarts. William's mother was the oldest daughter of the executed Charles I; Mary was a daughter of James VII & II. The Jacobite "cause" had become a cultural one of shared land, language, and values – an indigenous cause – not one of advocacy in general for Stuarts at large. In such a climate those who adhered to the old ways could all too easily be suspected of political opposition; and it was undeniable that the Jacobite cause, although forced underground, was very much alive.

In 1700, Sir Donald MacDonald left Skye to live in Glasgow, "holding no correspondence with his people in the Isles" during the years he resided there (until 1714, when, after a brief imprisonment in Glasgow, he returned to Skye). It is believed he maintained this silence "to divert suspicions that he might be secretly fomenting rebellion in his territory." Which, in fact, he was. "Like his father, he was always active in the Stuart cause, and he was privy to all the intrigues of the Jacobites." In the years after Mary's death, he would be a key player in preparation for, and in the implementation of, the Jacobite rising of 1715.

There was to be one more change of MacLeod chieftains before Mary's death. Norman died in 1706 and was succeeded by his second son, another Norman (Sorley MacLean's plaint about Gaelic naming customs resonates), whose older brother, a toddler, had died shortly after their father. The new chief Norman was an infant when in that same year of 1706 he became chief. Until he was of age, "the estates were managed by his tutor, John Macleod of Contullich [that is, Sir Norman's son John (Iain), already the MacLeod factor], an active Jacobite agent, in recognition of whose service young Macleod [then eleven years old] was created a baron in the Jacobite peerage in 1716."

The events that give context for "To MacDonald" began when Mary was in her mid-seventies. Somewhere roughly between the ages of eighty and ninety-two, she composed "To MacDonald" and other poems that remain in her canon. This was not a poet content with previous accomplishments, but one insisting on her right to be heard *now*. It is easy to marginalize poets, as Aonghas Phàdraig Caimbeul and I discussed in his wife's studio, but whatever the circumstances of her last years, Mary – elderly, outspoken, increasingly alone – was not going to let herself be silenced.

30.

"I have a treasure exceeding great," Mary begins, "my precious noble / guerdon [gift] art thou, my jewel of many virtues thou; the / king himself shall not sunder us, for since I have won [found] / thee, by my word I would not part with thee for gold."

Within the space of a few lines, Mary has set the subject of her poem within metaphors of wealth. She goes on, "There hath been a hoard these many years bestowed in / secrecy." It is "not wan silver and not iron," she tells us; it is – of course – MacDonald himself. There is more: he is "a boon" and "my shapely and beautiful gift, my ship of which many a history was told."

In the lead-up to jogging memories of MacDonald's renown as a warrior (at Killiecrankie and in other Jacobite battles), Mary's lines present a type of riddle. Rephrased as such it might be, "What is large, valuable, noble, a gift, a jewel of virtues that even the King cannot take away, even if he uses gold as a bribe?" Moreover, this "hoard" has been kept in secrecy. The rest of the poem is put in motion by Mary having found it – the treasure, MacDonald – as was intended and having decided – or been encouraged – to make MacDonald's leadership known and not leave him "in neglect." In that sense, it may be a poem about publicizing and timing a rebellion – thus the calling up of allies which follows; but it remains a puzzle, too. In these lines, the poet has situated herself with affection, even teasing, in intimate relation to MacDonald. In a verse included by Ó Baoill in his translation, but not by Watson in his, a line refers to MacDonald as "the fosterling my people have provided me with." It would be nice to connect dots: fostering was common; the relationship with a fosterling could be closer than that of a blood relative; Mary did look after children at Dunvegan … but it would be easy to misread cues and get the picture wrong. It would be logical but not provable, too, to link the poem's timing with MacDonald's period in Glasgow, apparently out of contact with his clan, but deep in Jacobite conspiracies.

There was a great deal going on at the beginning of the eighteenth century.

James VII & II died in exile at the age of fifty-seven in 1701. Not long before his death, an Act of Settlement was passed in the English Parliament to ensure that none of James VII & II's Catholic heirs could succeed to the thrones of England and Ireland. William, who had survived his wife Mary (d. 1694), died in 1702 following a fall from his horse, which tripped in a mole's burrow. This gave rise to the Jacobite toast to "the little gentleman in the black velvet waistcoat" (i.e., the mole). He was succeeded by Anne, the second daughter of James VII & II, who was, like William and Mary, a Protestant. The Scottish Parliament, however, did not accept the Act of Settlement, and in 1704 passed the Act of Security, which reserved the right to choose its own successor to Queen Anne. It was a time of volatility in which Jacobite plots flourished.

Whatever the political timing, the bardic timing in the poem requires the poet to remind its hearers of MacDonald's lineage. He is a noble, "a bough of the precious apple-tree," a man of "pure true blood" with rights to a rank of leadership. If more evidence were needed, it can be found in his titles, lands and possessions, and accomplishments. Mary presents Duntulm Castle, the MacDonald seat, as displaying Gaelic style with blazing candles, gleaming cups, wine, music, literacy, and hospitable maidens in silk. It is a generous court. And yet ...

Watson says that the metre of the poem is "unusual." Sharron Gunn suspects satire. In that light, is the reference to the "maidens" tongue-in-cheek? Ó Baoill translates the verse like this: "Your court where liberal giving was nobly done, and / handwriting among fighting men was good; your delight in / maidens was part of it: there were fringed gowns of silk held / down close about their stays; and they give unquestioning / support to any stranger who comes in exile."

Murmured endearments, secrets, treasure, unquestioning maidens, and wine "drunk freely": how are we to understand it? Is it a serious foray into politics by Mary? A satire of ambitions? A critique of the clans' accommodation to anglicization? Or something other? It is a theatrical poem. The display of Gaelic virtues is thin, each with a double meaning. Mary's comment on MacDonald's ancestry, "if it were trac- / ing thine ancestry I were, what I knew I should declare," could be read as a threat. Or not. It is a bard's job to know genealogy. The list of allies is long, with around two dozen individuals and clans of hundreds cited as supporters or potential supporters of MacDonald. The Irish would rise, too. Mary concludes the list: "woe betide any English-speakers who would take a shot at you when *those nobles* [my emphasis] were pursing them." It was said that Mary's satire could raise blisters.

The convention of a listing of allies by bards is a rhetorical device used to cement loyalties. Watson writes that "some of them [the allies] would have done less for Sir Donald than Mary would have us believe." Sharron Gunn observes that Mary is actually "listing the enemies of Clan Donald and those Jacobites who were neutralised [were made peace with and swore allegiance to the government] in this period. Some of the clans named in the poem were Williamite supporters and great enemies of Clan Donald during the Wars of the Three Kingdoms (a.k.a. English Civil War) and first Jacobite rebellion in 1689." To Watson's comment, MacInnes replies, "But this is precisely the point. One view of this is that these are propagandist appeals, not a direct reflection of political and military realities." A variation of his view is that the poem is a petition to those who should be involved, and that it employs the bardic power of naming – a common control practice in spell-making: as we have seen in Mary's work before, a poet may assert that something already is, in order to make it happen.

As it turns out, some former Williamites and many of the neutralized clans did go on to side with the Jacobites in 1715 and 1745. Such a listing of Gaelic clans that had not supported the Gaelic cause also possessed a shaming effect – a possibility raised by Sharron Gunn. The Dunvegan MacLeods were left off the list completely, an omission which some have argued means that Mary did not compose the poem at all. But everyone knew that Iain Breac, the MacLeod chief in 1689, no supporter of William and asked to join in at the time by Dundee and by the exiled King James VII & II himself, chose neutrality because his clan had endured great human and material losses through its prior support for the Stuarts. Leaving them off the list avoided controversy raised by either shame or undeserved praise. Mary's voice as a MacLeod poet drew in the MacLeods anyway. People understood for whom she customarily spoke. It could be argued that her song in praise of Sir Donald, a close relative and ally, as a potential battle leader positioned the Mac-Leods as instigators of rebellion, too. Such a public association would have created a problem whether the song was composed during Roderick's pro-English regime or after his death in 1699 when the MacLeods re-embraced Gaelic practices. It would certainly have provided fuel to those who believed that Mary had no right to express an opinion on serious matters at all.

Sharron Gunn reminds me that although Mary was related to chiefs and had high status in Gaelic society, she – as a woman – was not supposed to handle certain subjects in poetry or recite in public. If she had been a man, this wouldn't have been a problem – especially since by the 1690s she had great respect from her peers. "She was allowed to compose and recite poetry for children; she wasn't supposed to compose 'big' poems for the chiefs and their gentlemen. But she did anyway … Another woman pushing the envelope." If women wrote, they were supposed to stick to women's topics. These did not include fomenting rebellion, advocating for a leader, and calling – whether directly or through satire – on Jacobite soldiers to fight.

In lines I have never forgotten, the American poet Adrienne Rich speaks of "a woman of my time // obsessed // with Love, our subject: / we've trained it like ivy to our walls / … worn it like lead on our ankles …" Although this poem is now nearly half a century old, Rich's diagnosis of "our subject" as not only artistically limiting, but political in its stunting role of defining women, remains largely true. As readers, we want more of her life from a woman poet, more personal poetry, rather than the "big" subjects. We (lyrical poets and scholars, too) want Mary – as did Sorley MacLean – to have written more widely, when, in fact, by composing at all she was already a "woman pushing the envelope" to the limits of personal endangerment.

VI

The Place Longed For

down the path by the side of the hay field
down the path by the side of the flax
down the path through the corn field
puntrunpuntrun haugh!
down the path by the side of the kale patch
down the path by the side of the beet patch
at the turnip patch

little pig was lost!
snickhock snick
into the sack

We found the house
when the moon had set
No one home. He's not in
said the welcome mat
smacking its lips
over crackling and fat
– Tighnacraig

31.

My grandfather built the small white clapboard house in which he and
my grandmother lived, on one of two lots he had bought from the remains of a large orchard when they moved to Victoria from Winnipeg
in 1940. By the time we arrived in the 1950s, he had helped construct

houses for his two sons already living in the city, he and my uncles dig-
ging out the basement of one of them by hand. He had previously
worked with my father and mother on a house for us in St Boniface after
the Winnipeg flood. With the aid of relatives who had left Newfoundland ahead of him, he had constructed the house in which he and my
grandmother raised their children in North End Winnipeg. Before that,
he and his brothers had erected the house, close to the post office on
Coley's Point near Bay Roberts, in which my grandparents lived when
they married, and where my father was born. One afternoon, when El,
our small daughter, and I visited Coley's Point, we were driven round
while my father's cousin Muriel, who was blind by then, directed where
the car should stop and pointed out where each family member had
been born, lived, married, or died. Each house or empty lot or slope
or section of shoreline was a repository of stories. Some of them I had
recently heard from my father's Aunt Ellen, then one hundred years
old, in Vancouver. When I got out of the car to walk, I followed the
route she had taken to school on her pony, Forest. When I walked, I remembered the poems and stories I had heard as a child, spoken in my
grandparents' voices.

There were more houses: my grandfather and father built one in the
interior of BC with my father's youngest brother; much later, my father
and El and I and my mother built our house in Sooke, and my parents
built a house on Haida Gwaii with my brother. The links between generations were in wood and glass and stone. When the Scottish poet Liz
Lochhead visited us the first time, she slept in a room with a tarpaulin
for a wall. We were wrapped in blankets and sleeping bags finishing
supper, huddled next to a small air-tight stove, a northeast wind chuck-
ing rain against the tarp, when a flat-bed truck drove up the dirt track
in the dark, bringing windows. The driver knew how badly we needed
them. He said it hadn't felt it right to leave us in the storm without delivering them.

In the morning, Liz and El and I carried three fourteen-foot fir two-
by-eights up the stairs to what would be our bedroom. When it was finished, it had floor-to-ceiling south-facing windows, a skylight over the
bed, a tunnel greenhouse accessed from the deck, and a row of windows
in the low wall fronting west. It was a room in which to watch trees and

stars and the mist gathering over the sea. When we visited Liz in her Glasgow flat this time, on the way to Skye, her late husband Tom's architectural sense and open personality were everywhere because he'd designed the rooms, for her, to take in light.

32.

My brother and I share a room in the northwest corner of our grandparents' house. Our window catches the lights of the few cars travelling the gravel road from the airport or the village of Sidney. Our grandparents sleep in the room next door. Their window has a view of the roses at the front of the house and the crab-apple tree where I help my grandmother hang the carpets to air. Our parents sleep in a room in the basement that my father and grandfather framed in right after our arrival. When I go down the basement stairs to wake my parents, I smell the wood that fuels the furnace, and the bins in which my grandmother stores apples over the winter.

Giant fir trees, survivors of the original forest cleared for the orchard, form a border along Kenneth Street to the south. The wood-frame house with its ship-lap cladding and board floors was made from that forest. From the treetops, ravens watch over the fruit trees and the garden my father and grandfather dig together in the spring. Beyond the house are farms, grazing cattle, and greenhouses, which reach all the way to the wilderness of Christmas Hill.

33.

The song "Tuireadh" / "A Plaint," the first that Sharron Gunn translated for me, is the only work in which Mary (if the song is truly hers) speaks of her childhood. Watson refers to confirmation by reliable sources of a tradition that at the time of writing, Mary was in exile on the Hebridean island of Scarba, an island which, even today, is not easy to access. In the poem, which expresses intense longing for home, she says: "I have been depressed / For a week. // Here I am on the island without / Grass or shelter. // If I can / I will go home. // I'll make the trip / the easiest way // To Ullinish / Of white-footed cattle // Where I was raised / In my youth [Where I spent my youth] …"

Gunn says that the line "Where I was raised in [or where I spent] my youth" is "a well-used line, almost a kenning, to express longing in exile for the land of one's youth." It situates both home and youth in the category of irrecoverable time.

The place longed for – Ullinish – is a drive of roughly fifty miles north and northwest (about 80 km) from the B&B on the Sleat peninsula where I am staying. It is about half a day's walk southeast from Dunvegan Castle, spoken of in the poem as the "great house" where Mary, when young, was "joyful." Both places were (weather depending) always accessible by sea-road.

We have scarcely entered the Cullin mountains after the westward turn at Sligachan, when I find myself singing "Chì Mi na Mòrbheanna" / "I See the Great Mountains," a song I have learned in the Gaelic Choir. "O chì, chì mi na mòrbheanna," I sing, repeating the chorus too many times. It is just that the lyrics, written by an exiled Highlander, perfectly reflect where we are. We are, as the song describes, seeing great, lofty mountains, and corries and peaks under the mist, and sooner or later there will be the woods, thickets, and fair fertile lands the song also evokes. In this distance, on this road, more mountains hug cloud to their serrated vees; and then the low brush and heather of the roadsides give way to near slopes of small, planted pines touched with gold. A high watery light coloured somewhere between grey and grey-blue bleeds through the cloud. The road bends, throwing green moorland forward against a background of high-gapped peaks, and then the sea with its crab-fingered sea-lochs appears along with the islands and headlands that mark the southeast entrance to Loch Bracadale and the small settlement of Ullinish.

"I see right away the place of my birth / I will be welcomed in a language which I understand," the exiled Highlander sang. Mary's song "A Plaint" has no need to speak of language or landscape – these, she can take for granted. Her exile is an inexplicable one from the people, tasks, animals, and celebrations that shaped her identity. Watson uses "mournful" where Gunn supplies "depressed" in lines that make clear the intensity of Mary's feelings. From despair, the poem shifts quickly to an imagined return. "I will go home [*Thèid mi dhachaidh*]," Gunn says, "is a line out of a pipe tune by the MacCrimmons who were patronized by the MacLeods. A line with resonance." One of its resonances is its use in love songs, and another is an evocation of the aura of Patrick Mòr MacCrimmon / Pàdraig Mòr MacCriomain, who appears in another of Mary's exile songs, "Crònan an Taibh" / "The Ocean Croon."

A third echo, for me, is of Aonghas Phàdraig Caimbeul speaking of the importance of Patrick MacCrimmon's early-1650s "Lament for the Children," which is not only a lament for the deaths of seven of his eight sons, and the deaths of many other children, after a ship carrying fever came ashore at Dunvegan, but "real defiance of death: to stand up and look at it and defy." To summon childhood as Mary does amid abandonment and isolation, to conjure it vividly and to give it permanent form in this song, is also a defiance of death – a death of the spirit.

Mary's childhood home, Ullinish, in contrast to the barrenness of Scarba, contains both grass and shelter. The first half of this brief poem tells us it is an area where there are "white-footed cattle," but more importantly, it is where the people she longs for live: the "white-palmed women" on whose breast milk she was raised, "Over there in the household / of brown-haired Flora, Lachlann's daughter." We learn a little more about Flora, that she is "a milkmaid / about the cows," and that these cows belong to the Dunvegan chief, Roderick (Rory) Mòr, before the poem uses his name to turn from this first scene of childhood to a second scene in the Dunvegan castle hall. Here, Mary says, "I have been joyful, // Dancing merry on a wide floor." The Gaelic words used mean that it is a new floor of planks or flagstones. Rory Mòr died in 1626 when Mary would have been about eleven years old, but he had built Dunvegan's large hall between the castle's two existing towers as part of a major 1623 addition. If the floor were new when Mary first danced on it, she was probably about eight or nine years old at the time. This young self, sleeping and waking to the rhythms of the castle's music, had "The fiddle-playing / to put me to sleep, // The pipe-playing / to wake me in the morning."

The poet has taken us on a journey to her childhood home, "easily as may be," from the island where she has been stranded, but it is hard and wrenching for the reader or listener to meet the final lines: "Bear my greeting / to Dunvegan." Plain as this is, it precipitates us from immersion in immediate childhood experience into the sadness and privation of the deserted adult. The song's journey changes nothing because it is only imaginary: but it does speak loudly of the injustice of the poet's change of fortune. It is a simple song, its chorus filled with "vocables," the syllable-sounds that help keep the rhythm when women sing together through the steps of "waulking" woolen cloth as part of its preparation. It is a song designed to be remembered and repeated wherever women meet.

34.

Ullinish was cleared of its twenty or thirty families by the MacLeod chiefs in the mid-nineteenth century. Little is left of the village on the shore but a few crofts and holiday homes punctuated by a red telephone box, rough pasturage, and the view westwards across the loch to MacLeod's Tables, two flat-topped mountains on the Durinish peninsula.

We park the car and take a footpath toward Ullinish Point and the small tidal island of Oransay, an island used in Mary's time for "corne and gerssing" and which, I like to think, may have provided grass for the cows in Flora's charge. We jump back and forth from one turfy edge of the track to another to avoid heavy mud. Once through a gate and having threaded a knot of cattle before which a group of hikers has halted and clustered nervously, we are on boggy moorland where there is nothing we can do to escape getting our boots and socks soaked through. Nonetheless, a woman thrusts a pram at speed along the path towards us, balancing the carriage from tussock to tussock and trailing an exhaust of midges behind her. Once we are on top of the headland, we can see that the tide is moving quickly in over the stony link to Oransay where some children play. Above and behind us, about a mile away, an ancient broch surveys the coastline with us as we watch a sailboat beat its way up the loch in our direction.

From about the tenth century and on into the thirteenth, the Norse raided and controlled parts of this seaboard. Even before this, the broch was on the lookout. "Sharp is the wind tonight, and white tresses rise on the ocean / I need not fear the calm sea, bringing the fierce warriors of Norway," someone wrote in Gaelic marginalia on a Latin grammar in the early Middle Ages, in celebration of the relative safety guaranteed by foul weather.

At this moment, I am a little fearful for the safety of the playing children, and we wait until they cross the beach, seawater hissing at their heels, race up the path, shout greetings to us, and then call ahead to catch up to their mother.

Mothering, or more specifically wet-nursing, and likely fosterage, may have been what brought Mary to Ullinish in her early years to be "reared // On the breast-milk / Of white-palmed women." Fosterage was common in the Highlands and Islands until the eighteenth century. "Through fosterage, families like the MacLeods and Mackinnons ... reinforced family ties and added support to their family structures." In such arrangements, formalized by contract (Norman of Berneray's fosterage contract still survives), the foster-parents were "nearly always of lower rank than the natural parents of the child." The agreements included material and financial provisions and were a means of wealth redistribution and mutual care within a clan or even between clans. The bonds formed this way were said to be stronger than blood ties: "*Comhdhaltas gu ceud, is càirdeas gu fichead*: Fostership to a hundred and blood relationship to twenty."

In most cases the child – either girl or boy (another of the few surviving contracts is that of a young girl) – went to live with his or her foster parents at the age of seven or eight for a fixed period of about seven years. Fosterage itself is also described as "for the purpose of being nursed or bred"; and nursing and raising are certainly what Mary portrays in the poem.

It is getting late, the afternoon nearly gone. El and I hold hands as we make our way back across the bog and through the mud and up the lane to the car. The moor has lost most of its green and is now shaded in purple, the headlands and mountains soaking up dark. We stop for a quick coffee at Bracadale on the road back, and I browse the shop's used books and clothing. El persuades me out of buying a Welsh fly-fisherman's coat, the kind with a cape over the shoulders instead of sleeves

(I own many old coats already), and then it is back into the car, headlights on full, the day rolling itself up behind us until we leave its spool
and make the turn south from Sligachan and all the way back to Sleat.

35.

It is not the journey that disappoints: it has pulled us across prairie and
up and over mountains, stopping at lakes and hot springs and dams
until we finally meet the sea and take ship; but the island road we have
ended up on after so much travel is not even paved. I see no streets with
brick and stone buildings, there is no sunshine or snow, no outdoor
rink along the lane, just a gravel track, narrow and pot-holed, and a
grey sky. The windshield, cleaned as soon as we drove off the ferry, is
already smeared with grime; and it is drab dusk and raining. I don't
really understand where we are, and once we're inside the house, it is
too dark to see out the windows.

When I sleep, I find the house I was born in beside the Seine River;
and then the new house on Champlain Street, the one both my grand-
fathers helped build while my grandmother looked after me, so I have
been told. The colours of the rooms are muted, but each contains a
scene or two I have carried with me: the back doorsteps from the
kitchen; the walk past the sandbox to next door where my friend Char-
lene lives; the lower bunkbed in a room I share with my brother. When
my father was ill with acute appendicitis, he lay on my bunk while we
waited for the doctor. Nearby, a stairway mounts to an attic space
turned into a suite for my parents' friends and their son. The closet off
the living room is where the woman friend who looked after me in lieu
of rent used to shut me in as punishment. I have been promised I will
not have to see her again. Years later, the novelist and poet David Malouf
tells me of a film he had made about Rudyard Kipling. He and the film
crew visited the house Kipling was boarded in as a child and found the
basement cupboard in which the poet was often kept, the words "help
me" chalked inside.

Near the large living room window of the Champlain house are the
delicate glass animal ornaments – deer and horses, and birds – that my

mother collects. They glitter in sunlight, displayed on a bank of open vertical shelves.

But I am not there – not skating, tobogganing, or paddling in the Sherbrooke pool braced by water-wings, or even strumming the ukulele that I love despite its broken strings: all of it has been left behind. Instead, I am in a house I do not know, with my family and my grandparents, having come to the end of a long journey. I carry a small chalkboard and chalk with which I draw the same scene again and again of a house, smoke puffing from its chimney, a tree on either side, and a front walk on which a family stands in a row, the mother holding the little girl's hand.

It is days before I come out of the gloom into which I have subsided. My brother, who had crossed the road and gone through the pasture with me to meet a boy his age and a girl mine, has gone to school. I am not allowed to cross the road alone; and to be truthful, I am a little frightened of the cows in the field. My father starts his new job at BA Oil, and my mother catches the bus to her employment at a downtown legal firm. My grandfather leaves for his work building houses, and I am left with my grandmother.

36.

I am sitting on a stump in the backyard waiting for my grandmother to wonder where I am. She is an indistinct presence going about her housework indoors. She looks nothing like my mother and her friends, or my aunts, or the step-grandmother I left behind in Winnipeg. They are slim, smartly dressed, quick-moving women with cut and curled hair, and they wear lipstick and high heels and stockings. My grandmother is short and round. She braids her long grey hair, winds it into a coil at the back of her head and fixes it in place with hairpins. She needs wire-rimmed eyeglasses to read with, and her slippers have the sides cut out of them because of her bunions. I hear a call from one of the fir trees. Since all here is new to me, it does not seem strange that the caller, a large black bird, flies down and lands beside me on the stump. I know enough to stay still while we have a "talk." When after several minutes it leaves, I go inside the house where my grandmother is making lunch, and then, without being asked, I help put napkins and soup spoons on the table. She asks me to fetch the milk, so I climb onto the counter next to the sink and open the door to the cooler. The milk rests against a block of ice. Through a wire grate in the outer wall, I can see the stump where I was sitting, the dug soil of the vegetable garden, and a screen of fruit trees. The branches of the great fir, from which the bird flew down, are empty.

37.

A late dinner at the Eilean Iarmain Hotel, after finding nothing open nearer Sleat, means we are slow to get up in the morning and must hurry to reach the station in Kyle in time for El's train to Inverness. He is giving a reading there for a Highland Heritage Organization and will be away several days. I wave goodbye, climb into the rented car, and remind myself on which side of the road to drive. When we lived and travelled in Scotland before, I liked driving its single-track roads, but I am used to smaller cars, like El's mother's yellow Mini or our own green MGB or the pastel blue Citroën we had when we last lived in Edinburgh, not this broad-beamed generic rented white Ford. I head back over the Skye Bridge and north to Broadford, where I fill the car with gas and then go into the Co-op to buy wine for dinner tomorrow evening with another poet Aonghas MacNeacail has suggested I talk to.

Today, I am going to drive back along the route we took to Ullinish, but continue past, this time, to Dunvegan. I have been to the castle several times before, but never with Mary in mind. I doubt I will learn anything new, but it is where she is supposed to have spent much of her time from childhood on and learned her art in what Aonghas Phàdraig Caimbeul termed its "university." I expect the castle will be crowded with tourists, but since I can't shake the feeling that I have left something unfinished there, I relax into the drive and feel my spirits lift as soon as, once again, I've made the turn west at Sligachan where climbers gather and camp before testing themselves on the heights of the Cullins.

It takes close to an hour in the heavy rain and mist, which have obscured most of what I was able to see of the land and seascape yesterday, to reach the castle parking lot. It is packed with cars and tour buses, many of them from Germany and Spain: children flee their parents to splash in puddles and then sprint into gardens that did not exist in Mary's day. In that time, the castle on its basalt promontory – which no longer gives the sense of its being an island – was encircled by a wall. The only entrance was from the sea. "Mantled with cotoneaster and gay with dainty ferns and wilding flowers, the rock descends all round fairly vertically to the short scree slopes that blanket its base except in the indent on its north-western quarter, where there is a kind of 'slack' in the cliff, up which a double-curved flight of rough stone steps mounts to the sea-gate." And this gives passage through the thick rock wall into the courtyard.

Beyond the wall, the island was covered in indigenous woodland; and beyond that, on mainland Skye, was what Dr Johnson on his eighteenth-century visit called "wine-dark moorland," all of it overrun now with plantations. Most people leave their umbrellas outside the entrance and their soaked backpacks on the wet floor at the bottom of the indoor staircase before they troop up to a corridor to the left. This is divided by velvet rope so that the throngs, coming and going, do not impede each other. There are portraits and swords and banners to see and a splendid view of Loch Dunvegan from the lower level of the c. 1500 AD Fairy Tower. I am in the library where there is a desk at the window facing the sea, and looking out, when I become aware of the sounds behind me. The rustle of damp jackets, careful footfalls, and the respectful murmur of voices from Europe and Asia and the Middle East. Like the gathering of its lineaments from its ninth-century elements to new building ranging from the thirteenth to the nineteenth centuries, plus all the modern additions of comfort and marketing, the castle seems able to accommodate layers of interpretation and understanding and perspective, as if in the long run they will make as little impression on its substance as a change of weather. I move into the drawing room, once the great hall, advised by my research to mentally substitute the present plaster ceiling with another of oak beams and boards blackened by smoke from the open fireplace. It is a room in which more than one bloody deed was enacted. A dungeon entrance and a glassed-over trap door and a view of heavy shackles give these testament; but the mood is set, and the world's people drawn not by these – which, sadly, can be found in variation worldwide – but by the famous fairy flag, possibly from Syria or Rhodes, maybe the silk of a saint's shirt, perhaps brought back from the Crusades, or left by the fairies to save the chief and clan in time of peril. It is said there is one more use left in it, it having been raised twice before: and I wonder who will have the wisdom of the moment.

Aonghas Phàdraig Caimbeul has told of going to Dunvegan and hearing corgis behind him, "and then the current Laird appears: 'Are you the writer, Angus Peter Campbell?' he asks, and I say, 'yes'. He asks me what I am doing, and I say I am reciting a poem which is a prophecy about what will happen at Dunvegan. I begin the recitation in Gaelic again: it tells of the turning of the great wheel and refers to the complete loss of Gaelic culture and the ruination of the MacLeods. I have no sooner spoken more than a few lines than the Laird stops me, 'Oh, it is all gibberish to me!' he says. And thereby, in the moment, fulfills the prophecy."

And yet: there is an atmosphere of the permanence of the stone, and of music played and songs sung, and poetry recited. The bard is for permanence, for human permanence, as is the emblem of the fairy flag and its origins in a time touched by mystery. And there are some, like Aonghas Phàdraig Caimbeul, who do come with the language and poetry and replenish the castle store.

The hereditary standard bearers, those who carried the fairy flag in battle, were buried not far from Mary in the chancel of St Clement's Church at Rodel, Harris. "This tomb ... was provided with an iron grating, about a foot beneath the cover-stone, and on this grating the body of each dead standard bearer was laid. On every occasion when a standard bearer was buried, 'the coffin was opened, all that remained of the last who had been buried in it was shaken down through the bars of the grating into the bottom of the coffin, and the body of the new occupant was laid on the grating. In this way the ashes of successive standard bearers mingled in one coffin.'"

And this is how I discover a sense of Mary in this busy destination: through the voices of its diverse visitors for whom the castle is a university of its kind, and because of the burial practice for carriers of the fairy flag – the flag so many come to see – which speaks to the continuity within Mary's own burial story, and in Aonghas Phàdraig's tale, a fulfillment of the fate against which Mary warned.

From when first she entered through the sea-gate in childhood, perhaps to "dance merry," Mary belonged to all that came before and what is left to come and chose to join in its expression through her art. Despite the apparent indifference of memory, I believe there always remains the possibility of discovery and recognition; and when a foundation needs repair, of restoration.

It was "the custom for the children of the leading men of the clan to be received into the chief's household," but, although "the fact is well vouched for," we do not know "[w]hen she entered [Sir Rory's] ... household of Dunvegan in the capacity of *bean altruim* (nurse)." Mary was associated closely with Dunvegan through five chieftainships, and through her care of "the five 'lairds' of the MacLeods whom she nursed." Her position at Dunvegan "during her poetic career ... was one of privilege and prestige little if at all inferior to that enjoyed in a great household by a trained bard in the preceding period," but the evidence of the surviving songs is that she was most closely and "passionately devoted to Sir Norman MacLeod of Bernera[y] in Harris, the third son of Sir Roderick Mòr."

We have no idea how this devotion came about, or what may have started her composing. We do not know how often she left through the Dunvegan sea-gate or where or to whom she went or in what capacity, but we do know that she was there and she danced, and that when she was expelled from her life there, she mourned, and that when a courier came from Dunvegan to tell her "gently and kindly" the news that she could return from her island of exile, "it banished the pang" in her breast.

38.

I am back on the road, anxious to return to Sleat and change because I am wet through from the walk I took in the gardens in the rain after leaving the castle. In the last quarter of the drive to Sligachan, I slow down and try to pay attention to the district around the small village of Drynoch at the head of Loch Harport, and to Glen Drynoch where Mary's father Alasdair Ruadh was said to be from. The glen is low-sloped, open and green and typical with pasture, heather, gorse, and bracken, and with a river running along the bottom, its path marked by deciduous trees. For part of the way, the Cullins pop into view, sharp and serrated above the glen's southeast slope. They vanish as the road follows the river's dipping bow to its rise near the flat that is Crossal, at the end of the Glen.

What Crossal – only about three kilometres (two miles) from Sligachan – was like in the seventeenth century, I do not know, but now it is principally warehouses and parking space for a garage. Highland travellers, sometimes mistakenly called gypsies, used to camp here during the cattle market when their services as metal-workers, horse-dealers, labourers, and hawkers were in demand. The travellers, indigenous Gaelic- (and sometimes English-) speaking, have their own language, Beurla Reagaird, and old and deep traditions of music and story. One song, "Am Bròn Binn" ("The Sweet Sorrow"), collected by the folklorist and poet Hamish Henderson in 1957, is an Arthurian tale c. 500 AD. It is said that when they were first recorded, "[t]hey wanted to begin, as it were, at the beginning and pay respect to the deepest layers from which their gifts had come up to them." Other ancient songs were in the form of *caoineadh* (a wail or cry), "that ancient 'pibroch note'" that "had that special gift, that 'keening passion' ... that edge the Spaniards call the duende," although many of their songs were of their own experiences on the road, a period brought to a close by the motor car in the 1950s.

Without a shared form other than song itself, or courtly traditions, or a seat in a great chief's hall, these descendants of Stewarts, MacDonalds, Camerons, MacAlisters, MacGregors, and Macmillans held a thread – the "old and deep traditions of music and story" – which unwinds from the same source as bards such as Mary MacLeod. "They have a turn of phrase, pride in their archaic lifestyle and traditions. They maintain fierce allegiance to the places where they know their ancestors to have lived. Memory, familiarity, kinship are of central psychological importance: a harsh life has become a proudly borne addiction."

39.

Time, along the gravel lane in the house that sits bounded by orchard and wood and pasture, is like the wool I wind for my grandmother when it is cloudy or raining. She knits the colours into socks and sweaters, but you can still follow each hue as it makes its way through the pattern. After lunch, my grandmother fills the kettle and puts it on the stove. I sit in her soft lap in a chair in the sitting room and we wait to see who will come to the door for tea. It is not a knock at the door that draws us to the window, but the sound of an approaching horse and cart. My grandmother dons her cardigan and shoes, and we go out into the yard.

Behind the white two-board wooden fence that separates the grass from the road, a cart waits with three people in it. There's a man holding the reins of a small dark horse that nibbles grass from the verge, a woman beside him, and a girl about my age sitting in the back who does not look at me. In Winnipeg, I'd been friends with the milkman who delivered milk to the house with a horse and cart. It is a memory so faint its tones have nearly faded away, but the sister of a friend was run over by the cart and that is not something you forget entirely.

The woman opens a bag of sewing items on the kitchen table. We have been to Spencer's downtown for wool, needles, and thread, and there is nothing that my grandmother needs. But she picks out a tin needle-threader and a small silver thimble for me and gives the woman a quarter from her apron pocket. When they go, I am aware, from what they have said, that they will not return. There are too many cars on the roads, too few people needing to buy the goods they sell. Their visit was a farewell.

Whenever I have mentioned the gypsies, which was what my grandmother called them, I am told that what I remember is not possible: there never were any on Vancouver Island. But a child's truth resides in a person, and mine resided in my grandmother, and she said the people in the cart were gypsies.

One day, much later, I will learn that gypsies (English-speaking Romanichal) were transported by Order in Council from Britain to Newfoundland in 1603; and an uncle will tell me he used to see them camped at a Vancouver Island lake. I will take the trouble to search oral and written records and learn of the thousands of gypsies who moved across Canada with horses and wagons in waves of immigration and migration over decades – "there would be 10, 12, 15 wagons travelling together" – many gravitating to the west "where there were large populations of Slavic people from Eastern Europe and the Balkans, and [where] they were better received" than in the east. In the 1950s, in Vancouver, a police detective, designated the "gypsy specialist," charged gypsy women under the Criminal Code of Canada for fortune-telling and "pretending to witchcraft," but left non-gypsy tea-leaf readers, palm-readers, and clairvoyants alone. In Scotland, the travellers said of the 1950s, "our business went downhill so fast you couldn't see the smoke! It was the motor-car that did for the Traveller life," people getting out to what before "people couldn't get out to get!" It was the close of a way of life.

40.

It is nearly 4:30 pm when I limp the car with its badly damaged tire into the gas station at Broadford. Somehow, I have struck a rectangular chunk of concrete in the roadway. The tire has come away from the rim and it bulges ominously. "There's a place where you could get it fixed," a young man tells me in the Co-op grocery. The adjacent gas station is the kind that only supplies gas. "You could get it fixed, but it won't be open. You'll have to drive to Kyle." Kyle is where I dropped El off in the morning, across the Skye bridge, a good fourteen kilometres from where I am. I have been lucky to make it this far. "But I'll never get there! Where is this other place?"

"It won't be open," he says, but I press until he gives directions.

It is open. The tire cannot be repaired and needs to be replaced, and they don't have the unlocking tools for the wheel nuts. I scrabble in the glove compartment and hand out everything inside and find the un-locking tools. The mechanic hefts the tools in his hand: "We don't have the right sized tire."

A woman emerges from behind a reception counter. "Didn't some come in today?" she says.

"They're all spoken for," he says.

"I'll call headquarters and see what they say," she says and smiles at me. "You're the third I've had in the last half hour. The roads are shock-ing. I keep telling them!" She tells them again when she gets head-quarters on the line. A pale and shaken Spanish family of four hover near their damaged car and we exchange sentences of commiseration. And then somehow, expertly, I have a new tire and the bent rim has been hammered straight.

"It wasn't your fault," the mechanic tells me, "it was bent before."

41.

There's a knock at the door. I remain beside the chair where we have been sitting. The man who enters is slender and good-looking, a little taller than my father. He has dark hair and olive skin and wears a black wool coat which he unbuttons as he sits in a hard-backed chair near the door. He twists a black fedora in his hands. He is dropping in to see how my grandparents are. It has been a long time. He was in Vancouver (a long ferry-ride and then a drive away) and thought he'd come by. His new black car is parked on the verge, not in the driveway. He won't stay. Just came to say hello. They were neighbours in the old North End Winnipeg. "Do you remember?" he asks my grandmother.

"Are you walking with the Lord?" my grandmother says.

His sadness leaks from inside the coat between the breast buttons and through the ends of the sleeves; it moves in a cloud towards her as she speaks. *Are you walking with the Lord?* I have never seen a man cry before, but grief, sorrow, and a shadowed life have entered the room.

"How is your family?" my grandmother asks him.

He is no longer with them. He is working, that is why he is here, out west, a thousand miles from what he tries not to think of.

"You shouldn't drink so much," she says, kindly.

"I know, I know."

"I will pray for you."

He lifts his head. Her prayer makes a shape around his body. He wears such very good shoes. When he stands, she stands and holds him. Does he call her "mother"? Hold fast to good (the Bible says), be merciful. He has travelled a long way for these moments. Will they be enough? How can they be? I wait by the chair while she opens the door. He leaves and the emptiness he comes from closes over.

I could draw him if I had chalk: green light over his shoulder through the window; the good clothes he wears on top of his despair.

There's a knock at the door. A tall old woman in a long black dress and laced boots enters and sits in my grandfather's chair by the window. When my grandmother speaks, the woman holds a strange object to her ear. I lean against my grandmother and whisper, "What is it?" Decades of curiosity still cast their sun and shadow. The woman says, "Come closer." When I am near, I see that despite her great age, the hair showing beneath the broad-brimmed straw hat she wears is as dark as my mother's.

"Here," she says, and she passes me the curious black and gold instrument I have been watching her handle. It is heavier than I thought it would be. Black, with a filigreed metal band around the bowl. I put the small end to my mouth. She smiles and says, "No, like this," and shows me how, and lets me put it, by myself, to my ear. "You have to listen," she says, and bends and speaks quietly into the bell of the ear-trumpet.

The floral curtains are partly drawn. My grandmother, across the room, remains silent. The woman's words enter my ear and stay there. I would know her voice if I were to hear it again.

I close my eyes now and search for details. I find shiny buttons on the woman's dress and a black stick with a glossy top that leans against the bookcase. She had carried the ear-trumpet into the house in a carpet bag.

VII

A Gathering

Bhiodh teanal nan cliar
Ré tamaill is cian,
Dh'fhios a' bhaile am biodh triall chàirdean.

For many a day poet-bands would gather towards the
homestead whereunto friends would fare.
– Mary MacLeod, "Crònan An Taibh" / "The Ocean Croon"

42.

The drive to Meg Bateman's house, on the west coast of the Sleat peninsula, is a twisting single-track over a high pass and through low hills and moorland with sections where a mis-turn of the wheel could start the car on a plunge to a loch or into the sea. Highland cattle and sheep straggle across the road, inevitably appearing as I meet one of the few cars travelling towards me. I am a little out of practice in the negotiation of using pull-out passing spots but arrive a few minutes early anyway and stop at the top of the hill above the house. Meg Bateman is known for her poetry and scholarship in Gaelic. Hers is an unusual path for a person born into Scottish English-language culture, one that must have required considerable gifts and courage; and she is a friend of Aonghas MacNeacail. His son has been staying in her house to practise with his band while she has been away, and she has only just returned. I need a moment to think about what I want to ask her and the others she has invited to dinner to help with any questions I have about Mary MacLeod.

I am on two tracks. On one, I am researching the life of Mary MacLeod and trying to find my way into her poetry. That one is easy to talk about. The other is more elusive and may be a fool's errand. My friend, the artist Liz Rideal, calls the type of glimpse or intuition I have had a *feu follet* or "will-o-the-wisp" – the flickering lights sometimes seen in marshes. These were once, Mussgnug her co-author has written, "believed to be evidence of the harmony and mystery of relationships between humans, animals and spirits, and even to blur the boundaries between life and death." It is a good description of creative exploration and its risks. When pursued, the *feu follet* may lead to knowledge, restoration, and healing, or else to an endless wandering.

Liz also cites Italo Calvino, who called literature "a game of shadows." "Tracing the endless paths of a labyrinthine world," he wrote, "we play hide-and-seek with the elusive, ineffable order of the universe."

How can I talk about that? Calvino's words are too grand to help me now.

I put down my copy of *Gaelic Songs*. I have been flipping through its pages and watching golden sunlight slant across the sea and over the peaks of the Cullins. I start the car.

At the end of the driveway, I am met by a little tawny-headed boy running and jumping. He hangs onto my rolled-down window, then helps me park. His name is Calum. His mother is Veronica, a student and friend of Meg's. He picks up a black forgiving cat and carries it hanging upside down in front of him to the door where the poet is waiting to welcome me. Indoors, in a comfortable room that faces the water, we talk for a few moments. I pass on greetings from Aonghas and another writer friend, Sandy, and give her several of my books (a writer's credentials), one of which she has already read when it was up for a prize. She ushers me into the kitchen where the other guests are seated around the table.

At our home in Sooke, we do the same, gathering at the table, talking, eating, and drinking, watching for dark and stars through un-curtained windows, candles on the table. Meg opens a bottle of Prosecco, fills glasses and refills bowls of chips while introducing me to her Gaelic scholar friend Gillian Munro, just back and jet-lagged from lecturing in Canada, and Mark Wringe, another of Meg's colleagues at Sabhal Mòr Ostaig, the Gaelic College. Veronica, Calum's mother, slips in quietly a minute later. Gillian murmurs that she won't be able to stay long, and we begin.

"Mark will be able to answer any of your questions about the seventeenth century," Meg says. I mention that I had just visited Dunvegan and liked it more than I had remembered. Meg says, "Visiting Màiri's places?"

"The picture we have of Màiri nighean Alasdair Ruaidh," Mark says, catching sight of *Gaelic Songs*, which I have brought in with me, "is created mostly by Carmichael Watson's book and there is really no reason to think she was based at Dunvegan as he says or that she addressed most of the poems to the MacLeod [chief at Dunvegan]. Anne Frater [the Gaelic poet and scholar from Lewis] has written a thesis that argues strongly against this. It is more likely that Màiri spent most of her time at Berneray, Harris."

Several of the nineteenth-century scholars I have been reading, secure in their knowledge of Mary at Dunvegan, stir in their graves. Anne Frater is not the first to have had this idea, but she sounds more than ready to back it up against differing opinions. And it does make sense. Most of Mary's surviving work is associated with Norman MacLeod of Berneray, not the Dunvegan chiefs with whom some have suggested she had a non-professional court-bard type of relationship. There remain anomalies – Mary undoubtedly had an important connection with Dunvegan; but as I let the picture shift, I realize how vivid Mary is to everyone present. As Meg had commented when I had arrived, "Within Gaelic culture, Mary MacLeod is not ignored ... she is very well known." It is as if she is in the neighbourhood and might drop in to find Meg's melon salad on the table and take part in the discussion herself.

"Did she spend her childhood at Ullinish?" I ask, recalling the landscape I had explored, confident in Mary's descriptions and conveyance of feeling, and all the notes I had made.

"The best we can know is that it is likely, because of the landscape [mentioned in the poems] that she visited there."

Ullinish, as I had seen, is within striking distance of Dunvegan, so I ask Mark if he thinks Mary nursed the chief's children there as is usually said. Watson reported that Mary claimed to have nursed five MacLeod lairds in all. If so, she would have lived at Dunvegan for decades in the company of its bards and musicians.

"I think it unlikely," he says. "Màiri wasn't married as far as we know and as far as we know she didn't have children." There is a brief debate over whether the term "nurse" includes that of "wet nurse." In the end, I understand that Mark (or Anne Frater) is not saying that Mary was not a children's nurse and a poet with standing, just that she was not these things at the chief's residence at Dunvegan. In Frater's view, the five lairds could have been Norman of Berneray's five sons, all of whom Mary knew well, rather than a succession of five MacLeod chiefs as Watson reports. On the other side of the argument is the tradition that Mary was exiled for over-praising the MacLeod chief's children. Such praise could draw ill-luck and even encourage the fairies to take them; he may have feared the power of her words. Or was his children's well-being an excuse to get rid of her?

"The [bardic] line went from the Druids to the professional bards to a poet close to the chief," Meg says. "If Màiri was under MacLeod patronage – and their patronage continued long past [when] most other clans had stopped, and there were other poets – perhaps it wasn't thought as having as much status to have a woman poet? So, this was discouraged."

If that is so, and Mary had been accepted as having right to a voice in the bardic tradition by earlier chiefs, her demotion and banishment would reflect changes in what was acceptable within Gaelic court culture, changes perhaps driven by the chief's anglicization.

Or, "She may have overpraised Norman of Berneray, who was not the chief," Mark says. "In one poem she styles Norman as *the* MacLeod – which she shouldn't have done and which she would have known was wrong and asking for trouble."

"Màiri got in trouble certainly [for things she said]," Meg says, "but the blind bard [Rory Dall / Roderick Morison] also said what he had to say: it is the poet's duty to point out what he sees is wrong."

"There are other women poets at the same time – Sileas MacDonald [Sìleas na Ceapaich / Cicely MacDonald] is one I think of – who are very good," Mark says. "This is different from everywhere else, including Ireland, where there may have been one [Eibhlín Dubh Ní Chonaill] who was well known."

The mid-seventeenth to the eighteenth century is looked back on as a golden age for Scottish Gaelic women poets. Sharron Gunn had also spoken of them. Most were younger than Mary and like her were Jacobite supporters.

"Sileas MacDonald wrote a poem that warns young girls to be careful, to be chaste," Meg says. "She was criticized for writing a dirty poem when, in fact, she was doing the opposite; and [what she wrote] was in response to a truly dirty poem. [In response to the criticism] she became quite pious."

"There is no piety at all in Mary's verses; she rarely uses religious terms – would it have mattered?" I ask.

"In this period there was a kind of vacuum – the religious part just wasn't that important," Mark says. "And the Iona statutes – which attempted to close down Gaelic-speaking and to make sure all the clan leaders were to send their eldest son, or eldest daughter if there were no sons, to be educated in English – were often ignored."

Meg says, "There is a linkage going on: especially in the women poets, the conventional metaphor becomes a link or is linked to other things: feelings, meanings, so that rather than it being less powerful than an original metaphor [the lack of which Sorley Maclean complained of] it carries the weight and force of the tradition with it. Men composed formal court poems dealing with the big world; women didn't. Màiri had grander ambitions, we think; she felt her place to be there amongst the bards, not with the women doing the laundry, or waulking the tweed."

It looks like Mary may have been censured not only for the subjects she took on and what was between the lines but for what was thought to be between the lines because both subjects and undercurrents were in the voice of a passionate, outspoken woman.

Pipers I have talked to have their own view, their own oral traditions. They speak of the "bardic offense" for which Mary was sent away from Dunvegan and that the hereditary piper Padraig Mòr MacCrimmon was her lover. His son, the successive hereditary piper Padraig Òg MacCrimmon, composed the pibroch "Lament for Mary MacLeod" after Mary's death. It is a tune with a resonance and character that pipers continue to approach with caution.

To the idea of a lover Meg says, "I think that we now underestimate the passion for the clan, that we see only personal passion whereas this was something else."

The Gaelic mystery of "something else" is compelling, but it is not a romance, not reductive to popular culture's (or poetry's) elevation of personal passion above all else. Justifiably between the lines in Meg's words is the inference that to assess "something else" requires knowledge of Gaelic history, politics, social mores, and language. Aonghas Phàdraig Caimbeul had said much the same thing, but I think Meg's comment is also a warning that to focus on Mary's private life undermines her achievement, replicating damage done to her in her lifetime. It is a lot to unpack from a sentence, but it matters because that is not how I heard what the pipers said. I heard a tradition of love embodied in two giants of poetry and music, more iconic than romantic; but I do understand that speaking of it poses a risk.

It helps me to think of "passion for the clan" as a vanished species. Its loss severs a network of relationships from the world. Nothing can replace it; but art's ecological function is to stir remaining glimmers of it (the *feu follet* again!) back towards the centre of what it is possible to imagine. Mary and other Gaelic poets advocated for virtues in their leaders that encompassed responsibilities to people and land. These were not only idealized characteristics but were essential to the survival of a way of life. Art invites the re-integration of such virtues into a picture of the future and can help reset its direction.

"There are very few known named women poets; it was not the prescribed path for women at all," Meg says. "It was a Norse custom to bury witches face down [as Aonghas MacNeacail has told me] and this was done to Màiri. It was done with other women poets such as Margaret / Mairearad Lachainn. They were transgressive and not conventional and seem to have come into their own in middle age. The other tradition is that Màiri asked to be buried in this way, to close her lying mouth."

"Why would she have done that?"

"To symbolize the opposition she dealt with. I don't think for a moment that she thinks she is lying: the poet has to believe, otherwise the poems are dead."

I have one more Dunvegan question. "Without Mary having been a long resident there [at what Aonghas Phàdraig Caimbeul had called 'Mary's university'] as Mark and Frater have suggested, how would Mary have learned what she did of the genealogy and the forms, the strophic metres she composed in?"

"It would have been all around her," Mark replies, echoing Aonghas Phàdraig's words but widening their context.

43.

On my first visit to Harris, the day before El and I walked to the church at Rodel where Mary is buried, we had stopped at what was left of Clach Steineagaidh, a circle of twelve or thirteen stones looking out over the Sound of Taransay. Only one of the stones remains upright now where people have gathered since Neolithic times. The circle appears to have been important ceremonially or for navigation or as a calendar – or for all these reasons and others lost to us. Human remains have been found nearby. An information board suggests the stones had a link with two other sites around the Sound – a standing stone on the Island of Taransay and the MacLeod stone at Aird, which we had passed earlier on the walk. All three were made when a giantess struck a stone with a hammer and splintered off three shards. Between where the stones stand now was once dry land and I wonder if they are there as reminders of what once lay between them.

An earthquake and tsunami in 1700 – within Mary's lifetime – altered the coastline where I live. The toll inflicted on Indigenous villages and their inhabitants, and on the land and rivers, survives in oral accounts, but it is only relatively recently that examination of sediment layers, core samples from the ocean floor, dendrochronology (tree-ring dating), and carbon dating have "proven" the stories to be true. They were always true but were discounted by Europeans who did not arrive in the region until after the event. Thousands of years earlier, the space between the island where I live and the mainland was filled with sand. This was gouged out by glaciation and flooded by seawater, leaving islands, some of which came to be colonized by settlers from distant archipelagos such as the Orkneys.

Poets layer memories, history, stories, studies, people, art, and industry, each in their own way, into their poems. It is like placing artifacts on an archaeological museum table: the time for viewing is the present and yet the voices inherent in clay and tablets, cloth, and rings contain tremors of life. Visible and invisible assume shape and texture. Not all of it is discernable. Not all of it comes alive. Sounds rise within language to celebrate what remains and to recall what is missing. Like the Valley of Dry Bones in the Book of Ezekiel where the dead are gathered, bone to bone, tendons and flesh and skin, then breathed into from the four winds.

A great rock stood at the end of Whiffin Spit, the entrance to Sooke Harbour, near where I live, until it was blown up by dynamite in 1964 to assist navigation by large vessels. In the T'Sou-ke time of stories, a man had sat at the end of the Spit and asked the Changer to transform him into a rock which would be a watchman over the harbour. He wanted to guard the entrance and to protect the clams, an important food supply, from deadly red tide (paralytic shellfish poisoning). The Changer did as he was asked, and the man became a rock, which stood on watch for thousands of years. I must have seen the rock when I visited the spit as a child; but without the story, which I was never told, I could not hold on to its reality.

44.

There is no conditional tense in Gaelic per se, Mark says, so what is conditional and what is habitual (in the imperfect tense) use the same tense. It can be ambiguous. It is an open question.

In English, the imperfect is an unfinished action in the past. From the point of view of the present, it remains unfinished, it is ongoing, a form of the habitual. The conditional is also time-nuanced: it can mean that as long as – if – something happens, then it or something that depends on it can be done or be in the state of happening. What is being said in the Gaelic is dependent on context and still might be ambiguous. For me, trying to tidy this into what I find in the poetry, the ambiguity explains much about the refusal of Mary's lines to be bound by linear time.

There is also the question of a song Mary composed neither indoors nor out but on a threshold, which, as Meg points out, is a locale familiar from story.

"So, it isn't literal?" I say.

"Oh, it can be literal – more willingness that it be literal – that she had found her solution which would be recognized by others, I think, as her inhabiting a liminal space, a space of freedom, perhaps by circumventing a taboo: she lays claim to this place. Much of Màiri is, I think, to do with laying a claim."

45.

More than once while we are eating dinner (rice with raisins and a stir-fry with vegetables and mushrooms) Meg attempts to turn the conversation to what my connection is to Mary MacLeod. We have discussed much about writing and talked of an upcoming ceilidh at which Meg will read a commissioned poem that she intends as healing for the community; and about a libretto problem I solved by understanding that the text did not have to be sequential, it could move through a series of moments. Over crumble and foamy homemade ginger beer, Meg tries again: "You haven't told us what your connection to all this is?"

I begin my tale with the bookstore at Clashnessie where I first encountered Mary's poetry in the late 1970s, and my subsequent failure to cross paths with her work. I have reached my walk on Harris decades later, the visit to the church at Rodel and discovery that evening that Mary MacLeod is buried in the church, and I am just into the tricky part where I wake the next morning in a state of altered reality, when Calum runs in with a bouquet of daisies for Meg. This stops the story for several minutes, but when Calum settles, I must continue. At the end of my account, there is a pause. Meg says, not unkindly, "Well I can see why you didn't want to tell us because we'd think you were mad!" Her words hang in the air. But then Veronica says, "I don't think so. There is a pool that poets dip into; a shared place that they reach into. A commonality. Thank you for telling us."

46.

We are about to walk to the shore to view the waves a sudden wind has stirred up when the outside kitchen door bursts open. A smiling man with a beard and long, unruly black and grey hair stands like a manifestation of the outside roaring; or as if he had been long asleep in the peat and was awakened by the tumult. It is Meg's cousin, Justin. He has travelled over a thousand kilometres that day to visit her and to play his balalaika at the ceilidh in the hall on Saturday. He hands Meg a bottle of Laphroig. She heats a plate of dinner for him while we fill him in on Mary MacLeod. Gillian slips away after we have spoken about contemporary Gaelic communities in Canada; Veronica leaves to do her online course and to keep young Calum company. Both Mark and I are driving and so refuse the offered whisky. "The polis never come here," Meg comments as we compare our local driving laws. "Except once they came when they were looking out for someone who was ill."

When Justin has finished eating, the cat drapes itself over his shoulder like a plush scarf. Meg tells us that her grandmother typed out the manuscript copy of *Lady Chatterley's Lover*. Mark begins a story. His grandmother's husband was believed dead in the First World War, but then turned up some time afterwards. We wait to hear what happened next, but there is no conclusion, and so we go out to the cars.

I do not know where the headlight switch is on the rental car and cannot find it in the dark, but once I start the engine, a modest pair of sidelights turns on. I put the car in gear and follow Mark's car, which is speeding off into the night. A narrow ribbon of black within black twists and folds and upends beneath the wheels as I trail the red taillights ahead of me across moorland. The wind blows in drifts through the car's open windows; the grass of the verge flickers gold, and I catch a few silvery glimpses of the loch. A bat shoots from the trees. I cross a series of cattle grates, each one a surprise, gripping the steering wheel and leaning forward to squint through the windscreen at the increasingly distant taillights. Mark's car is leaving my slow crawl behind. Lamplight from two houses shines across a stone beach, Highland cows and sheep sprawl onto the warm paving; and then there is such a long way across a plain, and a descent in which, seconds before I finally find the headlight switch, I am sure I have lost my senses. Once I come to the T-junction and make the turn towards home, the road broadens, and it is not as lonely as it was in the deep glens where invisible mountains had their say while they imprinted their weight on my skin.

I had almost forgotten the moon rising over the Sound: just a hint through the cloud, but no big help when it was needed on the long winding way from Tarskavaig.

47.

My father turns on the porchlight. A face swims in from the night and blowing rain. Mr Speller stands at my grandmother's back door dressed in navy blue work-clothes and a dark wet jacket. He won't come inside. "Hurry up kids!" my father says. We run for our coats and boots. Our mother, behind us as we go to the door, is uncertain.

"Herb?" she says to my father. "It's already late."

"They'll be fine," my father says.

"Where are your tokens?" my mother asks us. We run back in to look.

I don't know what tokens are for except that they come with our milk bottle tops. We are supposed to keep them to take to the gathering at Marigold Hall where they count as points for our team. Perhaps, like the stamps my grandmother cuts from envelopes, they will help the missionaries?

We follow Mr Speller down the driveway along the path of headlights to where he has left his van running. He opens the back doors and lifts me up the step inside. My brother follows and we join half a dozen other children, most of them boys with scraped skulls and thin clothing, on the wooden benches that run along the sides. There are no windows.

Marigold! Marigold! I chant. It is still a favourite word. The dark is complete except for the little light that leaks through to us from the front where Mr Speller drives. A wet road, the smell of old lunches, the children silent. Several times, when the van is full, I sit in the front seat next to Mr Speller because I am the smallest. Mr Speller's thin knees lift and fall as he works the pedals.

At the old wooden hall, we go inside. Someone is playing the piano. We will not see Mr Speller again until it is time to leave. We sit on folding chairs below a stage and sing Sunday school songs we already know.

There is a Bible story. All of it is familiar except for the tokens and these children who do not speak to us. When I tell my mother that I want to stop going, she tells my father, who explains that he was trying to help out Mr Speller. With what? Why?

Mr Speller stops calling for us. There is no van. No Monday night journey in winter darkness. No answer to the questions I have tried to frame.

VIII

Metaphors for Poetry

The pagan Celtic belief system had no transcendent worlds: Tir nan Og [the
land of the young, an island in the western ocean] and the otherworld were
very much part of the globe, albeit out in the ocean or below the surface.
The two worlds, the world known to man and the otherworld glimpsed in the
wilderness, are two ways of seeing our world, the one from our socio-historical
perspective, the other mythopoetically, from the timeless perspective of the
natural forces of death and regeneration.

– Meg Bateman, "The Landscape of the Gaelic Imagination"

Taken on a sledge
drawn by a white horse
led by an old woman,
soft underbellies to the shrinking moon,
we were weaponless

calling out,
Is there a friend?

May god be gracious,
we are not avaricious
(born from a fast river
flung restless back into it),

we would fasten
our loose bones together;
we would speak to a friend.

– "Is There a Friend," Tighnacraig

48.

I am not sure I need – or want – to talk to anyone else about Mary Mac-
Leod. But I have arranged to see the Gaelic poet and children's book
author Maoilios Caimbeul / Myles Campbell while I am on Skye. I pick
El up from the Kyle train station on the mainland, re-cross the bridge,
and drive north through busy Portree and onto single-track roads.
Views of the island of Raasay off the coast to the east recall our night
on the cliff above Applecross with our daughter when we looked westwards across the Raasay heights into a storm. We stop at a café where
we are hurried through lunch by a woman rushing to a Zumba class. A
tourist information card on the table gives information about the Gaelic
language and how to discover who you belong to and where, but all the
voices in the café are English. Not long afterwards, we take a turn down
a hill towards the sea.

Many authors are unrecognizable from their photographs, but I've
no doubt it is Maoilios Caimbeul who comes to the door of the second
house at which we call, although he looks younger than I expected. Like
the striking Meg Bateman, whose appearance combines a transparent,
almost otherworldly quality with sharp intelligence, Caimbeul's face
conveys complexity. Unfortunately, some of this is because he has been
expecting a woman from Australia, with whom he has also been in contact, and not me. She is interested in William Ross, a poet born on Skye
in 1762, more than half a century after Mary's death.

It takes a few awkward minutes to straighten this out.

Maoilios invites us indoors for a dram, and Margaret, Maoilios's wife,
brings in tea, buns, and cakes while he pours Famous Grouse, and we
sort out where to start the conversation. Maoilios says that he is not
that comfortable talking about Mary MacLeod, whose work he knows
primarily through John Mackenzie's nineteenth-century Highland
poetry anthology, but he mentions how it was unusual for a woman of
her time to be a bard, and speaks of the reputation she had, alluded to
by William Ross, for a liking for whisky in her old age. I take a sip of
the Famous Grouse, a favourite from Glen Lochay days. He retrieves the
anthology from a shelf and reads Mary's poetry aloud in Gaelic, paying
respect and setting a tone; and then he answers my questions about the
poetry's strophic form.

In general, each line of the strophe contains two stresses, and there is end rhyme, which often works in chain fashion and can include repetition. Watson's analysis of Mary's metres discusses variations within this realm: only four of the poems in *Gaelic Songs* can be described as "regular strophe." The others involve changes in line length, the fall of the stresses, how the rhyme works inside the lines as well as at the ends, and the role of repetition. Each variation introduces what I think of as a small amount of new organic material – the poet's ear and influences – but not so much as to totally change the form's signature. He reiterates, as I had learned, that Mary's poetry is more formal than normal song poetry but is not as formal as the syllabic forms that the highest poets knew. There were also village poets – those known locally. Were these a little like, I venture, some of my Newfoundland forebears who recorded community and personal events in verse? One of these family poems tells the story of the shipwreck of the schooner *Swallow*, captained by the poem's author John Bowering, and how the crew, which included women and children, were rescued by a steamer, and taken across the Atlantic Ocean to Stornoway on the Isle of Lewis. It is the only historical connection I have, as far as I know, to the Hebrides.

While Maoilios is out of the room looking for a book of Nova Scotia Gaelic songs to follow on from my Newfoundland reference, I talk to Margaret.

Maoilios was born in northeastern Skye but lived "all over," Margaret says, because his father was a home missionary for the Free Church. Margaret was brought up on Lewis and Harris where Free Churches dominate, and the Sabbath is strictly kept. (El once ran into trouble on Harris when he turned the television on in his B&B one Sunday to watch motor-racing.) The Campbells met in the early 1960s, dated for two or three months, and then parted. Margaret studied nursing in Inverness, nursed throughout the islands, and met the man who became her husband back on Lewis in Stornoway. They moved to Suffolk and had two children. Maoilios attended university in Edinburgh where he knew and drank with well-known Scottish poet Hamish Henderson at Sandy Bell's pub. He married, had a family, and was divorced in the early 1990s.

After Margaret's husband died, she returned to Lewis to be near her family, lived in the family croft, and worked as a nurse. At a low point, after a builder took her money without completing the work for which she had paid him, she had a dream. "I was a Christian," Margaret says; "I am a Christian."

In the dream she saw a tall grey-haired man at a gate. When he turned to look at her, it was Maoilios, whom she hadn't seen or thought of for more than thirty years. In the dream he took her hand, and they went through the gate into a green place where there was great happiness between them. When she woke up, she was upset because she was no longer there with him. The dream would not leave her alone. After several years she found out where he was and called him "in order to get rid of it." She had said to herself, "If he takes this call then we'll see. But if not, that's it."

Maoilios answered the telephone.

"It is a long story," Maoilios says coming in. They have written a book about their relationship, the supernatural events in their lives, and his conversion from an agnostic Gaelic poet to a Christian one. They are interested in miracles, science and religion and synchronicity. For them, their experiences of the supernatural are evidence of the active role of God and Christ in their lives.

I ask Maoilios if he thinks such intuitions can be trusted. "There is also intellectual 'stuff' to it," he says. He reads religious philosophers and scholars such as Rudolf Otto and Mircea Eliade who have developed frameworks for their explorations of the numinous. When I tell my story about Mary MacLeod, it makes sense to them in those terms.

Many poets look for means to unify the rational and irrational in their thought and writing. Others receive without concern the dreams, words, lines, whole poems, even music that appear to arrive from elsewhere, needing only to accept the gift with gratitude. Some I know have felt haunted by subjects with which they have engaged closely. It is as if an act of creative empathy expands to reach an understanding that "all ages are contemporaneous."

Poetry, by its nature and tropes, grounds the unknown in the known in varying degrees. A way to distinguish poetry tastes and styles is to take the measure of the balance. In Mary MacLeod's verses, the ground is underlying cultural knowledge (which contains a measure of the mythic and irrational) tied to a record of clan genealogy and history, and then to contemporary events. Reception of the work as authentic depends on the listeners' acceptance of the poet's legitimate access to bardic power's source. Traditionally, bards lay in the dark with a stone upon the belly, to wait for inspiration. Meg Bateman writes that their gifts, like those of pipers and fiddlers, were "bestowed on them when in contact with the otherworld in the wilderness." The fairies, intermediaries between the Upper and Lower Worlds, Bateman says, are the donors.

The problem for Mary and other seventeenth-century Gaelic women bards was that as traditional structures decayed and the overall influence of bards waned, the chiefs adopted English social customs and language that did not recognize the female poet's residual right to standing. Any contact she did have with the bardic "source" was likely to be re- and mis-interpreted as socially disruptive and worse.

We finish our conversation, whisky, and tea, Maoilios makes copies for me of materials about Mary MacLeod that he finds in books, and we leave to drive round the north end of the Trotternish Peninsula. It is grand scenery, made of cliffy broken mountains and dramatic sweeps of moor to the sea. A hawk turns and keens above a field. We stop to watch it for several minutes and in the way of these things, several other cars pull up behind to see if we have discovered anything interesting.

Some cultures are more inclusive of the non-rational than others. Scotland is known for a population in which the gift of second sight is not uncommon. Symbols in Margaret's dreams play a role in her and Maoilios's lives, helping to guide their decisions. The capacity to see remote or future objects or events may be an inherited way in which information is received and processed by the brain; or, more generally, part of a larger creative mental process. It could be Scottish culture that helps Maoilios and Margaret find no conflict between written church dogma and "the unknowable [which is] present whether we would like it to be or not."

My deeply religious Canadian mother, on the other hand, was made uncomfortable by what she felt was incompatibility between her beliefs and her ability to foretell death. She spoke of her precognitive abilities rarely because they worried her. Only once, as far as I know, did precognition bring her happiness. It was when she had dream-foreknowledge of a birth and knew of my pregnancy before I did.

49.

Everyone here at the breakfast table in Martin's B&B in Uig, where we have stayed before when heading for the Outer Hebrides, is a traveller. The weather, grey and blowy, the sea whipped into racing horses, is going to affect us all. People padding around in warm socks and wearing heavy sweaters make toast at the counter or pour cereal from plastic containers into bowls. Nearly all of them stop for a moment to gaze out the window. Not even the younger ones have cellphones or iPads out because interest in the rest of the world has waned during a night when the wind slipped fingers inside the B&B's garret windows and rattled the glass. I was cold in our room, and once we are on the ferry, I know I'll be colder. The Minch isn't the smoothest crossing in a blow. Experienced travellers or not, each of us feels an inherent need to prepare for the unknown.

Mary MacLeod recounts an incident in the Minch in one of her poems: "a great roaring sea leaping about thy boat; thy / self and thy stout crew, when your sails ripped ... a drowning wave came upon thee." Windowpanes rattle; I drink cold coffee. But before I can go further with these thoughts, El remarks that there is little to no Wi-Fi reception here, despite the promises in the brochure, and that's the reason for the absence of personal screens.

Still, I can't help but feel there is something about a lodging in which travellers pause to rest and eat, even these days, that makes them look for a little bonding, someone to notice them, put them on record, just in case. El speaks to a couple on their honeymoon who have careers in international diplomacy; I overhear an account of a long walk that swiftly reminds me of a time I was trapped at a formal dinner in Edinburgh by a man whose only conversation was to recount, pace by pace, his marathon runs.

I turn to the woman beside me and introduce myself. She looks relieved to have someone to talk to, and once I ask her where she is going, immediately begins to tell me her story. We are not in *The Canterbury Tales* or *The Decameron*. There isn't enough time for lengthy narrative. We have ferries to catch: whatever we must tell each other has to be brief.

She was a primary teacher who married at nineteen for nineteen years and had two children. At the same time as her husband left her in their twentieth year together, her godmother died, and she inherited an eighteenth-century cottage in Buckinghamshire. When she married again, it was to a much older man who dropped dead at her feet when he was sixty-seven. After his death, she could no longer afford to keep up the cottage, and so, since she and her late husband had liked travelling in the Hebrides, she had decided, against the advice of her children and her friends, to move there. Everything she owns is in the small trailer she is taking with her on the boat. Her destination is Sollas, a tiny crofting village on the north coast of North Uist, known for its sand dunes and made famous by the resistance of its women during the Clearances.

"Do you know anyone there?"

"No," she says. She is resolutely cheerful. Determined that this will work. El, who has been to Sollas, has told me that its white beaches are beautiful, but there is little else there. A string of crofts each widely separated from the other, a grocery store and a community centre. Not an easy place for an outsider to move to on her own.

"Have you been there before?"

"No," she says.

She smiles, finishes her tea, checks the time, and gathers her breakfast dishes. "See you on the boat!"

If there had been time, I would have told her Aonghas Phàdraig Caimbeul's tale of the Big Woman who rode the length of the Uists to St Kilda and returned with hazelnuts. I would have said that the Big Woman must have passed close to Sollas on her journey, and that the woman changing her life should remember this. I would have said that hazelnuts represent wisdom from the otherworld. When they or the salmon that feed on them are eaten by bards who find them in the streams that run from a pool surrounded by hazelnut trees in the otherworld, they gain poetic and prophetic powers. I would have said that perhaps the Big Woman was a poet, or just any woman who risks the unknown. I would have told her how much I admired her courage. I would not have pointed out that with few trees left on the islands now, there is little to give shelter from the violent winter winds. I would have admired her courage and helped her believe that she would find a way to make the old stories true.

50.

For the last several days I have been grieving the death of a friend. News of her passing reached me as I began this journey to the Hebrides. Most nights since, I have awakened to the music of a river, its sound slow, cold, thick, and syrupy. This should be no surprise since the first night after I heard the news, I was sleeping beside a river, my window open just above it. It should also be no surprise since this Liz – Elizabeth Gorrie, the third of my friends with that name whom I have spoken of – had a gift for imagery and belief in magic that she displayed in her ingenious productions for theatre. I dream of her and get up and write without stopping: "*It must be the river darkling, the bodies of fish in a cool slide of current; the light enough to show the tops of the hills. It must be the song of the river, all the remembered voices. The ones who passed by or who stopped to mark a stone; or to throw a stone into the water. It must be her, her feet wet, her shoes in her hand, thoughts calm as she feels the river's pebbles under her feet, can count them, can remember them like words, each with a tone that describes what the river says, who it has seen, where it is going. It must be the night like thin beaten silver, like a memory of planets: a room and the river and Liz in it, without shoes; it must be she who wakes me to listen.*"

51.

Last time I was in Uig, we sailed from there to Tarbert on Harris where we started our walk south, the walk that led me to Mary MacLeod, and returned to Skye from Lochmaddy on North Uist. This time, we will cross the Minch to Lochmaddy first, take the bus north to Berneray, and then retrace our steps back to Skye. We have only a few days for this loop, but I had promised myself I would return to Berneray, which we had visited accidently on that first trip and which I had liked so much.

At the time, I hadn't known of Mary MacLeod's association with it. Now that I have read Mary's poetry, I would like to see what else I can learn on the small island. Watson's introduction to *Gaelic Songs* includes a paragraph that intrigues me. It is about the ruins of a house on Berneray that Sir Norman gave to Mary. The ruins could be seen when the book was published in 1934 and I am curious to see if anything is left of these buildings after the passage of so much time.

As soon as we get off the bus from Lochmaddy to Berneray, we drop our packs at our B&B and head to the former Nurse's Cottage, now the Visitor Information Centre, which houses the Berneray Historical Society. I am in a hurry because it is Friday and I've been warned that the centre closes soon for the weekend. We are only here for a day and a half. Inside the stone cottage are several rooms of photographic displays, information about the Historical Society's cultural and genealogical projects, and natural history information and maps. As soon as he is finished with another visitor, the curator, a small man in a red pullover, asks if he can be of help. When he hears I am interested in Mary MacLeod and wonder if there is anything left of where she had lived, he leaves at once to hurry to his house and bring back a copy of her poems. We look through them together and he takes me through the verses that mention Sir Norman.

"You will never get to the bottom of the mystery of Mary MacLeod," he says to me when we have finished talking, and then he takes us to a window and indicates where the ruins of Sir Norman MacLeod's house are to be found, on a point at the far side of the bay. "You'll know it by the carving above the lintel: *Hic natus est illustris ille Normanus Mac-Leod de Berneray eques auratus*," he says. He locates the house for us on a map – and indicates where the MacLeod well was, nearby, to the southwest. Close by it, too, is where Mary's thatched house, Tobhta nan Craobh (Ruins of the Trees), also known as Tobhta Màiri (Mary's house), once stood.

I look at the map, confused, and trace my finger along the adjacent roadway to its end. But it is El who understands what has happened before I do. When we'd stopped and gotten off the bus and waited for the driver to eat his lunch when we were here before, we were there already. El had walked down the lane to Norman MacLeod's house, and I had crossed the field to the well and to where Tobhta nan Craobh, Mary's house, had been. I had climbed up the hill beside it, the sun out and wind blowing, and felt that I was home.

This time the weather is wet and stormy – sheep take cover in the bus shelter at the end of the line – and a lid of cloud presses towards the sea. Still, from the shore near where Mary lived, I can look across the water and see, just as she describes in one of her poems, the hills of Skye and the tower at Rodel and the white sands of Scarista on Harris where we had been.

We spend the rest of the day exploring the island, trying without success to fit our walks between showers. Our B&B host at Seal View signs me up to receive the Historical Society's newsletters. One of their current projects is to trace the culture – songs, poems, customs, genealogy, memories, and artifacts – that left Berneray with the Clearances. The Society is making connections with people in South Africa, Australia, and Canada, attempting to map some of what vanished along with the displaced people. We walk to a small fishing loch, then back past Seal View (and a great many seals lounging on the shore) to take the path to Borve, passing many little farms. The community hall when we reach it (hoping for more information) is locked, so we veer off down the road and across the machair, the sandy grass-covered soil strewn with purple and yellow wildflowers, which stretches all the way to the beach. Across a burn, and into a boggy section of land where mushrooms plump up from cow pats and sheep droppings, to strike uphill, the turf springy and uneven, trying not to get our feet soaked. At the top, I lean against a Neolithic standing stone for shelter from the blowing rain. From there I can see the entire island, and the sea and so many other islands that were part of Mary's world. Pabbay, where Mary's brother lived, one of several islands where she may have been exiled, where she may even have been born, is only a few miles to the north. And there are other islands, in every direction, the steppingstones along sea-roads by which people in the Hebrides – in Berneray, the Uists, Harris, Lewis, Skye, and others – had travelled for thousands of years. By 1000 AD, the archeologist Dr Kate MacDonald has said, the Hebrides were linked by boats that travelled to and from Orkney, Shetland, Ireland, Scandinavia and even as far as the Mediterranean.

These are the continuing sea links mentioned in Mary's poems. When Sir Norman slipped in and out of the Hebrides on missions to Europe to promote the Royalist fight against Oliver Cromwell, he travelled ancient and familiar routes. Cromwell's soldiers, camped on a hill that overlooked Sir Norman's house, were perfectly aware of what he was doing, but they did not know how to stop him.

The driver of the bus we flag down, to return us to Lochmaddy in time for the ferry, is at first taciturn, but after we cross the Berneray causeway to North Uist, he begins to chat. He talks about the change in the weather: the winter is longer and not as cold; the storms are greater, the sun rises and sets in a different place, the moon rises now in the northeast instead of the east – although there was an exception the other day at the full moon when it was back in the east. I tell him that the Inuit believe the earth has shifted on its axis. "Finally, someone who sees the same things I do," he says. He is from North Uist and lives on the west coast. He tells us that he sold a piece of his croft to a man who built a log house there. Imported the whole thing in two big containers from Canada – this on Uist, the once-forested land. These days, it is on my home island that you can watch the forests decline. Only a small percentage of the great old-growth trees remain.

"Two men came over, too, to do the building, although the weather was so bad, they couldn't finish it and had to go back, so it was completed by the local boys."

It is a windy day; waves break onto the outer Lochmaddy harbour islands. The ferry arrives half an hour late. When we're at last onboard and ready to leave, we watch a man in his shirtsleeves wrestle with the gangplank and nearly catch his arm in the winch hawser; and then, having waited to cast off until the last moment with the ferry nearly underway, he leaps across the gap to the dock, lifts and hoicks the stern line from the piling, and sets us free.

IX

Cauldron

I reached   into the niche
of the cliff
I eased grass   aside

and there   under the brood
lay a shattered   bowl

Sometimes   when you look
inside   the nest
there's an egg

sometimes there's an egg
still   whole

and gold   and alive

– "Cauldron (of Vocation)," *Threshold*

52.

The stories I have from my grandfather are narratives. His tales are of
fishing and ice-fishing and ice-sailing, shipwrecks, and drownings. They
cluster around him, forming a personality along with the many anecdotes
told about him – such as the winter he built a fishing boat in the kitchen
and removed a wall in the spring to get it out. The story my grandfather
tells that I like best is of his first sight of my grandmother, who walked

one evening from her father's fishing camp in Labrador to his father's camp to borrow an axe. "I see her / on the ice / moving in silver / bringing stars down ... like a girl / becoming a bride," I write, re-imagining the moment in my first book. She gathered the eggs of seabirds. She picked berries in the bogs and marshes to dry for the winter. She liked bakeapples best, she told me. I know them as cloudberries.

Afterwards, they spent any free time they had together. As soon as they returned to Newfoundland at the end of the season, he went to Canada to seek his fortune so they could marry.

What I learn of my grandmother, I learn differently. When we rest and wait for visitors after lunch, I sit in her lap or on the floor leaning against her legs. In the quiet I notice several photographs on a shelf. I have seen them before, but never *looked* at them. One is of a young woman in a white high-necked blouse. She has upswept hair, a smooth round face and large, beautiful eyes. My grandmother tells me it was taken when she was sixteen and working in Montreal. Working? Where? She and one of her sisters had gone there together. Another photograph is of a baby. Tommy, she says and takes an in-breath. The boys in the other photographs are Wilbert and Clifford. She does not need to tell me that they and the baby did not live out their childhoods. My father and uncles, but not my grandmother and only a few times my grandfather, talk about the dead boys. In this way, all the children remain part of the family.

After the postman hands my grandmother letters, she and I go through them together. She reads them first to herself and then reads parts of them aloud for me. Most often the letters are from her sisters, Dorcas in Boston and Zelah in Saint John's. The letters are filled with names and places I will remember and identify in what I learn when I visit Newfoundland years later. Many of the names repeat through the generations. The reading of the letters opens a door I cannot pass through, but listening to my grandmother's voice lets me peer through a window at her once separate life. The gardens running to the sea; the kitchen in a jut at the back of the house her father built; the bluffs, "the Bars," where she and her brothers and sisters played.

She recites the poems she learned in school – Wordsworth, Coleridge, Keats, and poems for children such as "'I love you, Mother,' said little

John; / Then, forgetting his work, his cap went on, / And he was off to
the garden-swing, / And left her the water and wood to bring ..." time
after time without complaint when I ask her to.

I learn, when helping my grandmother select a new dress in Eaton's,
that she does not wear the colour green. She was wearing green when
news came of the death in 1901 of her fifteen-year-old brother in an accident in Boston. A few years later an uncle and cousin drowned when
caught in a storm while pulling up cod traps offshore the family fishing
camp near Holton, Labrador. Just under a decade after that, another
brother was castaway – drowned at sea. Yet the green dress is the only
way she ever indicates her grief to me – a grief that could not be expressed and must instead be housed in a dress and stored or given away.

Once she leaves Newfoundland at the age of twenty-seven (the same
age I am when I meet El), she does not return until the 1950s. By then,
both her parents are dead. Her father, Azariah, was the seventh son of
a seventh son, a sea-captain and lay preacher in the Methodist church.
People came to him to be cured of headaches and toothaches. My
father's cousin tells me that his aunt, my grandmother's sister, said
Azariah would just touch the spot and they'd say they were cured. She
said that people believed in it – not as if *he* did. The cousin lived in the
family house with his parents, along with my grandmother's mother
until she died. He remembers the old woman seated in a rocker beside
the stove in the kitchen in which there was also a couch and chairs.
"People lived in the kitchen back then," he said. She wore a big black
dress and a white apron, a brooch at her neck, her hair scraped back
in a bun. She looked serene and would criticize her daughter-in-law
saying, "I see there's not much done today."

This is most of what I know of them.

Even this is no longer knowledge as easy for me to access as it once
was. To find it again, I unfold the only survivor of all the hooked rag-
rugs my grandmother made. Its sacking back is disintegrating, and
some of the hooked materials have come loose. I touch the faded blues,
reds, golds, and yellows of its sunflower-mandala design. I remember
her stirring rags and old stockings in pots of dye on the stove; and remember, too, that I am not to tell grandfather that after washing her

hair in the sink she rinses it with bluing. She dries her hair and winds it into a thin air-dried towel. I climb onto the short counter to the left of the sink while she removes her apron and lean my back against the ice-box pantry door to wait. Soon the iceman will arrive with a block of ice and load it through the outside hatch, and I will help my grandmother reorganize the milk and butter. If it is hot, she will chip off chunks of ice for me to suck.

Her presence suffuses me. My father and uncles have a share of it. If you could bottle it, a cousin told me, you would make a fortune.

And now, as my fingers follow the rug-pattern, we are once more downtown in Eaton's. There isn't enough time, really, before we must catch the bus home, but she lets me persuade her down the stairs to the basement so I can run through the underground tunnel between the two large buildings that make up the store, with the lights off.

53.

Of the three Hebridean Islands – Mull, Pabbay, and Scarba – thought to be those to which Mary was banished at one time or another, either individually or, as Watson suggests, as a *cuairt* (a journey through a given list of places), the only one named in her surviving songs is Scarba. This time, when she sets the emotional ground of the poem, she tells us exactly where she is and not only names the island – a never-much-inhabited one in the southern Inner Hebrides – but her precise location on it as she composes. Her story is characterized by such gaps, silences, puzzles, and erasures that it is a relief to discover something this specific. But what can be so special about where she is and what she can see from there that she wants the hearers of her song to think about it while they listen? Scarba is more than one hundred miles (161 km) south by sea from Dunvegan, or closer to one hundred and thirty miles (209 km) south from Berneray. Even by the most direct sea-road, Mary is a long way from home.

In the song "Luinneag Mhic Leoid" / "MacLeod's Lilt," Mary begins this way:

Sitting here on the knoll, forlorn and unquiet, I gaze
upon Islay and marvel the while; there was a time I
never thought, till my times took a change, that hither
I should come to view Jura from Scarba.

I hurabh o i hoiriunn o,
i hurabh o i hoiriunn o,
I hurabh o i hogaidh ho ro,
hi ri ri rithibh ho i ag o.

Hither to come and view Jura from Scarba! Bear my
greetings to the land that lieth shadowed by the rugged
peaks, to the young renowned Sir Norman that hath
won headship over an armed host ...

Throughout the poem, the first line of each verse repeats the last line
of the verse before it in the same – or a variation of the same – words.
This makes a chain of sound and reinforces the content of the repeated
lines. Here, in the beginning, Mary's astonishment at what has happened to her and where it has brought her is impossible to miss. "I /
never thought, till my times took a change, that hither I should come
to view Jura from Scarba. // Hither to come and view Jura from Scarba!"
If we weren't sure at first hearing, by the second time through the point
has registered, helped by the vocables – rhythmic non-semantic syllables between the verses – that invite the listener to join in.

Mary's response to the bewilderment of exile is to appeal to her
patron Sir Norman MacLeod. She asks that her greetings be sent to him
through this poem, which celebrates his achievements as a leader in
battle, his noble lineage and kinship, and his practice of the Gaelic
virtues of open-handedness and hospitality. His character, she tells us,
is his inheritance as one of the sons of the great Rory Mòr (the chief in
whose hall she had been "joyful, // Dancing merry on a wide floor" as
a girl). All Rory's other sons are dead.

In Ó Baoill's translation, Mary describes Sir Norman, the surviving
son, as "a treasure among men" and hopes, although she has "been

parted" from him, that she will never hear news of his death. Watson uses the word "sundered" instead of "parted" for what has happened, a word that suggests an aggressive separation. Both translations convey that the parting was against her will, although there is nothing to indicate if it were or were not Sir Norman's wish. What Mary has been divided from includes Sir Norman's physical body, which she describes as "fair of form without flaw of fashioning." His "manly and generous" heart, his ruddy cheeks, blue eyes, and curling hair are listed, a catalogue that along with "fair of form" is conventional in praise poetry, but in her rendering conveys an intimacy, yet is no infringement of Sir Norman's exalted fitness as leader.

The poem moves on to the leader's well-stocked weapon-rack and armoury. Powder-horn, shot-horn, sword-blades, rifles, carabines, bows with hemp bowstrings, and arrows "fledged from the plumage of the eagle and the silk of Galway" make up a mix of hunting and fighting weapons. Sir Norman's prowess at hunting with his well-armed men, the young hounds inciting the old ones – which results in "blood on the deer" – may be analogical as well as conventional, especially in the context of the poem's ending, which has these armed men "read the day and speed over the ocean," men who are "fit to sail the vessel to the haven wherein she would be beached." Accompanying references to Sir Norman's alliances with Ireland and throughout Scotland further hint that in the guise of praise, Mary has armed resistance in mind, or even – given the mix of personal and formal, emotion and rhetoric in the poem – her own rescue. Either way, or both, and even if neither of these readings is valid, it is important that Mary mark her location as she sends her "greetings" to Sir Norman. But why? I am sure the answer matters, but even the eminent scholar and translator of Mary's work Colm Ó Baoill, who draws attention to Scarba as a medieval site of pilgrimage, only notes that "[t]o judge by Ordinance Survey maps, it is probably impossible to see much of Islay from Scarba" because the mountains – "the Paps" – of Jura are in the way.

54.

The materials I have asked for are waiting when I arrive at the Maps Reading Room of the National Library of Scotland in Edinburgh. I spread current and old maps and books, files, and papers around me on a large wooden table I have to myself, and settle in.

The island of Scarba, part of an archipelago of hilltops and dividing ridges between drowned valleys, is about three miles (4.8 km) long and close to the same across. It rises steeply from the sea in a knob of rock to a height of about fifteen hundred feet (450 m) in the centre, giving it the appearance of a single mountaintop rising from the seabed. Scarba's north end is separated from the island of Lunga, the southern-most island of the Slate Islands group, by the Gap of the Grey Dog, two channels divided by islets. One of these channels is unnavigable and the other passable only with local knowledge. Scarba's south end is just over half a mile, at the narrowest part of the channel, from the north tip of Jura across the Gulf of Corryvreckan and the Corryvreckan whirl-pool, the third largest "maelstrom" in the world.

Scarba is not an easily approachable island.

The Gulf, I read, is likely part of an ancient seaward extension of the valley of the Add River. A 719-foot-deep (219 m) hole in the irregular seabed and an underwater shelf ending in a basalt pinnacle near the channel's western end create "an impetuous current, not to be matched anywhere about the isle of Britain." The surging tide is forced up and over the pinnacle, where it drops down into the chasm as an underwater waterfall of intense down-currents. It has been shown by experiment that if someone fell in there, they could be sucked down to the seabed and dragged along the bottom for several kilometres.

Martin Martin goes on to observe in the late seventeenth century that at Corryvreckan "[t]he sea begins to boil and ferment with the tide of flood and resembles the boiling of a pot; and then increases grad-ually, until it appears in many whirlpools, which form themselves in sort of pyramids, and immediately after spout up as high as the mast of a little vessel, and at the same time make a loud report." Some say the noise can be heard six to nine miles (ten to fifteen kilometres) away.

Locally, the whirlpool, which can be clearly seen two hundred yards offshore, is called the Cailleach (old woman) after the elemental Gaelic goddess-hag said to be present in the Corryvreckan vortex. Only at or near slack tide is it safe to navigate the channel. Even for modern craft it remains a fearsome passageway to which the lifeboat is called out frequently.

I examine the ordinance survey map. Across the Gulf of Corryvreckan on the much larger island of Jura, Scarba's quartzite ridge becomes "The Paps," mountains between 2,408 feet (734 m) and 2,575 feet (785 m) high. I have to agree with Ó Baoill that Mary might not have seen much of Islay, if at all, from Scarba since Jura's south/southwest-lying neighbour is tucked so closely into Jura's side behind those mountains.

I turn the map and test the angles: there is a point from which it looks like Mary could have seen both islands. It is at about two hundred feet (sixty metres) up on the southwest heights of Scarba overlooking the Gulf of Corryvreckan near its western end. I reach for another map of the island, an older one, and squint at the Gaelic names printed on it in tiny antique lettering until I can decipher them well enough to write them down.

I have been working for hours. A small round soft-spoken brown-haired man in a green tunic, one of the librarians, stops by my table. "Are you not taking a break?" he asks. I look around and see that the chairs at the other tables are empty. Those labouring at them have left their materials spread out to await their return. It is nearly 2 pm. "Do you think I should?" He nods and gives me directions to a nearby coffee shop where I can buy rolls. As he is about to go, I see him glance at my open book of Mary MacLeod's poetry.

"Are you a Gaelic speaker?" I ask him. No, but he organizes ceilidhs about once a month, the next one unfortunately not until September, when, as I tell him, I will no longer be in Scotland. "I don't speak Gaelic," I add – I am not sure why – "but I have been singing in a Gaelic choir where I live on Vancouver Island."

"Oh! Then you must know Mabel, the woman who started the Vancouver Gaelic Choir!"

It is a tiny moment, hardly worth remarking, but for me it underscores how much I like encountering links between my disparate lives. "Can I leave all this?" I ask him. I have notes and book-marked pages and articles arranged in what appear to be (but are not) chaotic piles.

"I'll keep an eye on it for you."

I buy tea and rolls and take a short walk that brings me to the former Edinburgh Geological Institute. Books, maps, records, and collections of sketchbooks and rocks are the real reasons for cities, in my opinion. The building isn't old by Edinburgh standards, not like the historic houses and tenements near where we lived for several years at the top of the Canongate on the Royal Mile, but it is well-designed with sandstone ashlar brought from a local quarry, architectural details such as columns and bays, and with grey slate roofing from Scotland's west coast; and there's a skylight. Below it is a palm tree, and on a platform below that – this is all high up, giving a view from there of the street – a sunbed lounge chair.

55.

"The person you need to talk to," Jim Battison, our host at the self-catering chalet near Oban on Scotland's Argyll coast, tells me, "is Shane Cadzow. He farms in the island of Luing, but he has the grazing rights on Scarba. He's been over every foot of the island looking for his animals." We are in Jim's office next to a metal-sided barn where there is also a small bar and a café, both closed now. I thank Jim and tuck the phone number in my pocket to follow up a little later.

On our way here, we had checked in with Coastal Connections, the small charter boat company operated by two brothers, which will take us out to Scarba in the morning. One of the brothers was at Corryvreckan when we stopped by, ferrying a woman who was being filmed swimming across the gulf for a charity. It is a feat purportedly done first by George Orwell's brother-in-law when Orwell was living on Jura and writing 1984. On a different occasion, Orwell and several companions, including his small son, nearly lost their lives in the Gulf when Orwell misjudged the tides, their boat's engine shirred from its pins under the strain, and they capsized as they rowed towards an islet. With difficulty, they reached safety and were rescued from the islet by fishermen who saw smoke from a fire they managed to light. Since we hope not to swim, our captain is not only monitoring tides and currents but keeping an eye on the weather. It doesn't look too bad, although there is a forecast of a low-pressure centre coming in and delivering rain.

After we drive into Oban for groceries and to buy waterproof gear for the trip, we return to the chalet, a basic two-room log cabin nestled with a few others in a narrow valley between low treed hills. El makes supper while I walk up a hill to see if I can get cell-phone reception. When I do, I call the number Jim has given me. I explain my reasons for visiting Scarba, and Shane Cadzow agrees to try and answer my questions.

We talk generally about the island, the wildlife found there, and that the entire island and Kilmory Lodge near the island's northeast corner are privately owned. These days the lodge is mostly used for shooting and other recreation, and by the owner's family in summertime. Shane Cadzow says that the last time there were year-round inhabitants was in the 1950s and '60s when a shepherd and his family lived on the island. Historical accounts note that at the end of the eighteenth century (1797), the island supported fourteen families. By the mid-nineteenth century, most of the fifty or so people who had remained were gone. Ruined crofts at the island's northeast end – the only arable area – are all that is left of the settlement now. There is also an old graveyard, last used in the nineteenth century, and the overgrown remains of Cille Mhoire an Caibel, a chapel dedicated to the Virgin Mary notable as a destination of pilgrimage. Both are below the lodge not far from the eastern shore. In 1389, the Scottish chronicler John Fordun said that the chapel was "*Ubi capella beatae Virginis, qua multa fiunt miracula* [a chapel of the blessed Virgin at which many miracles are performed]." Although the chapel is said not to have been maintained after the Reformation (in the sixteenth and into the seventeenth centuries), this is a flexible enough period in the Hebrides that the chapel may still have been in use and venerated during Mary's sojourn.

There is another detail that draws Mary a little closer. One of Scarba's earliest chroniclers wrote of a woman of the island who in about 1700 was around 140 years old. Although she would have been fifty or so years Mary's senior, the two women were likely on the island at the same time. The chronicler adds that the old woman had "enjoyed the free use of her senses and understanding all her days."

"Let me read you what Mary MacLeod says in the poem she wrote when she was on Scarba," I say to Shane. I read the lines containing the poet's feelings as she views Islay while also looking at Jura. "Is what she says possible? Not everyone thinks it is."

Shane says, "Yes. You would have to be at the southwest point. I have seen Islay from there myself."

I had encountered a further piece of information when I was in the Edinburgh Maps Library that I want to ask Shane about. It was part of a series of notes about the island made by the Geological Survey of Scotland in 1909. "There may have been a processional way running from steps cut in the rock on the east side of the island along a winding path to what is called the Point of the Maidens above the Corryvreckan."

"I know the steps," he says. "They are about a half-mile south of the pier where there are some fir trees. You could go there, but the path is very overgrown, and you'd be struggling through the undergrowth the whole way."

"What about the Point of the Maidens itself? What's the best way to get there?"

"It's possible to go in right at the point from Corryvreckan and scramble in from the boat onto the rocks, but what is better is to land at the pier and walk up behind the house – Kilmory Lodge. A trail goes up the hill; a track winds all the way down to the Southwest Corner. It would take one and a half hours or so to get there."

"In another part of the note about the Point of the Maidens, it says there are the stone remains of three circular buildings nearby. And 'a womb shaped lochan' that 'empties its waters into a stream that flows out towards the whirlpool.'"

Shane pauses. "Yes," he says after a moment. "I think I have seen a building there, and also another; and an old stone bench."

Early in the morning, I pack lunches and put out the wet-gear we bought yesterday. El has found a jacket and rain pants and I am pleased with my rain pants, a tin of dubbin for waterproofing my leather shoes, and a pair of waterproof socks, a luxury I had not known existed. I take my coffee and sit in the lawn chair out front while El finishes his preparations. Jim, the owner, waves at me as he goes into his office. The only other living creature I have met on the premises so far is a duck with a beak and face like marbled endpapers. It wanders in and out of the office and comes to stand beside me next to the lawn chair as it did last evening while I drank a glass of wine before dinner. A few farm workers arrive in trucks and drive out again, and I have a few minutes to ponder what must be one of the last red telephone boxes in Scotland before El is ready.

56.

We meet Struan Smith at Loch Feochan where we board one of his and his brother Cameron's Coastal Connection RIBS. It is a fast, powerful twin-engine machine. I take a seat in the front beside Struan, El behind, and more quickly than I had expected we are out of the loch and through the Sound of Insh and passing the Slate Islands, some of them so small and exposed and hollowed out by quarries that they were over-whelmed in the late nineteenth century by storm and tides. Belnahua, the smallest of them, is uninhabited. Its low ruins blend in with the grey sea and sky heavy with cloud, but when I look back, after we pass the Fladda lighthouse, a shaft of sunlight paints a small swath of the shore-line moss green.

There have been changes – emigration and the Clearances, a different kind of re-settlement related to resource extraction, and open-net fish farms that have devastated wild fish populations – but the sea-roads re-main the same. Yet even in these I have to admit there must be differ-ences, not only in the types of craft plying the waters and the speeds at which they move, but in the campsites fringing them where people halt between stints of swimming from island to island. The "wild swimmers" are well-supplied by boats that carry their food and gear. They swim in colourful wet-suits and with rescue near to hand, the technology beyond imagining in Mary's time.

After we pass between Luing, where Shane Cadzow lives, and Lunga, the island just to Scarba's north, Scarba looms large and dominant, a dra-matic contrast to the low-lying islands through which we have been travelling, its heights caught in cloud. The northeast coastline's deciduous woods, of oak, birch, rowans, and willow, spray olive-green and red against hillsides woven in swatches of pale green bracken. Although we will be landing at the pier here and walking overland as Shane Cadzow has advised, I have asked Struan if we can first circumnavigate the island before he drops us off. We continue southward. Scarba's trees thin out and then there are none. Stark cliffs rise sharply from the ocean, and caves pock the rock all along the shoreline as we veer westwards into the Gulf of Corryvreckan. I glance up and discover a string of goats along a cliff top to welcome us. Below it is a glen with a bothy, and an upturned red boat and a tent nearby on the beach. Struan tells us that the fellow camped there had a problem with his engine: the boat could only go in reverse, and so he ended up marooned there near the entrance to Corryvreckan. The fellow has been there five weeks – he says the government is after him. He doesn't look like he's going anywhere and no one has shown an interest in moving him on.

More goats – three white and one black – populate the rocks as we enter the Gulf proper. The boat rolls and stirs in the cross-currents of tides and rips. It is near slack tide, but even so, the turmoil of the water catches at our craft in clutches that challenge the engines.

Once we are well into the strait and near Scarba's southwest point and the location of the whirlpool, we reach a zone where Struan says Islay should be visible in the distance: but the distance is veiled in mist. I look at Jura, near and green and steep; and then west to the island of Colonsay. Even it is more of a suggestion of purple in the haze than a solid presence. To come all this way and not see Islay ...

After voyaging north along the west coast with its cliffs and caves and high benches, we get ready for the tidal race in the Bealach a' Choin Ghlais / Pass [or Gap] of the Grey Dog at Scarba's north end. Struan is even more watchful here than he was through Corryvreckan. The boat slips and skates across the rough pitted boil before he puts on more power and we're through to quieter waters. Like Corryvreckan, the tidal race here has the effect of a door that swings open and closed unexpectedly. Safe passage depends on timing.

With its rocky shores, southeast and south-facing cliffs, a west coast too open to the winds to offer much in the way of shelter, and its challenging tide races, Scarba – a single massive rock for its heart – is an island to access on its own terms. I cannot know what was in Mary's mind when she was put ashore by those who brought her here or what was said to her or for how long she thought she would be left; or how she was received by the families who lived on the island. There would be no question of their help to escape. Who would risk the wrath of the clan chief? Where could she go, anyway? How was she ever to return home?

The opening lines of "Luinneag Mhicleòid" / "Macleod's Lilt" (cited in Section #53) leave no doubt about Mary's homesickness, misery, and isolation. At one time, as the lines proclaim, her life was so different that she could not have imagined the present situation. Her reputation, kinships, and overall status throughout the Hebrides would have protected her. They do so no longer.

As we slow and approach the pier, a little speedboat zips out to meet us, piloted by a younger member of the family that owns the island. He and Struan know each other; it is fine for us to land. The speedboat zooms away. I think about the landscape I have seen from the RIB as we circled the island and try to calculate how much time it will actually take us to reach the southwest. Shane Cadzow had estimated about one and a half hours, but it will depend on what the trail is like, and on the weather. How long we can stay at all is governed by the tides.

It is late morning, cool with the threat of rain by the time we are walking uphill along a lane bounded by firs, oaks, and rowans, past scattered farm equipment and gates. The sun emerges briefly. When I look back, the view eastwards across the water is placid, milky blue and white with a stretch of the low, pale hills of Luing for a horizon. To complete the illusion of a watercolour, a sailboat etches its way northwards.

Kilmory Lodge is a traditional steading, the buildings constructed around an open square. The owner's family – three grown children and the father, a middle-aged man – is packing up, putting away gear for the winter, planning to leave the next day. We introduce ourselves, saying hello again to Struan's acquaintance. I explain where I wish to walk overland, and why.

"It is a very long way to go to the southwest," the father says, "but you are welcome to it."

"Do you know where you are going?" one of the boys says. He points up the hill. "It's the donkey track, over there." I brandish my ordinance survey map and smile.

In Victorian times, he tells us, the women went that way by donkey for picnics. The men would go up to a shelter used for shooting and stay overnight, so as not to disturb the stags; fresh horses would be brought up for them. It took a great deal of organization and employment.

The father asks about my last name, which is a familiar one from where he lives in Lancashire, but I know of no connection. We shake hands, thank them for their assistance, and they wish us luck.

Grasses blow, fence lines appear, and wildflowers in yellow and mauve sprinkle the verge as we head on to the lower levels of a turfy path. We have just reached a sheepfold, higher up, when the rain hits, a downpour so cold, heavy, and hard I am sure there is ice in it. I am wearing my jacket with hood, waterproof pants, and waterproof socks; El raises the large black corporate golf-umbrella Sam gave him in Edinburgh. Rain and wind continue their assault. I dig in my pack for my waterproof poncho, unfold and put it on and belt it to protect my camera: El hunches his shoulders and struggles with the umbrella until I point out that he has a poncho, too.

The rain stops and starts; the ground is boggy and often deep in mud. Wildflowers give way to heather and burned-over ground and bracken. There isn't much wildlife – a few swallows and gulls, two bees (one walking, one flying), two caterpillars, and one struggling white moth. We see no sheep except for a carcass, nor any cattle, although there is dung to tell that animals have passed this way. There's not even a glimpse of the herds of red deer the island is known for. They, more sensible than we are, are likely sheltering.

My damp map reveals that we have skirted a boggy stretch called Blàr Nan Sìth (Plain of the Fairies). Martin Martin, in the 1703 account of his travels, may have found an alternative explanation to fairies for there being a race of little people in the area. Of nearby Colonsay, he writes, "The Natives have a tradition among them of the very little Generation of People that lived once here, call'd Lusbirdan, the same with pigmies." More popularly, though, Scarba is said to be a place where "myths abound and the island is considered the haunt of ghosts and faeries." One way or another, much of Scarba appears to reside within its vanishings.

After an hour and a half of walking, we stop in a lull between showers and eat lunch. When we return to the trail, the path shifts direction, and we face a freshening wind. At the two-hour mark, given that we have the same distance to cover in reverse and must meet Struan by late afternoon, El starts to worry. He wants to strike overland to the west shore and call for Struan to pick us up there. Not only is this likely to be difficult, but it would mean we would not reach the southwest point where I think Mary composed her verses. This is not what I have come here to do. We argue a little; but after passing a lochan that may be the one I've been looking for, we agree to climb to the next landmark, a cairn, about another half hour on. A little past the cairn, we come over the brow of the hill to a view of land and sea spread out below a clearing sky. We are high above Corryvreckan, with Jura green and purple, full of shadow and colour, straight ahead across the Gulf. I advance to a small rocky knoll close to the ledge and sit. The sky clears to bright sun. Beyond Jura, Rubh' a' Mhàil, Islay's northeast point, is a gnarled dark-blue sunlit length on the horizon. I move from the knoll and test how far I can go before losing sight of Islay. It isn't far. We have found where Mary set her song, with Jura the view and Islay beyond at which to gaze.

We haven't much time to celebrate with tea and chocolate; soon we must hurry back. The weather has closed in, the blue skies have disappeared, and it is no longer possible to see Islay. The Cailleach, the goddess-hag of the Corryvreckan / Coire Bhreacain whirlpool, is making her presence felt. She stirs in her deep rock hollow, the coire or cauldron, whirlpool, or kettle. Foam heaps and swirls at the surface. White water leaps against the rocky shores on both sides of the gulf. She may be washing shrouds and plaids, as some say, more gently now than she will later in the year at the great tidal flows that presage winter. Then, she will prepare more vigorously, ready to spread the clean garments over the hills as snow.

As I sit a little longer, I absorb more of why it may be that Mary wanted us to know where she composed her poem. El and I have hiked here from Scarba's northeast shore, beginning above the ruins of the chapel and pilgrimage site sacred to the Virgin Mother. From there we followed a path south and west, crossing above the Point of the Maidens, which can be reached more directly from the eastern shore by steps cut into the rock and what appears to have been a processional way. We have seen the womb-shaped lochan with its stream bleeding into the Gulf and have ended here on this knoll above the whirlpool that is home to the Cailleach, goddess and crone. It would seem reasonable to conclude that we are in a region which was sacred to women long before Irish monks established a handful of beehive cells above Lurach Bay on Scarba's west side.

The Paps (mountains) of the island of Jura, thought to obscure Mary's sight of Islay, are noted by the writer Mairi Hedderwick as the mythical habitat of women with magical powers, and by others as home to priestesses associated with an ancient deer-goddess cult.

Mary, I would suggest, has situated herself within a context of women's legitimate and ancient power as she composes, because she is in exile for having over-reached the role prescribed for women by a culture that has increasingly lost its way. It is, for those who are paying attention, a reminder of the fundamental nature, necessity, authenticity, and eternal role of the sacred feminine in the Gaelic world.

And then there is Islay, the island at which Mary notes she is "gazing." For centuries, Islay was the seat of evolving Norse-Gaelic (Gall-Ghàidheal) and Gaelic control, laying the foundation for and then establishing the Lordship of the Isles under the Macdonald Lords of the Isles, the epitome of the values and sovereignty for which Mary advocates in her songs. Islay represents the inheritance Mary evokes with her praise of Sir Norman. In this way, by accident or by design – and surely it is by design – Mary's verses are rooted in and spring from her foundations. In her hour of greatest need she speaks from within this strength.

So many layers of time are close to the surface here. Geological time is shown in Scarba's high quartzite ridge, terraces of marine alluvium, dyke fissures, caves, raised beaches, rock notches, and great boulders. These tell of the movements and climate that produced the island. Human and mythic time reside in the ritual practices of ancient times indicated by place-names and tales, and in the accounts of saints and travellers, and in the hard evidence of a scattering of ruins. Mary's song plays its part, too, by pinning this place to her story of exile in the light of Islay's political power and Corryvreckan's unquenchable resources.

As we hurry down, knowing the way through the bogs this time, I find a rhythm from all that is around me. From the way the heather crooks near the base of its stem before it branches and flowers; and how cloud and sun uncover panels and caves and doors in the mountain;

from the heaps of fresh dung on land shared with animals; and the flint rock, and the spongy moss and the threading wildflowers in yellow and white and pink and gold; and by the way I walk quickly and the varying ages of my body as I walk; and by the strength the rain and the sun pour into me – such simple things that it is easy to forget them when elsewhere, and impossible not to be aware of them here.

In the bar at the chalets where we are staying, we eat vegetable and feta pie and drink wine. Not many locals come in, most customers are transients like us, although there is one old man, a farmer, formerly in textiles, who is still upset by "the accountants who didn't understand how things were done and destroyed the business [his] father started." He speaks favourably of the Chinese who control the textiles markets these days but laments the loss of quality and that he is only allowed to drink wine and not whisky by order of his doctors.

In my tiredness, I tune out of the conversation. A line drifts into my mind: "If the sea-roads are open and the wind continues …" The voices around me blur. A few ducks, and horses on the way to their feed, pass by the bar's open door. The twilight gaps between them fill with images from the day. My feet know their way on the paths of Scarba. At the top of Cruach Scarba, where the ice sheets of the last ice age moved simultaneously but in different directions, I am as much at home as I have been anywhere.

If the sea-roads are open and the wind continues …

57.

Every night, after I am in bed in the room I share with my brother, after our mother or father has read us a story and the lights are out, I begin my own tale in a world that belongs to the nighttime. In it, I meet friends in the woods across the road. I don't think of the leader of our gang as a boy, because when he speaks it is me speaking too, and I am a girl. He lives high in the trees, but he waits for me at night and comes down when I call him. He/I and the rest of the gang – there are three others, boys, and girls – gather fruit from the orchard, or nuts the squirrels leave in hollows, for food. We run along paths we have made, climb trees to swing from branches, tree to tree, covering great distances. I am good at letting go and leaping. One or more of us is always on lookout.

Lying in bed, looking up at the ceiling, holding a square of worn green blanket to my chest, I narrate our adventures aloud, sometimes as C, the leader, at others in my own voice telling everyone what we are going to do. At the same time, I hear my brother smothering his laughter with his pillow. Our mother has told him he is not to laugh as I tell my stories. His laughter does not bother me as long as he does not speak and interrupt.

In the daytime, in the life I have with my family, I never think of C. Once or twice my brother teases me by saying C's name to others, and this does offend me. My friends in the woods are mine, our time there is private, and I can do anything I need to do – run the fastest, jump the furthest, make plans depending on what needs to be done, who needs our help, who we must hide from. I do not have words for the feelings I have in the stories. The woods can be dangerous: there are people who do not want the gang to live there. They would take us from the trees. They would make us go forever. Yet we have always lived there and love it more than anything.

In the daytime, I am a little afraid of the actual woods across the road unless I go there with Diane or Sherry. We like to walk all the way through the trees to Mr McColl's field. There is a swing there, but Mr McColl chases us away if he sees us. When he puts a scarecrow in the field, we don't go near it. We remain at the edge of the woods and talk about who it is supposed to be, where the clothes came from, and if it is dead or alive.

The rope on the swing breaks and is not replaced. The crops are overgrown. Fall and then winter. Christmas. My grandmother suspends the hundreds of Christmas cards she receives on red and green thread looped from the picture rail in the living room. Filigree frost on the windows. I ask my father what makes such beautiful patterns. "Jack Frost," he says.

X

A Weakness for Whisky

... and her behaviour in her old age must have made a great impression on her
contemporaries. She was much given, it is said, to whisky and snuff ...

– J. Carmichael Watson

58.

Every time I think I am getting somewhere with Mary's story I find
another riddle. It isn't so much like water leaking through my fingers
now, although there is still a scarcity of facts, but that as I gather pieces
of Mary's world, they form different pictures. In one, she is a gifted
and valued poet, a woman who is pushed aside as her culture is colonized and its beliefs are undermined from within as well as without,
and political and social compromises are made by – or forced upon –
the Gaelic polity for political and material advantages. These compromises displace Mary and others like her. To be fair, and depending on
who is chief, the changes are also tactics for survival. In the other picture, constructed mostly of anecdote, the "it is saids," Mary is a trouble-
maker, coarse in nature especially as she ages. She is deservedly a figure
of fun.

A weakness for whisky, evident in the hue of her complexion, is said
to lie within an exchange between the elderly Mary and another woman
as they greeted each other:

Mary MacLeod:
Welcome to yourself, Mary Smith,
Although you are growing sallow and grizzled.

Mary Smith:
You are the one who is swarthy and sallow,
Although you are under the year's manuring.

Sharron Gunn observes that "[t]anned skin was not admirable in this era," putting a different slant on the dialogue's usual interpretation. Mary travelled the islands on foot or horseback, visiting and performing her songs from place to place when she was no longer welcome at the chief's court. In Mary's era, the palest of complexions was a mark of women's prestige among well-born English and Europeans. Mary's face showed the effects of time spent outdoors. That is, the exchanges of insults may have been about rank and social standing rather than drink. And, of course, it plays into stereotypes (we don't know whose) with no acknowledgment of Mary's bardic power or noble descent.

John Mackenzie, in his influential 1841 anthology of Gaelic poetry, tells of "the celebrated Mary McLeod, the poetess, who is said to have been a little dry in her last years." If, when visiting friends, she was not immediately offered a drink, "she feigned to be suddenly seized with colics – raising such lugubrious moans and shrieks as could not but alarm the inmates … Mary, who was musical even in her distress would reply in the words of the chorus – *Hò rò gur toigh leinn drama* [O how we like a drink]."

Watson writes, alternatively, that Mary, who "was much given, it is said, to whisky and snuff," is said to have composed a song, "*Hò rò gur toigh leinn drama*" / "O how we like a drink," on her deathbed. This is the song that Maoilios Caimbeul told me is referenced within the eighteenth-century poet William Ross's poem "Moladh an Uisge-bheatha" / "The Praise of Whisky."

"Hò rò gur toigh leinn drama," he begins, quoting Mary. Sharron Gunn's translation takes up the rest:

O how we like a drink,
O how we like a drink,

O how we like a drink,
Many a man [person] is pledged to it [or is addicted to or longs
for it].

Further on in the poem, Ross presents himself as Mary's follower in
having a taste for whisky and writing in praise of it. It is a kind of bardic
inheritance. He says he is no worse than she – "the old woman ... in
Harris" who "got pity" for liking a drink. "Pity," Sharron Gunn says,
"can also be translated as 'pardon' or 'compassion.'" When Maoilios
spoke of Ross's lines, I was a little stung on Mary's behalf, feeling that
an old woman in the damp of the Hebrides would have need of a dram
or two for her arthritis and should not be made fun of for it, as some
have done. Ross's lines pull in two directions. In one, he has a laugh at
Mary's expense – at the "old woman in Harris" – while coupling himself
to her fame; in the other, he suggests by implication that she – and he,
too – merits pity/compassion/pardon.

But the pity that the old woman got
Who was once upon a time in Harris;
It is no worse when I praise you
Although I followed her tune.
[or Although I continued the tune]
She chose this tune and sang your praises.

Ross's poem describes whisky's benefits – courage, pain relief, warmth
in winter – and its costs – poverty and dissolution – in brief portraits
of lads, maids, wives, cowherds, clerics, philosophers, and others; strong
drink can even be a lover. The verses are often humourous. He reiterates
that bards are devoted to it and spread its fame – as he is doing – and
ends with brave-faced lines about it not mattering that he loved drink,
but that he *loved* (my paraphrase and emphasis). In Calder's 1937 translation, pity (or compassion or pardon) becomes "the ease she [the crone,
Mary] got in worries." Ross had many worries. He was influenced by
Burns and was thought at times merely to be a Burns imitator. He died
when he was only twenty-eight years old, his affair with whisky seemingly arising from his disappointment in love and from illness, nothing
to do with the infirmities of age, like Mary.

Obviously both tales – one with Mary singing her whisky song as she importunes friends for a dram, the other with her composing the song on her deathbed – cannot be true; but if she did praise whisky, singing as she lay dying, it shows wit, practicality, and defiance.

In another anecdote, Mary is said to have fallen from her horse at a stream that runs from Loch Smeircleit in South Uist to the sea. The horse's leg was broken in the fall. The stream is called Sruthan a' Bhàird (Bard's Stream) after this event. Tradition says – whether at the same or a different time isn't clear – that she "lost" a horse at the stream and said:

> It's no surprise that I am without wealth
> There are many ways it was taken from me.
> I paid for my half dozen bottles
> Pulling (dragging) your corpse to the grave.

The verse encapsulates the condition in which Mary finds herself. Poverty, exclusion, social disapprobation, and age stalk these grimly funny lines. Their exact context is lost, but does the mention of "bottles" mean she was a drunkard? Gunn's opinion is that "[i]t looks like she lost her bottles [probably in the river] when she was on her way to bury someone or go to a funeral … She seems not too worried about it." Gunn notes that the verse "is phrased in a manner which is humorous" and comments, "I read what was ordered for a funeral in the 18th or 19th century and it was a prodigious amount." Mary's whisky consumption was likely, she concludes, "[n]o more than anyone else['s] in that time." Yet her reputation as a female poet who drank too much (for which there is little evidence) has been one of the historical reasons for a patronizing attitude towards her work.

59.

My shoulders tense as I drive in the weekend traffic heading home to other parts of Scotland from the Oban Highland Games. We have said goodbye to our host at the chalets and are returning to Edinburgh. An ambulance rushes by on the road past Lochawe. Soon we come to a bus and a crushed red car, the paramedics loading the injured into the ambulance. At Tyndrum, I pull up beside the tour buses and stop to buy honey, Poit Dhubh, and take-out coffees. Back on the road, my spirits lift. I know these hills by heart and believe that these scrolling bands of trees and flurries of scattering sheep could belong nowhere else. Like a skein of wool winding onto my hands, which are the right distance apart for the task on the steering wheel, memories gather, too densely packed to distinguish them all, but an accumulation nonetheless of faces and places and intentions. Friends who built a house from a ruin while they lived in a small caravan with their new baby; a night journey down a track to a river pool in which at one time the mad were immersed, then chained and left to be healed or not; the train station where El and I, in our green MGB, jammed in visitors to take home with us to the cottage. One of them was El's father, come to have a look at me and what I meant to his son.

We say hello to Tighnacraig where we had lived, then drive through Glen Lyon and up the back way into the National Trust for Scotland's Ben Lawers reserve. You can see Tarmachan Ridge from there; and Corronaich, and behind that Beinn Ghlas. We park near where the now-demolished visitors' centre used to be, to walk up the stony Hydro track towards Tarmachan and Craig Cailleach, the heathered slopes singing with bees. We're wearing sandals because our boots are soaked from Scarba. When we stop for a picnic, midges bite and bloody our ankles, and we quickly pack up: but in any moment of stillness, this other life, stored in this land, comes awake. It is like a film that starts and stops and starts up again without notice. An artist friend, Paul, paints Glen Lochay and its mountains outdoors, while in the cottage I make vegan meals for him using Mrs Beeton's nineteenth-century sick-room recipes; our little cat, Solon, accompanying us on the sly, dashes from tree to tree while we pretend not to see her on the mile-and-a-half walk to the pub to play billiards with Rob and Betty. Once more, Celia in the woollen mill in the village unlocks the grate that secures the niche housing St Fillan's healing stones and lets me hold them, and I touch them with the handkerchief Aunt Daisy sent me in hopes of a cure for her many years' affliction of shingles. At the post office, I write a card, seal it and the hankie in an envelope, and mail it back to her. In this slice of glimpses, in the years before she dies while I am living in Spain, I return the wedding ring she had given to me so it wouldn't be stolen from her in the "home." By giving up the ring she had unwittingly untethered herself from herself and suffered because of it, until, worrying about this myself, I sent it back. My dearest cousin, Linda, the only person to be there for the funeral, has the ring in her keeping now.

Each memory fragment – impossible geometry! – lies at the permeable boundaries of fractals adjoining parallel worlds.

We are in the dining room of the hotel where El's father and I waited over drinks one night for El to drive through a rainstorm from the hospital in Edinburgh where his stepfather was dying. Rob, our neighbour at Daldravaig, had brought news of the emergency to the cottage (we had no telephone). He had driven El's father and me to the hotel that evening to wait for El and news, dark falling, branches cracking and breaking in the wind. On another night, Rob drove me and our sick and shivering puppy to the vet in Aberfeldy, the Range Rover splashing along narrow flooded roads, frogs streaming in their thousands from the hills, hopping through shallows (or drowning if they misjudged), to cross the road and spill down grassy banks to the loch. The vehicle was a green capsule in green water, the windshield wipers without effect. Even this linkage of kindness, long unthought-of through distance and lack of burnishing, has thinned to paper.

The dining room has become a sunroom packed with bus tourists, but we have the Poet's Bar to retreat to. Robert Burns had visited in 1787 when he was on a "reading tour" and had written a poem in pencil on the chimney-breast. You can read it and feel Burns, cool and handsome, gaze slantways at you from several portraits. His praise for drink in his work is well-known and has come to represent a vigorous strand of Scottish nationalism. Burns's lines "Freedom an' whisky gang thegither! / Take aff your dram" have become a toast we might hear from one of the drinkers near us.

But where is there a "poet's bar" for Mary MacLeod?

60.

The lens through which Mary is seen is her reputation, and it comes up throughout her story. John Mackenzie, who has given us the portrait of Mary when "a little dry," passes on the description of her wearing a tartan tonnag fastened with a large silver brooch, and carrying a silver-headed cane, a picture echoed in several sources. Mary is a striking figure, however usual, in fact, her manner of dress may have been. More damaging, and often repeated, is Mackenzie's assertion that as well as being "much given" to snuff and whisky, Mary was "much given" to gossip. To me, this implies that we should not trust what she has to say: Mary's communications should be taken with a grain of salt.

Juxtaposed to this, like a nugget of gold in the literature, is an earlier nineteenth-century poetic reference to the polish of Mary's work shining from her language. Nothing – not life or death, from the time of her youth on, Iain MacGriogair wrote – would lock Mary's mouth. He and others valued what she had achieved and celebrated her for it. A current of regard stayed active even though the effects of opinions such as that of the widely read and taught Mackenzie may have influenced experiences like those of Aonghas Phàdraig Caimbeul, who had regarded Mary as "a figure in textbooks" until he reread the poems with attention and found they were "so deep and deeply full of the culture."

Whether or not Mary was a gossip as an old woman, she was much gossiped about. In a soundtrack recorded in 1968 by the fieldworker Morag Macleod, a contributor says that he "heard traditions relating to the MacLeod bard, Màiri nighean Alasdair Ruaidh, from older people. She was apparently exiled by the chief because she was pregnant with his son's child." If true, this could account for an exile – possibly on Pabbay – which was earlier than that on Scarba. If untrue, it is a rumour that would linger, however accommodating people were to Mary's noble heritage or the practicalities of custom.

As a female bard, Mary was especially vulnerable to gossip. An outsider in what was primarily a male world, acceptance by her chief and community was vital if Mary were to carry out poetic responsibilities. Without it, she could not praise or criticize her chief and community or offer support to a communal identity. As well as praise and criticism, satire was part of a bard's toolkit: "A scathing, rapidly spread satire was ... a thing to be feared." A satirical poem could strike at the heart of a chief's authority. Fear of it could be visceral: "there are several reports in Scottish oral tradition of people breaking out in boils as the result of a satirical blast." Mary MacLeod evidently "raised boils with a song."

Writing on Mary's younger poetry contemporary Sìleas na Ceapaich / Cicely Macdonald (born c. 1665), Colm Ó Baoill observes that "Gaelic society, either during their own lives or in retrospect, seems to view women poets with suspicion ... When women whose names we know stepped out of line and became to compose 'bigger' songs [high-register Classical poetry and Ossianic ballads – the stories of Fionn mac Cumhail], they came to be suspected of evil intent, witchcraft, and the abuse of power."

There is an account, less frequently mentioned than others, which offers a view of Mary so far out of line with accepted mores that it is no wonder she was exiled, nor that she grieved deeply and looked to her roots for strength on Scarba. In this tradition Mary "was given to composing satirical or even obscene songs" until she "was finally prevented" from composing these unacceptable verses by her exile.

The tale associates her to an anecdote in which she bests a group of wandering bards who are defecating publicly, by engaging them in coarse, sexual repartee. The anecdote is told in similar words in different regions and times in the Hebrides, but its specific relation to Mary is recorded in Lochaber and in Cape Breton where it was "likely derived from North Uist." The oldest version of the story is in an Irish manuscript dated 1638; but there are earlier accounts of parallel engagement by women with bands of disorderly bards who drain their hosts of food, drink, and patience – bards who if displeased will wreak vengeance on their hosts through widely circulated satires.

"A legacy of frequent (but not total) association between women and the darker aspects of poetic activity" runs through Scottish Gaelic popular culture. Women poets share characteristics given to "satirists/ buffoons/entertainers ... [I]n addition to a strong association with satire ... they are portrayed in various ways as existing on the margins of society, or as being accorded at best liminal status." It is an astonishing contrast to the literary leadership to which Mary aspired and in which she was supported by Sir Norman of Berneray. It is as if women poets, by their very natures, harboured a sub-literary stream of filth that sooner or later would be revealed.

61.

In the morning, up the hill onto the moor where the wind ferries clouds and mist and a shiver of voices less heard than felt as a tingle on the skin. It is a moor where I have stopped and walked and listened and sheltered behind drystone dykes a dozen times. It isn't a place to ask questions, but, with luck, to open to what may happen when gaps between speech and thought are left unfilled – "if we have the courage not to move, / say nothing, idle between the folds of the world."

62.

To celebrate the arrival of a messenger bringing news of her recall from exile – although we do not know with certainty to which island he came, or when this was – Mary wrote a song, "Fuigheall" / "A Fragment." Likely, this was after the 1699 death of Roderick / Ruairidh Òg, who "aped the manners of the south" and had no time for Gaelic culture, and the succession of Norman, another of the sons of Iain Breac (c. 1637–1693), a chief whom Mary had loved. This Norman, like Iain Breac himself, was a patron of the arts and reinstated the ancient customs his older brother, Roderick, had dismissed from the Dunvegan court.

It is a relief, after reviewing some of the innuendo attached to Mary, to learn from the poem that news of her coming restoration had "banished the pang" in her breast, those painful feelings the same or very like those she had expressed on Scarba. In "A Fragment" (in Ó Baoill titled "Thèid mi lem Dheòin" / "I will gladly go"), she says, "I will sing a song about MacLeod's clan and about that place / of waving satin banners, the refuge of poets, clannish and / loving, hospitable to long-established friends," conjuring the life she has missed and can now look forward to again. The last verse begins, "I will gladly go to Dunvegan of the drinking horns, where I / used to be found at the beginning of May ..." It is a spring song, whether the news has arrived in spring or not, as Mary reminds her listeners of her fixed station in the customary progress of the year. Her expectations are high; but if it is 1699 or after when she composes the verses, Mary is well into her eighties, and it is not a springtime for her.

63.

We follow the sea front – sun and clouds in their rolling play, clouds boiling along the Firth of Forth – to the mouth of the river·Almond. No ferryman waits to be called from his cottage on the far shore to row us across in a small open boat to walk the shore, as there used to be, so we follow the river-path past descendants of the swans we knew when, after we returned from two years in Spain, I raced from our riverside row-house up School Brae with our daughter past the sweetshop to her primary school. I had failed at coffee mornings and the baby-sitting co-op and the church jumble sales and car-rallies, but had made a friend of the other "literary" mother, a niece to Brendan Behan, both of us fish out of water in Cramond. Yet I loved the swans and the stone-carved green man in the churchyard and the fourteenth-century tower nearby and my runs along the river past Dowie's Mill and inland to make a circuit back to the village. After school, my daughter and I went swimming at the pool or wandered the seafront and, if the tide were low, walked the causeway to Cramond Island – all of this surfacing later when I came to write the story of a Scottish immigrant doomed to hang in Canada.

But now, we keep on the path past the weir to our friends' cottage at Dowie's Mill, hoping to find them home or up the slope on the insecure terraces of their riverside garden. There are layers here, too: the first time here was to a different family with a story not mine to share. It was dark and cold indoors, candlelight on damp stone and the thick blonde hair of a woman; her husband's face in shadows; and there were children.

XI

Plovers and Chicks

'S e m' fheadagan is m' eòin thu
'S e m' fheadagan is m' eòin is m' uighean
'S an luachair bhog far an suidhinn

You are my plovers and my chicks,
My plovers and my chicks and my eggs,
And the soft rushes where I would sit.

– Mary MacLeod, "Hilliù-An, Hilleò-An"

64.

All morning we sweep and polish. After lunch (tomato soup and crackers) my grandmother makes salmon, cucumber, and egg sandwiches, cuts them into triangles, arranges them on plates, and covers them with damp tea-towels. I help carry teacups and saucers and teaplates to the dining room table, which is spread with one of my grandmother's embroidered linen cloths. She fills the sugar bowl and milk jug. I lay out little spoons. Teapots and tea cosies remain in the kitchen. The kettle is filled and ready to put on to boil.

We bring extra chairs from the bedrooms and group them with the settee and armchairs and the dining chairs. My grandmother changes her slippers for shoes. I watch out the window. Will it rain? Will anyone come? My grandmother, in a silk floral dress (size 18), twiddles

her thumbs. I sit and copy her, then jump up when I think I hear someone coming.

The ladies arrive at the door in twos and threes and carry plates of
cake and squares straight to the kitchen. They shed their coats in the
bedroom. A few unpin their hats – small dark straw lid-like shells that
all look much the same – but most – those whose hats display a feather,
a velvet band, or a rhinestone pin – keep them on. The ladies say hello
and "How is your mother?" but I recognize few of them. Recently, I had
asked my mother why the daughter of one was called "Vulva" and my
mother had explained that her name was "Belva." That lady is nice to
me, but I am newly shy of her.

They settle on chairs, take out their knitting, and chat while they at-
tach sleeves to sweaters, or finish off a toe or a cuff on a sock. A basket
fills with completed projects. I sit on the floor and cut stamps from envelopes the ladies have brought with them in paper bags. A lady arrives
late, and I move to make space for her chair. One of the group has
brought this month's Missionary Paper for my grandmother. She gives
it to me so I can look for the children's story in it. I cannot read, but I
turn the pages until I find a silhouette of a child – a boy – at the top of
a column. Soon, the ladies step over me, filling teacups, fetching sandwiches and napkins, and sitting down again. One of them tells me to
take sandwiches and cake for myself. A lady prays for God's blessing on
the food and the hands that have prepared it. I leave the crowded
dining/sitting room. It is cloudy and raining. I am not in my play-
clothes and must stay indoors. I sit on the steps to the basement and
listen until the ladies finish their gathering with a prayer.

As soon as they have gone, I ask my grandmother to read the
children's story to me. She puts on her slippers. I sit in her lap. The sitting room is back to normal, the project basket and bags of cut out
stamps are gone, the coats removed from the beds. Teacups and plates
are stacked on the kitchen table for later washing-up. Rain slips lightly
in streaks and droplets down the windows. From where we sit and look
out, my grandmother and I, our space expands to include the fruit trees
and the giant firs, the woods and pastures, the farm, and its barn across
the road, and further along, the Chinese greenhouses, their wood-fired
chimneys smoking. It includes the vacant lot where each child in the
neighbourhood "owns" a tree that no one else may climb. Diane and

Brian next door, and the Rouses and the Sabeys, and the bulldozer operator's sons, gave my brother and me our trees. Grass grows long at the foot of them, the orchard untended and unpruned. My tree is a pear. It is reliably safe, unlike Christmas Hill, home of poisonous snakes; or Mr McColl who chases us from the swings; or the bulldozer operators' boys, who draw Diane and me to the back fence to coax and whisper.

65.

Sometimes a memory is like a dark room in which a few lights burn. El and I have driven from Tighnacraig, leaving behind the rowan trees – said to keep witches away – that flank the front gate and are full of berries, their leaves turning orange; and the circle of beeches on a mound; and the Scots pine on a rise nearby, which makes me think of A.J. Casson's painting "White Pine" – both pines signalling "home." The rest of the drive is forgotten, perhaps through familiarity, but next I am getting out of the green MGB, parked at Edinburgh's George Square. I have come to the Centre for Canadian Studies invited by James Wreford Watson, the geographer and poet who is the Centre's director, to give a reading. For months, the trees, the glen and its mountains, and the little village nearby have been my references. It will be my first reading in Scotland, and I am nervous. Then I am indoors, waiting to enter the lecture room, welcomed by Wreford Watson with whom, it turns out, I share a publisher. The room is full – geographers, historians, editors, and students – people who, like Wreford Watson, include literature as part of, not separate from, other studies. When the power goes out after half an hour and I stand at the lectern in the dark, Wreford Watson's voice lifts and we begin a conversation about poetry and landscape and language and myth, and the audience helps me weave a citizenship in which I find the call and response of my poetry practice – born on the Prairies, begun on Vancouver Island and in years in Greece and on Haida Gwaii, and now in the Highlands – as distinct and open to variation on a theme as music.

Later at dinner, El and I talk with William and Norah Montgomerie. William, a poet, edits *Lines Review* and has published some of my poems. He and Norah, an artist, are known as collectors of Scottish folklore and nursery rhymes. Another pool of illumination finds us sitting on their living room floor drinking whisky and examining books and reading manuscripts. In his first letter to me at Tighnacraig, William had asked, "Where did you come from?" At the reading, in the dark, I had given my answer.

66.

At the School of Scottish Studies on Edinburgh's George Square, I follow Dr Cathlin Macaulay, the archives curator, up the stairs to the library. Dr Macaulay – Cathlin – knows something of my quest already from Meg Bateman, whom she knows well. We discuss what I hope she can help me with and begin to delve into the archive's catalogues of collections and recorded materials, including tapes that go back to the early 1950s. While I examine collectors' notes, she finds books for me to look though, and does some data searching. The books help to contextualize Scarba, as well as Jura and Islay, in the period of Mary's exile, as alliances between clans and control of territory shifted, and authority in the islands passed from one clan to another. It is easy for me to become sidetracked here. There are many remaining puzzles about the where and when of Mary's exiles, and I am drawn by the intricacies of Scottish history. Just in time, Cathlin pulls up information about two songs I have asked her to look for: both are closely associated with Mary MacLeod but are rarely included in her canon. Neither is in the bardic style, dealing with the big subjects: instead, they are personal and rhythmic, the type of songs sung by women as they worked.

"Siuthadaibh siuthadaibh, a mhnathan" / "Come on, go on ladies ..." is also called "Gu Dè Nist a Nì Mise Ma Bhristear Mo Ghlùin" / "What to Do Now if My Knee Is Broken." The collectors' notes say that the song, "full of repetition and with a mouth-music chorus," may be a waulking or even a rowing song. "In the first section ... the composer asks what will happen if she fractures her knee. She reveals that her little house is in need of thatching, and a drip is falling on her. In the second section, there is a change of subject and the composer asks those with her to waulk [the cloth] vigorously. She says 'Four of us are here, one more than three. We would really need eight and one at the helm plus a helmsman or woman. We would call on Rory, son of Iain in Dunvegan.'" The implication is that fault for Mary's poverty – she doesn't have the means to fix her roof – lies with Rory (Ruairidh), as does its remedy. He is the chief who expelled practitioners of traditional Gaelic arts from Dunvegan. Not only that, but if Mary could, she'd get a crew together to row to his dwelling and call on the chief, presumably to admonish him and present her case in person. When the song came to his ears, Rory could not have been pleased: it may have played a part in Mary's expulsion. Whether a banishment was deserved or not would depend on who you thought Mary was – a proven poet with bardic-type responsibilities who should tell the chief what he needs to hear; or a woman who doesn't know her place and needs to be shown what it is.

The other song I have asked about is "Hilliù-An, Hilleò-An," a song associated with the tradition that Mary MacLeod composed on the threshold, "the piece of wood at the bottom of the doorway," after she was banned from composing indoors or outdoors. "That was where she would stand, and so she was neither out nor in and she made that little song."

The story goes – with caveats about the uncertainty that surrounds where and when Mary was in exile – that on hearing the song "Luinneag Mhic Leoid" / "MacLeod's Lilt," the piece Mary composed on Scarba (and which must have travelled mouth to mouth all the way to Dunvegan), the MacLeod chief sent word that Mary could come home if she agreed "to make no more songs on her return to Skye." Mary agreed, but once safely back she got around the ban by song-making on the threshold. Mackenzie writes (without mention of a threshold) that when Mary was challenged by her chief who remonstrated with her for again attempting song-making without his permission, Mary's reply was, "'It is not a song; it is only a crònan' – that is, a hum, or 'croon.'"

The song begins: "There was a time when I could sing a song / I could sing a croon just as well / Today I can just croak to myself." These lines establish the context: there has been a change; it used to be that Mary could sing any kind of song (*òran*) including singing to a child (*crònan*). The inference is that people liked to hear whatever she sang. Now she is out of voice – literally because of age and/or metaphorically because of being banned – and her audience is only (permitted to be) herself. It is a cheeky thumbing-of-the-nose at the chief who put her under restriction. And then the poem shifts into a lullaby:

You are my plovers and my chicks,
My plovers and my chicks and my eggs,
And the soft rushes where I would sit,
My little child who has not yet spoken.
With my little bow and my little quiver,
Hiri my love, hò my love,
Hò my love, Fionnghala
I would not give you bread,
Hò my love, Fionnghala,
Without butter on top of it,
Hò my love, Fionnghala.

Mary's stationing herself on the threshold to compose is "the second most famous anecdote about her." Her stance is both method and strategy, a message to the future as well as to her contemporaries. Dòmhnall Uilleam Stiùbhart says, "Her work was a synthesis: both public, in the sense that it dealt – overtly and covertly – with political themes; and personal … Màiri herself is neither entirely in the domestic nor in the public sphere."

Meg Bateman had commented that the threshold was Mary's solution, one which would be recognized by others, to the restrictions imposed on her; and that it laid claim to a space of freedom, the in-between world which is mediated in traditional lore by the fairies.

Stiùbhart continues, "Màiri nighean Alasdair Ruaidh's position in tradition is thus emphatically liminal, not just between the public and the personal, between male and female, but indeed between this world and what was to come."

A different form of the lullaby was collected in Nova Scotia. This one is apparently sung by a fairy, its vocables suggestive of the song's otherworldly nature, although the feelings it conveys could be those of any woman who cannot be with her child. Kate MacDonald's version (above) is said to share fairy themes in some of its verses with this other song. "There is also an interesting similarity in the supposed origin [site] of the song's composition, a door frame, which may represent liminal and thus unearthly territory often given up to the fairies."

Something else intriguing may have gone on here. Stiùbhart is "relatively certain" that the poem "also refers to a specific method of *dèanamh na frìthe,* a procedure of divination in which the diviner walks in a circle about the fire reciting a rhyme, goes to the threshold, opens his or her eyes, and then interprets the future according to the first living creatures seen." This is old bardic practice, one not so distant from poetry exercises where students are asked to try a version of the same thing and to write a poem about it. Where I live, a first sighting could be of a deer, a cat, a raven, or a quail and her chicks crossing the rocky knoll and meadow where I like to sit. I give it a try: open the door, open my eyes, and wait. A slight stir of the trees in the wind, a few leaves in the air, but no living creature – not even an insect – to be seen. After ten minutes I go back inside and sit at my desk. The tree outside my window fills with birds.

67.

With the piece of bread my grandmother gives me to keep in my pocket and protect me from the fairies when I go outside to play, I do not mind if I must play alone when my friends are at school. My grandmother's mother gave her bread to keep in her pocket when she and her sisters gathered bakeapples from the marshes and bogs to store for the winter. I am not sure what bakeapples are except that my grandmother loves them and wishes she had some. I climb the wet wood pile, its bark-on fir slabs wide and glistening, slip and jump back down and climb it again, as many times as I can without stopping. My father and grandfather will split the wood and take it into the basement to dry, but for now the woodpile is mine. When my woollen mittens are soaked and my hands are cold, I go back indoors.

68.

The late Peter Narváez, a folklorist friend at Memorial University of Newfoundland, told me that in Newfoundland, the predominant belief was that the fairies were fallen angels, those who were driven from Heaven by God at the time of Satan's rebellion, but arrested on their fall through the universe towards Hell when He showed mercy on them. Those who fell onto the earth account for the indigeneity of fairy inhabitants. He has written that fairies might be regarded as "liminal personae." They "set boundaries which demarcated areas of purity, liminality and danger" – areas such as muskeg bogs, barrens, and marshlands.

In such territories people disappeared, lost their memories, and turned up later with no explanation of their absence. One of the accounts he cites refers to a relative of my grandparents from Clarke's Beach who was almost lured away by fairies who were leading her into the woods. It was only because of the intervention of her friends that she was able to return home safely. In his writings, Narváez quotes the French anthropologist Arnold van Gennep, who observed that "whoever passes from one zone to the other finds himself physically and magico-religiously in a special situation for a certain length of time: he wavers between two worlds."

To me, Peter said that the European folklorist assumption that fairies have not existed in North America, that they failed to take passage with the emigrants sailing for America, is wrong.

The poet Sean Virgo, who said he saw fairies in Ireland, mentioned that his mother saw fairies and that they went with her when she lived abroad in India and Africa. He said that "the fairy world turns us; it provides an entrance to seeing with new eyes. Art, itself, is the language of fairies." When he first came to Canada, the first place he felt "fairy air" – air of the same density as around fairies in Ireland – was at a site sacred to the Hurons. He felt, there, the same sense of a layer of the old world, of ancestors, ghosts, and fairies. He noted, "There are no fairies where there have been no people."

"Little People" accounts are found worldwide, including in most North American Indigenous cultures. Like fairies in the Old World, they are often seen beside or near water (riverbanks, lakeshores, marshes, etc.). They play tricks or pranks, such as braiding the strands of hair on the tails of domestic animals, but they may also bring healing, good health, and good fortune. The Little People known to the Iroquois live deep in the forest and help control the forces of nature, guard the gates of the underworld, and protect mankind from chaos and disease. The Little People of the Cherokee, who live in rock caves, are well-shaped and handsome, helpful, and kind-hearted. They love music, they bewilder strangers who disturb them, they gather corn or clear the forest when people need agricultural land.

69.

After my mother dies, I ask Dad about fairies. He says that "Dad" – his dad, my grandfather – was against all that, the superstitions were against the teaching of the Bible. He used to scold my grandmother for her small rituals. When he is drifting, dreaming in his chair, my father says: "The only way to assess a thing is to step outside the theories in which you exist," and "As you construct something according to a theory, you affect the result. So that you cannot assess the results," and "The world is made of mixes – it is difficult to separate from the mix," and "Material world is all mixed with the spiritual. Difficult to separate." And finally, he said, "Did Mum really die, or do we only think she did because we no longer hear of her?"

70.

Last night, in a dream, I saw one of the tribe of dogs that sailed in the dory with my grandfather. The craft steered north through the ice floes, away from the family. My grandmother's dog swam to catch up to the stern.

My grandmother stood in the garden, a hoe in her hand, and lifted her head to await their return. But the oars of my grandfather washed in on the tide, alone.

She took hold of my hand, and we entered the water, dogs at our legs to save us, and plunged through unfastening nets of seaweed until nothing had happened, no one had died.

I returned to combing her hair: a thousand strands of light to braid through my fingers while the trees of the orchards set fruit which would fall through the rest of my years.

XII

When We Speak of Eternity

we think of   blowing grasses
and banners   of white flowers

and an open boat   heaped
left to drift

The mountains   once between us
are only stones   and they tumble away

When you sleep   it is beside me
and it is   for always

– *Threshold*

71.

It is said that Mary was on the island of Berneray when Sir Norman died there on 3 March 1705 at about the age of ninety-six. She, who had known him all her life, was then about ninety years old. From her songs about him and his support of her, it is clear that he was her foundation.

In Mary's poems, Norman embodies the ideals of Gaelic manhood. He is physically strong and attractive, of noble lineage, a generous host who keeps an open, hospitable household in which the arts and learning are celebrated. He has demonstrated skills as a hunter, and his bravery

and abilities as a soldier have brought him a knighthood and wide renown. He is trustworthy and reliable in all ways – the much-beloved
leader in the land and of the people that Mary loved.

But Norman was more than a Gaelic figurehead: the virtues Mary
praises in him are supported by his biography. He was fostered near
the Forest of Harris where he acquired his hunting skills. His father,
Rory Mòr, sent his sons away to study in English as prescribed by the
Statues of Iona. Norman attended Glasgow University in 1631 and 1632:
he was literate in English, Latin, and Gaelic. He was known to have possessed books including Thomas à Kempis's *Imitation of Christ* (written
in Latin c. 1418–27). To learn the genealogy of the clans, he studied the
works of the classic Gaelic bards. Bards and pipers, into whose company he welcomed Mary, were welcome in his Berneray house. Neil
MacVurich, the Clanranald bard, described him as the "Lamp of true
history" and the "Protector of true learning." Duncan Ó Muirgheasáin,
of the bardic Ó Muirgheasáin line, described Berneray House, Norman's home, as "the halloed banqueting hall of Fionnghall" (a reference
to Norman's antecedents in Norse and Irish mythology). He was only
a few years older than Mary and had told his son that her blood was
not inferior to his own – although what he meant by this remains a
mystery. In his service to the Royalist cause, he fought against Cromwell.
He was imprisoned in and escaped from the Tower of London. He offered refuge to defeated Royalists fleeing the Commonwealth armies,
and, despite the risks, undertook missions on behalf of Charles II between the Hebrides and the Continent, raising money and troops and
delivering weapons. After the restoration of Charles II, he was knighted.
When as a reward for his sacrifices he was offered estates that had become available through the impoverishment of another Stuart loyalist,
he declined them.

It may be that the songs Mary composed in his honour were sung
on the island in his dwelling or in the house he had built for her nearby;
they may have been sung when his body was conveyed across the Sound
of Harris by *birlinn,* or after he was interred in the MacLeod burial
ground on Harris in the churchyard of St Clement's at Rodel, where his
enclosure can still be seen. Two of these songs can be listened to in mid-

twentieth-century recordings on the *Tobar an Dualchais* (Kist o Riches) website. It can seem, at times, that there has been no break with the past at all.

Mary had written other death laments, but those for Sir Norman are different. In verse after verse, they convey a deep personal grief, yet neglect nothing of Norman's having inhabited – and having left bereft – the heart of his culture. The poems are anguished, yet dignified, as they convey a loss that widens from Mary's mind and body to the entire community. How is it, Mary asks, that at the same court wherein she used to hear new and pleasing tales, she is now sleepless and tearful?

"A great heaviness is this that hath come upon me and / left my veins without vigour," she says in the poem "Marbhrann" / "Dirge." The verse continues: "I have lost the key of my treasure-house; / in the company of music-makers I will not go." Her strength and power have been "bestowed under boards" with Norman since they are inseparable from his being.

The feelings of depression and desolation Mary describes are familiar to anyone who has suffered great loss, but Mary's acknowledgment of Norman's death is also literal. She gives us his coffin boards, how it felt to see him dead, and the inescapable knowledge that "Under a gravestone the dust doth lie upon my / treasure." Out of this union of the felt and seen, Mary shapes a summation of loss:

Much we long for what we lack, for what is closed within
the grave, our treasure and triumph, our care and our
boast, our glee without gloom. What I myself have
received thereof I shall remember long.

The last line of this verse, especially when read in Ó Baoill's translation (below), sounds as if it is both spoken and overheard from the next room: "I will long remember what I myself have received of it." It is a private thought – a whisper to the self – made public, one in which the courage to continue is grounded.

In another song for Norman, Mary describes more of her reaction to the death of her loved one:

With no will for anything useful, without hope of recovery;
my joy has vanished forever.

My body has lost its energy, the cause of my grief each day,
as I go on recounting the ways of my dear one ...

It is thinking of you that has tortured my body ...

"[T]hy nobility, dear one," she says, "is no longer my support."
The depth of Mary's expression in poetry is as far as I can imagine
from the voice attributed to her in her old age by some accounts. Did
these poems mean nothing? Did she lose her way subsequently? Forget
who and what she was?

72.

Sometime after Norman died, Mary accompanied the body of her sister,
with whom it is thought she had been living, as it was taken from Aird
in Benbecula, where her mother's family held land, to be buried at
Rodel, Harris. While the funeral party was travelling through North
Uist, "a professional 'bean-tuirim,' mourning-woman, accidentally met
the funeral procession and instinctively joined in weeping and wailing,
like to break her heart."

After some time at this, this woman, not recognizing Mary, asked her
the identity of the dead person, a question which, given the excesses of
the woman's professional grief, might almost be comic. In reply, Mary
invokes the Supreme Being and repeats the question:

But, O King of the world [also King of life; or King of virtues/powers]
And King of wondrous power [also King of the universe/elements],
What was the clan-name
Of my utter burning?

Mary's anger is formidable, the invocation "King of the world" gives
its scale, and the grief of "my utter burning" is palpable. She goes on:

Wert thou, my dear, in Kilmuir,
Or in Eynort of the solemn processions,
Or in Rodel of the bare tombstones,
It would not be asked what was thy surname!

By listing MacLeod burial sites, Mary asserts her sister's and her own identities and excludes the questioning woman while inviting her to imagine herself as present in these graveyards whether (in my reading) living or dead. The encounter could have taken place only a little more than thirty miles from the house Sir Norman had built for Mary on Berneray. This is territory throughout which Mary and her songs had been well-known. Once she was famous. But Mary has lived long enough to find herself being forgotten. She wrote some of her most beautiful work in her old age, but who was left to champion her, and to listen?

For a poet, an artist, to fade from awareness is bitter. It is not art if it cannot continue to speak. Norman had been the repository not only of Mary's past achievements, her house and security, but her value and continuing potential. He had been the glass behind which she could display her love of Nature and of learning, her role within the Gaelic community and her knowledge of the interconnectedness of language, land, and time – a positioning she underscores through poems such as the one she wrote on Scarba. The tropes of the poems – conventional ones of deer, fruit, bees, fish, trees, hills, and so on – the figures used by Mary and other praise poets – communicate this implicitly. The poems, as repositories of Gaelic culture, are also expression and store of "the social and non-social parts of the individual." Another way to think of it is that Mary and the form, ground, and imagination of her work are indissoluble. For art to last it must be beautiful and/or carry emotion and/or story, and it must be coloured with a gesture by the artist so striking it cannot be forgotten. It is not the thing itself that is recalled this way – that is too complicated – but a signpost which may lead to it. A time capsule in an act, a phrase, a gesture, or an image that becomes a *feu follet*.

73.

The door from the hallway to my grandparents' bedroom is closed. It is after supper, almost bedtime. I do not know where my grandparents are while my brother and I wait for my father to open the door. When he does, I see my mother sitting propped by pillows in our grandparents' bed. She wears a peach-coloured bedjacket, her cheeks are hectic red, her black hair is a splash against embroidered white pillowslips. The bedtable is crammed with water glasses and bottles of medicine. My father pours a tablespoon of cough medicine for her, and she takes it. As a joke, he offers the same – it is Buckley's Mixture, notorious for its strength – to us. I refuse, but my brother takes a swallow and then coughs until his eyes water.

Then, and shortly after when we visit her in the hospital where she is treated for pneumonia, jugs of orange juice on a wheeled metal table beside her, it is as if my mother is behind unbreakable glass.

74.

I sit on the counter beside the sink where I can pass items from the cold pantry – eggs, butter, milk, meat, and vegetables – to my grandmother as she works. But this time she doesn't ask me for anything. I open the pantry door: there is no block of ice inside; a sheet of wood has been nailed over the outdoor hatch. On the shelves, instead of foods that need to be kept cold, are tins of creamed corn, peas, and tomato soup.

"When is the iceman coming?" I ask her.

"We have a fridge now," she says.

The white fridge with its rounded shoulders shrinks the porch space between the kitchen door and the back door. We peer into the fridge together, but there is nothing there that could not be kept just as well in the icebox except for a brick of Neapolitan ice cream in the little freezer. As well as the iceman, we no longer need the milkman, breadman, or vegetable seller. My mother writes a list, and we go in the car and buy whatever the household needs at Safeway.

The uncles and my father buy my grandmother an electric washing machine. There is no mangle in the basement now and no reason to go there together to sing and tell stories and for me to ask her over and over about how when she was a girl, she caught her fingers in the rollers.

We still pin out laundry on the clothesline, but with the new hoover, we do not have to hang carpets over a line or rail or tree branch and beat them with the carpet beater.

The uncles and my father have the wood stove and wood furnace removed and replaced by an oil stove and an oil furnace. My grandfather no longer gets up early to light the fires. There is no pile of wood, no wood to chop, no kindling to splinter. When years later he forgets and puts paper and kindling in the furnace and tries to light them, it is taken as a sign of his decline.

75.

Valentine's Day. I am making cards from red construction paper, white paper for lace, scissors and paste in the kitchen. With a little help, I print Mum, Dad, Grandpa, Grandma, and To My Brother in pencil. The front door opens. My father is in the hallway although it is only afternoon. A large truck enters the driveway. My father tells me to stay out of the way and he goes outside again. I peer around the corner and watch two men, helped by my father, bring in a large object covered in padded blankets. They manoeuvre it into the living room. I'm not allowed in there, but I can hear my father and grandfather shifting furniture.

"You'll have to wait to see until Mum gets home," my father says when he comes out, shutting the door behind him.

We wait. She works in a law office downtown and travels to and fro by bus. On the mornings I go to kindergarten, we travel by bus together. She opens the front door. A wool three-quarter-length jacket, gloves, boots. My father says, "Happy Valentine's Day!," kisses her and opens the living room door. He lifts the blanketing from the bulky object.

There is not enough room for a piano. The leaves of the dining table have been folded down and the table shifted beneath a window. There is scarcely enough space for all of us to listen to my mother play. My grandparents sit on the couch, which has been pushed against another window, while my brother and I and my father gather around her at the piano stool.

76.

It snows. I love snow. Yet, sorrow is hunched like a winter bird in my heart, a knotted string in my entrails. I had loved to go to school, walking with my brother from the new house.

At the new house's picture window, I watch snowflakes fall, pull the drapes my mother made around me, stand over the warm air vent. I will not eat. I will not speak. I will not go to school. My mother, hurrying to work, has no time to see; and then she does.

She will go to the school the next day; other parents have gone to the school already, but the principal shrugs – the teacher who disciplines a classroom of six-year-olds with a yardstick is near retirement. She'll be gone in a few months. The principal smiles. Ricky's wrist bleeds where the metal edge of the yardstick strikes it. Some of us wet our pants. Some of us go to the hospital for tests to find out what is wrong with us.

At lunchtime, my mother brings her lunch and eats with my grandmother and me in my grandmother's kitchen. My mother's beauty is as sharp as pain in this simple house. My grandmother is quieter than I remember.

There is just enough melting snow for me to slide down the gravel hill three times on the new red sled my mother has brought for me. She, who has discerned my heart's desire.

I shake branches and catch snow on my tongue. I look up to the top of the fir trees: snow slides off in wet heaps onto my head and shoulders.

I go indoors and sit with my grandmother at the kitchen table. She watches the clock. When my grandfather comes home, we have toast and tea and wait for my mother to come and take me back to the new house. On Sundays, my grandparents walk the side of the newly paved road to church and back. They do not drive; they have no car. Does my grandmother take the bus downtown all by herself?

How does someone disappear in plain sight? At family gatherings my grandparents sit together on the couch, or if it is a beach, on a log, or in a park, on a bench. They drift further and further from the rest of us, and we let them go. I let her go.

XIII

Mirror

What is the name   of the ship
and what   is the coast

a sweet   small ship
a ship that   out-sails

all others

Do you know   who is on it

A thousand   coastlines
and they are all   seal-haunted

over all of them   birds   sweep
near all of them   are mountains

and I keep on asking
where   is there anyone

to look   at me
by the water's   edge

– *Threshold*

77.

I am in London for the afternoon to visit Liz Rideal, with whom I have been friends since we met at an artist's residence in Spain. We had bonded over a love of walking, and swimming in the sea, and browsing vintage and hardware stores. She is the one who writes of images – *feux follets* – that are "intangible, complex and fleeting." Along with many other accomplishments, Liz is the author of *Mirror/Mirror: Self-portraits by Women Artists*; and *Insights: Self-portraits*. Both are published by the National Portrait Gallery.

I find her at Somerset House installing her work for a Macmillan charity exhibition, but she takes time for lunch and then to give me a quick tour of her favourites in the Courtauld gallery. First is an exhibition of self-portraits by Jonathan Richardson (1667–1745). After we finish our tour and Liz goes back to Somerset House, I return to the Richardsons, interested that although their circumstances were very different and he was born half a century after she was, his and Mary MacLeod's careers overlap for about twenty productive years for both.

While Mary's world was the Hebrides and revolved around clan relationships, Gaelic history, myth, and contemporary military and political struggles, Richardson lived an urban English life in London. His reputation as one of the best portrait painters of the seventeenth century continues to this day. His peers were influential, and he was influential, not only for his painting but for his writing about painting and his skill as a collector. He never travelled, and he relied on his son for reports of the artistic world abroad, which he incorporated into his writing, and for his success in acquiring Old Master drawings.

The exhibition is of dozens of self-portraits Richardson made as he began to retire from public life when he was sixty-one. He drew them with chalk on sheets of blue paper – butcher's paper, Liz said – while looking in a mirror. The images weren't meant for display, but for himself, family, and friends. He continued with them for a decade, carefully dating each one. They record a man whose face could belong to any period and who does not seem to be looking in a mirror, reflecting himself to himself, but making a record – scratches on a window-pane – of an existence. Unlike most self-portraits I know, these convey no desire to be seen and rated or to have a story to tell. His gaze throughout the years is unchanging and conveys the unnerving sensation that as much as I watch his face, he is watching mine. It is not so, of course, but the feeling prompts reflection not about who Richardson was, nor who I am, but that he and his viewers inhabit the same fabric of time. That what is going on is not as much about art as it is about mutual acknowledgment.

Mary MacLeod's gaze, which has captured me, is not located in a face but in a place and in thoughts and experiences linked to it that assume contours I recognize from my life in poetry. Just as Richardson's eyes do not follow when I move from the self-portraits in the gallery, Mary MacLeod's presence does not accompany me from the Hebrides, although I can summon a memory of it. Her songs are (in part) an aide-memoire for Gaelic speakers; and they have become so, differently, for me. If I had been younger and not aware of the losses that come with age; if I had not earlier found generous love in a similar landscape; if sea and stone and sky and immersion in notions of an otherworld had not been mine since childhood, had not been my language, I would not have found her.

There is no portrait of Mary MacLeod for me to examine for what it may reveal. She left no letters or diaries. What there is of her is taken from recollections noted years after her death, and from the compositions that have survived and were transcribed and later still, some of them, recorded. She exists in her poems and in the Hebridean environment that encompasses them and which she travelled on foot and by sea-road.

"We crave the story but the ghost denies us a reality," Liz Rideal writes as she contemplates pursuit of the *feu follet*. To this, I would add that it is the craving that matters. "Much we long for what we lack, for what is closed within / the grave, our treasure and triumph, our care and our / boast" are Mary's lines in "Marbhrann" / "Dirge." From loss and longing for what we no longer have; and through the pain of craving; and from accepting that some closed doors will never reopen, we are given means to remember what we did receive.

The point of the ghost's refusal to be real or to tell its story in full is our return to life.

78.

In the two years from Sir Norman of Berneray's death in 1705 until Mary died in about 1707, Mary composed one more song that we know of. It is an unusual and moving "thank-you note" to Sir Norman's oldest son Iain (John, b. 1646) for the gift of a snuff mull.

Iain qualified as a lawyer in Edinburgh, and in 1700 he became factor (managing the estates) for Norman, the MacLeod chief who restored Dunvegan to traditional Gaelic practices after his 1699 succession. (He was the chief who may have facilitated Mary's return from exile.) In the year of Iain's advancement (1700) Sir Donald MacDonald, the Sleat chief for whom Mary had written the poem "Do MhacDhòmhnaill" / "To MacDonald," left Skye to live in Glasgow, from where he began "secretly fomenting" Jacobite rebellion. Iain, like his father and Mary, and Sir Donald, was a Jacobite, as he would demonstrate during the subsequent years of Jacobite risings.

The "Snuff Mull" poem is believed to have been written in 1706, following Sir Norman's death and at the end of Iain's employment as factor. In that year, the MacLeod chief, Norman, died and was succeeded by his infant son, also Norman. Iain was appointed as the infant chief's tutor, a responsibility that gave him authority to administer the domestic affairs of the clan and direct its policy, which he did from Dunvegan and from his home at nearby Claiginn until the young chief reached his age of majority. In recognition of Iain's services in the unsuccessful 1715 rebellion, James III & VIII would make Iain's charge (the young MacLeod chief) a baron in the 1716 Jacobite peerage.

Iain was influential, and his relationship with Mary was, by all accounts, affectionate. That she might compose a song for him is not extraordinary. It seems likely, given his prominence, his life-long knowledge of Mary and her songs, and her association with his late father, that he helped support her in her old age. Her death is said to have occurred at Dunvegan where Iain was in charge. But why would her song for him have been instigated by his presenting her with a snuff mull? Logic, poetry, and human nature would suggest that the snuff mull was less a nod to an old woman's snuff-habit than a token that held meaning for them both.

79.

The Stuart King Charles II, for whom Norman of Berneray had fought and who had rewarded him with a knighthood after the 1660 Restoration, brought fashionable elements of the French court at Versailles with him when he established his own court in London. Among these French manners was the habit of snuff-taking. Snuff boxes, carried or displayed by those who used them, "could be used to demonstrate a person's wealth and social status and also their political affinities." The habit became widespread, eventually to all classes, but it continued to be associated with the French and with Royalist Highlanders, especially after King James II & VII fled to France in 1688 and was replaced on the British throne by William of Orange and Mary. "From 1689 the Jacobite court in exile was based in the palace of St. Germain-en-Laye, Paris, a court to which many Scots flocked." At the court, loyalty to the cause was encouraged with "gifts bearing a royal image or cypher." These objects included "rings, medallions, fans and snuff boxes."

A Jacobite gift snuff box might be like one in the collection of the University of Aberdeen that was taken from a prisoner after the Jacobites were defeated at the battle of Shirramuir / Sheriffmuir in 1715. It is made of silver and engraved with a Jacobite rose. Or it might be like an earlier silver box, dated to the end of the seventeenth century, which "hopefully suggests the restoration of the Stuart line with visual references to Charles I and II, as well as a hidden scene inside showing dogs worrying the bones of their owner's enemy." The association between Jacobitism and snuff boxes continued throughout the eighteenth century.

In the University of Aberdeen's collection, as well, is a snuff mull "inscribed with two entwined hearts and 'Rob Gib's Contract' (Jacobite passwords)." The words – the passwords – refer to the story of Rob Gib, a master of horse to the Stuart King James V of Scotland. When the King asked Rob why he served him, Rob Gib answered, "for stark love and kindness," an expression that became proverbial in Scotland. It became associated further, as a motto or toast, with Prince Charles Edward after the Jacobite rising and loss of 1745.

I am not supposing that Mary's snuff mull was like any I have described, but a snuff mull given as a gift between Jacobites in Scotland, at a time when such boxes were being presented to Scottish supporters at the Jacobite court in exile, is likely to have included Jacobite iconography. This would help explain why although the record makes the poem's inspiration clear, the poem is not about the gift, but about the bonds between Mary and Sir Norman's son, Iain.

80.

The song for Iain begins with Mary's sleeplessness. The water that drives her mill is in flood (normally good circumstances for grinding), but her mill is "unshod" – lacking the iron parts that drive the motion of the millstones. Even so, she must pay the mill-due – the grinding fees (multures) charged by the MacLeod estates for the building and maintenance of mills. This is a worry that keeps her awake because "the mill due / is to be paid if this year is not to ruin me, and get it / I must, though it be that I borrow it." Iain, as factor, was "presumably ... responsible for the charges and repairs" of the mills, which had begun to be erected on the MacLeod estates around the year 1700. In other words, the condition of the mill – and Mary's worry over it – is his fault! Where Mary was living to have had such a mill as her concern is an open question.

The poet expresses her love for this "mason that has satisfied my spirit." He is "silent" but "eloquent" with his "sweet-speaking mouth." So sweet-speaking that "I would get castles if I merely asked for them: / despite my state that has placed debts on me." The tone of the poem makes it plain that Mary is teasing. Yet she gives Iain and his heritage their due, praising his lineage and status as a "true MacLeod ... comely, prudent, wise, and generous ... good as a host to poet bands." The rest of the poem – apart from a verse that appears to reference Iain's son, Roderick, who is "a pure and gentle blood-drop ... a bright and gentle countenance withal," and who has brought stirring (Jacobite?) news – is a series of blessings on Iain and all his descendants: "[M]ay every year prosper / thee, to give success to thy descendants and increase / to thy prosperity; and for the rest of thy sire's children / in every way they shall fare, may the fruit of my good / wishes be accomplished for them as I would desire."

As the poem continues, Mary specifies Iain's success in the hunt with his hounds at his heel and a "slender sure gun ... tough and straight, with no bend in it" in his hands. She seals her blessing with: "Safe faring to thee, Iain, may good luck befall thee," and closes the song with an image of Iain, fit in body and accomplished with weapons, in the saddle and ready for what he may be called upon to do.

With stark love and kindness, Mary has set a course for the future. Thereafter, unless we believe that she composed a song in praise of whisky as she lay on her deathbed, Mary MacLeod, from the point of view of poetry, falls silent.

XIV

A Drowning Wave

... you chewed   the water
the air   was smoke

No one could reach   into the waves
where you glissaded and   gleamed

– Threshold

81.

The islands of Lewis and Harris, together known as the Long Island, are joined by an isthmus less than half a mile wide. The village of Tarbert (the name means crossing point or isthmus), with its ferry landing from which we walked on my first visit to Harris, lies on the peninsula between East and West Loch Tarbert, oriented to the shore of East Loch Tarbert. This time we are driving, not walking, having travelled first by ferry from Ullapool on the mainland across the North Minch to Stornoway on Lewis, where I was researching a family story. Now, we are headed south. The drive down Lewis is hypnotic, the road a passage across wet moorland between small lochs until the land includes low grey and olive-toned rises and then higher hills casting shadows over larger lochs, and the blue and white sky spills into the blue of bird-rippled water. We come to the isthmus and drive through Tarbert, up the headland and past the spot where El and I exchanged backpacks on that former walk.

Where the road splits, we take the east fork, not the west branch to Scarista and south as we did before. That landscape was green, the beaches curves of white sand, but the terrain through which the east road twists and turns and rises and falls as it skirts deeply indented lochs, or veers for a period inland on its way south to Rodel, is rocky and barren and heathy. Until 1897 there was no road at all by which to access the small settlements along the coast. The high cost of building this one has given it the nickname of the Golden Road.

Near the village of Geocrab – a portion of the lands on Berneray in the Sound of Harris and districts on mainland Harris that were granted to Norman of Berneray by his father, Sir Rory Mòr, around the time he left university (c. 1633) – we stop at a café that has a view of the water. Several fishing boats, tied to buoys, bob in the cove below. A few crofts thread the shoreline, anchors for what was once a run-rig system of agriculture on the upland. Eastwards, across the Minch, the Isle of Skye presents a blue profile. It looks easy to reach on this calm day, yet the stretch of water is treacherous, home to the mythical storm kelpies, *na fir ghorma* (the blue men), found only in the Minch, who rise twisting from the waters, and who, diving like dolphins, capture drowning sailors from ships the blue men have themselves capsized.

In a song, "Marbhrann do Iain Garbh" / "Dirge for Iain Garbh," which Watson includes in his collection, Mary memorializes Iain Garbh ("stout John") MacLeod of Raasay, who in 1671, when she was about fifty-six years old, drowned in the Minch with sixteen of his kinsmen on their return from a christening on Lewis. Iain Garbh had "married a daughter of Ruairidh Mòr MacLeòid (Rory Mòr Macleod) of Dunvegan (1573–1626)." Rory Mòr was the MacLeod chief on whose "wide planks" Mary MacLeod danced as a girl, and he was Norman of Berneray's father. Iain Garbh, married to Norman's sister, was Norman's brother-in-law. The death struck at the heart of Mary's circle.

"Son of Mary!" she exclaims, "it is my hurt, that thou art in the seals' pasture and / shalt not be found."

The fault for the storm that drowned Iain Garbh was not ascribed to kelpies but was reported to be because of a witch. In one version, this was Iain's own foster mother who was living on the islet of Trodda just off the north of Skye. It was said that the witch may have misunderstood something she overheard, believing it was a wish for Iain Garbh's death, and mistakenly raised the storm that killed him, using spells known to her; or she may have been bribed and enacted her spells for money.

Another record of the disaster, preserved by a minister from near Inverness, provides the alternative explanation that it was "Drunkness did the mischeife." Iain and his men embarked on their sea-journey home after a drinking bout, having failed to heed a warning from a ghostly voice in the night and/or to appreciate the approach of bad weather.

Additional traditions cling to the tragedy. One links a companion of Iain Garbh to a fight with a female monster from Skye or Harris that had killed his mother. The companion cut off the female monster's head. If Iain's companion was one of the men drowned with him, the drowning may have been one of revenge. Sharron Gunn's account of Iain Garbh lists three witches who were said to have played a role in the deaths. Their names were Spòg Bhuidhe (Yellow Foot) of Màileagair in Skye, Gormshùil (Blue Eye) from Cràgaig in Skye, and Doideag Dhubh (Black Hand) from the Isle of Mull. Sharron also tells how "a storm came up and three ravens settled on the mast of Iain's galley." This was thought unlucky – perhaps the ravens were witches in another form. "Then one settled on the gunwale beside him, and he drew his sword to kill it. He missed and the sword split the gunwale right to the keel where the sword stuck. Then the *birlinn* of Iain Garbh turned over and sank into the sea with all sixteen men of the crew lost."

These stories portray actions rooted in envy, greed, gluttony, pride, vengeance, and wrath. Of the seven deadly sins outlined by the early Christian church (fourth to fifth century onwards), only two – lust and sloth – are missing from these narratives, although these might be found in fuller tellings. The counterparts of the sins, the seven capital virtues, mirror qualities Mary MacLeod praises in Scottish Gaelic leaders. As capital or heavenly virtues these were chastity, temperance, charity, diligence, patience, kindness, and humility.

There was enough congruence between Scottish Gaelic beliefs in witchcraft and fairies (which included such nature spirits as the blue men), the organization of clan culture, and the Celtic and Roman Catholic churches before the Reformation that they were able to coexist fairly comfortably. For the most part, indigenous folk beliefs were tolerated.

After the Reformation, though, with the Kirk in charge and different ideas of what constituted acceptable spirituality enforced, this changed. But it changed more slowly in the remoter Gaelic-speaking areas where people continued using the practices to which they were accustomed.

In traditional Gaelic regions, the primary supernatural forces at work, more than witches, were fairies of one of two kinds: either a subterranean society of non-human people, "with its own queen, dwellings, and industries," like that described by the Rev. Robert Kirk in his 1691 book, *The Secret Commonwealth of Elves, Fauns and Fairies*; or "creatures associated with natural features of land and water." These ferocious land and water spirits were the natural inhabitants of the "wild, imposing, and dangerous" geographical features of the Hebridean world – exactly like the blue men who haunted the Minch and caused shipwrecks.

Mary's poem attributes Iain's death to "a drowning wave." In a verse that carries her feelings, she envisages the scene as it happened, shifting from speaking of Iain Garbh as the poem's subject to addressing the dead man directly:

It is hurt and sorrow to me, that which hath befallen
him; a great roaring sea leaping about thy boat; thy-
self and thy stout crew, when your sails ripped, that
you could not bend your might upon them.

Magical action and/or the existence of storm kelpies or witches are not excluded by the verse – you might read them into the sea leaping about the boat – but if there was magic in "that drowning wave" which even stout John could not prevail against, it was intrinsic, not extrinsic to the environment.

82.

The schooner *Swallow*, which was captained by my grandfather's cousin John, left Domino, Labrador, for home in Bay Roberts on 25 October 1915 with six crew and eleven passengers including four teenaged girls.

It was the end of the summer fishing season, and the ship was heavily loaded with salt fish. *Swallow* was seen at Seldom-Come-By on Fogo Island where it waited two weeks for favourable winds. It left 15 November. Not long afterwards, a great storm struck the northeast coast of Newfoundland. *Swallow* and six other Newfoundland schooners were reported missing. It was assumed that *Swallow* had been caught in the storm and driven out to sea. The minister of Marine and Fisheries launched a search, but nothing was discovered of Captain John Bowering's ship.

For a few weeks, the families of those who had been onboard the schooner, all from villages around Conception Bay, hoped *Swallow* might still be found. But it was wartime, and they would have known that the Germans had launched an unrestricted U-boat campaign against merchant shipping. Even if *Swallow* had managed to ride out the storm, the Atlantic shipping lanes held risks. From February to September 1915, "U-boats sank 470 ships totaling some 715,500 tonnes, including the large British passenger liner Lusitania on 7 May 1915." The first news, too, had come in of the deaths of Newfoundland soldiers serving at Gallipoli. The battle there had begun in mid-September and would continue for months.

There was hope when, near the end of November, *Swallow* was sighted, but when she was towed to shore, she was found to be without sails or rigging, filled with water, and with no sign of her crew. On 29 November 1915, the Bay Roberts newspaper *The Guardian* published the names of those who had been aboard the schooner and were now presumed irretrievably lost.

And then – on 1 December 1915 – a telegram came from Mr Bonar Law, secretary of the colonies, to the governor of Newfoundland, Sir Gordon Davidson, at Government House in St John's. It read: "The crew and passengers of *The Swallow* were saved and landed at Stornoway (Scotland) by the Norwegian Steamer *Hercules*. Please circulate information." The telegram was signed "John Bowering." Yet, this is not how the story has come to me.

What I know is from the privately printed poem "Trip of the Ill-Fated 'Swallow' by her Captain John Bowering." It is not a sophisticated poem, but it has a story to tell. Unlike the written accounts Bowering gave to newspapers in early 1916, the poem includes ship-handling details in step with Bowering's feelings as he and his crew worked to save the ship and her passengers, and, following their rescue, to bring everyone home. This was no easy task because of wartime regulations and the hazards of another winter ocean-crossing in danger of U-boat torpedo attack.

83.

John Bowering's Tale

Within hours of the ship's departure, near dark, from Fogo Island where *Swallow* had broken its homeward journey to wait for better conditions, the storm struck.

> ... just before the daylight broke
> The wind had veered right down;
> The Cabot light was on her lee,
> We thought we would get around.
>
> But no; the wind was blowing hard,
> The seas were rolling high;
> And everything looked dark and sad,
> Beneath the angry sky ...

They reefed mainsail, foresail, jib, and jumbo but the foresail began to tear. They tried to get the foresail down but with Cabot Island straight ahead they had to tack or be driven ashore. They did get around the island and "headed her off the land," but

> The 'jumbo' it began to tear;
> The jib that would not stand.
>
> We lowered our mainsail – all seemed dark,
> Crushed, hopes of getting home;
> We ran her then before the wind;
> We knew not what would come ...

They thought of running back to Seldom for repairs, but the wind veered to a west gale. They were running east, "With double reefed fore-sail." The wind veered further, forcing them to go southeast in a very high sea. It was snowing.

> We tried her, if she would lie to …
> She seemed as if she would sink …

> A dreadful night was coming on,
> All wondering what would be;
> The wind was blowing fiercer still,
> With very heavy sea.

> While trying to keep before the sea,
> Our foresail came around;
> It burst the rigging, then it tore,
> We could not get it down.

> A dismal night that seemed to be,
> When we found to our dismay,
> Not only had the rigging burst,
> The mast had given away …

All during that dark night, they thought

> … the mast
> Would go right overboard;
> We found the step had broken out,
> And had to be secured.

> The foresail then had blown away,
> A dreadful sight to face;
> Some casks had broken loose, and knocked
> The wheel out of its place …

A huge wave had "breached the deck, smashing a small boat on the deck and carrying a puncheon of molasses over the rail." It was one of the "casks of cod oil lashed on the quarter deck" that had "broken loose," rolled aft, and damaged the wheel.

They managed to secure the wheel again; the casks rolling around the deck went overboard, but now

> The mast was going to and fro,
> The deck was opening fast;
> We thought 'twould soon go right down through
> And then she would not last ...

Captain and crew considered cutting the foremast away, but a "large wire jump stay" held it to the mainmast. They fixed a brace to try to stabilize the mast against the side of the ship. When dawn came, they

> made some tackles, and commenced
> The rigging to secure.

> In vain we tried while heavy seas
> Would make the vessel roll;
> 'Twould burst the tackles, and that mast,
> We could not then control.

> Three days had passed, and still the storm,
> Seemed even growing worse;
> The vessel shipped a heavy sea,
> And the main rigging burst.

> The mainmast then began to sway,
> And heave the deck abroad;
> With halyards and tackles all set tight,
> We got it somewhat secured.

> Our vessel then began to leak,
> So heavy was the strain;

We scarcely could let go the pump,
And then commence again.

We still kept pumping looking out,
Steering and all the rest;
Although our hopes seemed very dark,
Each man did do his best.

But still the water seemed to gain,
For help we all did wish,
We set to work to lighten her,
By throwing out the fish ...

It was 18 November when they surrendered the food supply accumulated all summer and meant for many families – this was about 300 quintals or 33,000 pounds of fish – to the bitterly cold Atlantic.

But all seemed dark, while angry waves
Came washing o'er the deck;
We knew we could not reach the land,
On such a helpless wreck.

On the fourth night, just after dark,
Our hearts with hope did beam;
While working hard to keep afloat,
A steamer's light was seen.

We saw that she was going West,
And thought she soon would come
And take us from the sinking wreck,
And carry us toward home ...

We made a flare-up, blew our horn, –
Did all that we could do;
She did not notice us at all,
But on her course did go.

Our hopes seemed blighted, when we saw
That steamer had passed by,
But kept on pumping still, the wreck
To keep afloat did try.

The night passed on, and still we hoped
To see another light;
But morning came, and not one thing
Was visible to our sight.

The day advanced, and every eye
Kept watching all around,
But not one object could be seen,
Before the night came down.

A long night then was coming on, –
A night so lone and drear;
All seemed so sad, when we would think,
Perhaps not a soul is near.

But still we had not time to think,
But pump, look out, and steer;
We knew this was our only chance
And life seemed very dear ...

And so it was with us that night,
The clouds seemed hanging low,
We feared the "Swallow" would soon sink,
And down we all would go ...

At ten o'clock the night of 20 November, the lookout shouted, "There's
a light."

And soon the news went through the ship,
"A steamer's bearing down." ...

We lost no time, a big flare up
Was soon held up to view;
While firing guns at intervals,
To attract the steamer's crew.

Oh my! What an exciting time;
For fear she would pass by,
And crush our hopes, same as before;
And leave us perhaps to die ...

With the sky clearing, they kept a musket firing and "made the flare-up glow." This steamer saw them.

They lowered the life-boat, came 'longside,
To see what they could do,
They took the baggage, then the girls,
And likewise all the crew ...

With all aboard we rowed away,
The steamer then to find,
I thought it hard, to go and leave
The old "Swallow" far behind ...

The rescuing ship was *Hercules* bound to Kirkwall and then to Norway, but before it reached Kirkwall, it encountered strong winds and "could not make much headway, / so in Stornoway did go."

The poem goes on to tell of the struggles of the passengers and crew of shipwrecked *Swallow* to return home in the midst of a war in which travel was restricted and despite the dangers of a return Atlantic crossing through U-boat patrols.

I am glad to have both accounts – the prose tale given to the newspapers to provide the outlines of the story, cover its key events, and include some details such as the nature of the cargo and the composition of the rescuing crew, which the poem omits. It does so, I believe, because the newspaper report was meant for a public interested in the wider implications of the shipwreck, and the poem – homely, composed of circumstances, practical actions, and feelings – was a service. It would replace the helpless imaginings of families who'd had no news of the seventeen onboard *Swallow* for nearly six weeks, and even then had had to endure the uncertainty of their safe return as they took ship through hostile North Atlantic waters. During its recitation – and it would have been recited – the poem would have solidified bonds between those who had waited and worried, to a story of courage, hope, and God's grace, and to the community at large. Virtually everyone had prayed for the lost ship; and many believed they had been heard.

There were layers beneath *Swallow*'s story for my grandparents. One was the drowning about ten years earlier, which I have mentioned, of my grandmother's uncle and cousin. I have a copy of a poem written to commemorate them. It tells the tale of what happened when, with two others, they went to check their traps outside the harbour at Holton, Labrador, as a violent wind "came on to blow." That layer gains poignancy when I put it alongside a letter in verse written by John Bowering, *Swallow*'s captain, to his wife from his Black Island fish camp only a few weeks before the Holton drownings. He tells her that it hasn't been an easy season. When the fish were plentiful, there wasn't enough salt; when the salt cargo arrived, there was little in the traps.

My grandfather was a small boy when his maternal grandfather and many others in his mother's family died in the terrible storm of October 1885, in which more than eighty fishing craft and more than seventy people were lost. But in his family – my family – even this tragedy contained a thread of hope.

My grandfather's sixteen-year-old sister, Mary, the oldest child in the family, had spent the summer working with their father at their Labrador fish camp. The schooner *Excel*, captained and crewed by several of their mother's relatives, was loaded with fish and ready to sail home with a complement of men, women, and children, including Mary. The ship was anchored and planning to sail. Mary's father was staying behind to finish clearing up the camp but did not like the look of the sky and rowed out to the ship to say so. He argued with his father-in-law. The story goes that the older man said they knew what they were doing, they could wait it out where they were, but Mary's father took her and her chest of belongings back to shore anyway. This saved her life. At least twenty-two others perished on the ship when the violent gale drove *Excel* onto the rocks.

The wooden chest that held Mary's belongings has survived to the present. In the 1980s it was taken to Labrador each summer by family members who carried it to and from their fish camp "for luck." In 1915 when *Swallow* went missing, Mary had a fifteen-year-old son. By 1915 my grandparents had three children. My father was five years old, the same age my grandfather was when *Excel* went down. This time, though, for *Swallow*'s passengers and crew, there was a storybook ending. "At ten o'clock on Christmas night," John Bowering and all who had been aboard *Swallow* with him "to Bay Roberts came."

In the Stornoway library, helped by Margaret, the librarian, I work back and forth with the poem, local newspaper accounts, and period photographs that show a Stornoway harbour much like that of St John's or Bay Roberts at the time. There are sailing ships at anchor, the wharves are packed with goods and barrels, men and women unload, gut, and wash fish on the docks. Stornoway people, inheritors of "the drowning wave" of Mary MacLeod's poem, would have understood every detail of *Swallow*'s story. News of the miraculous rescue is printed alongside notices of the deaths of soldiers on the battlefields of France and Belgium and announcements of awards for gallantry under fire. A Corpl. Malcolm Macleod was awarded the Croix de Guerre, "the French V.C.," for action at the battle of Mons. His father, of the Island of Berneray, was in command of a minesweeper in the Dardanelles. A sailor was in court for drunkenness; school children were supplied daily with a cup of hot cocoa.

On the windowsill of my study at home is the wwi entrenching tool of my maternal grandfather. In my study, too, are photographs, telegrams, certificates, and letters, artifacts relating to stories told around the dinner table. Small boxes harbour baby teeth, locks of hair, and rings – mementos that help to draw the stories close.

They cut my grandmother's long hair and curled it before putting her in the coffin. I had difficulty recognizing her. I said to the aunt sitting beside me, "It's not her! Where is she?" When my mother died, I laid my head on her shoulder and wept, my cheek wet against her flannel nightgown. Her body quickened, her heart restarted, the icu monitor displayed its beats, and so I sat up, stopped my tears, and said

I would be fine. We would look after my father. And for the second time, she died. My brother, a doctor, was there, too – but there are not always mementos, poems, stories, or explanations enough to help us understand what happens.

84.

At Moniak Mhor, the Scottish Writing Centre where I taught immediately before coming to Stornoway, there was a little boy, son of another tutor, who laid a pattern of baby wipes on the earth in front of the door to the cottage in which he and I and his parents were staying. He would not or could not explain their meaning, but if his parents removed them, he replaced them as soon as they were out of sight. His parents thought he arranged the baby wipes "to keep away bugs." Although I cannot know what the ritual was meant to accomplish or see inside the private world from which its necessity and design came, he allowed glimpse enough of an inner world from which he could not be dissuaded, that I will not forget him.

85.

We return to the car from the café at Geocrab, the sky darker, the wind a little stronger, the boats at anchor, restless. It isn't far from here to Rodel and St Clement's church where Mary MacLeod is buried and where I began my journey with her. The remaining 13.3 km drive won't take more than about twenty-five minutes.

86.

There is a gap between the end of the deck outside my study and the rocky hillock beside it. From indoors, in spring, I look out my window at daffodils in the steep turfy bank where El has planted them. But to cross from the deck to the rock isn't easy. Even the dog doesn't like it:

the plank we use for a bridge is unsteady and often slippery with rain; the ground is a full storey below; and the "bluff" end of the plank is balanced on an uneven ledge. Little on the property is level, except for a cleared swath at the back where there is soil enough for a septic field. Back there, too, El dug a trench through rock and clay with a pickaxe to make space for a waterpipe. It runs two hundred feet (61 metres) from the house to a slope down through a wedge of rain forest and fern to the streambed. The pump is installed deep inside a concrete caisson that lines a hole blasted into the bedrock. Boulders buttress the pipe and electrical lines where they emerge from the ground between the stream-bank and the caisson. In winter, the stream's usual trickle becomes a rage of white-water that tumbles stones and carries boulders and whole fallen trees towards the sea. When trees drop on the hydro lines in seasonal storms or the fast water washes out sections of pipe and damages the pump-connections, the power goes out and we must fetch all household water from the stream in buckets. One day we will install water storage tanks and a carport to shelter them, and we will solve all the other inconveniences of a cedar house built on a hill in a forest so that it looks as if it might have grown there.

I like to sit in my chair on the bluff and look over the Basin to the hills of the opposite shore or across the staggered rooftops of the house and into the forest. Ravens in the tall Douglas firs growing close to the house *pock-pock* to each other from their lookouts. After we build a bridge from my study deck with a little money left to El by Auntie Florrie, the dog and I cross whenever we like. We go there even at night when the view becomes ancient, and the hills form a bowl for scratched restless water under moonlight. From there, El and our daughter often with me, we watch a pivot of stars; and when the time is right, meteor showers and comets. Always crossing safely, over the bridge and back.

XV

Rodel of the Heart

Mar táid dúile agus daoine
's na Hearadh d'a égcaoine,
ó'n mhuir-si a bhfoltaibh na bhfiodh,
's gan tuigsi ar foclaibh fileadh.

Sad the state of creatures and of men in Harris ... / for that this sea (is risen)
among the foliage / of the woods: men understand not poets' phrases.

– Anonymous, "Marbhrainn sior Tormóid Mic Leoid" /
"Elegy of Sir Norman MacLeod"

87.

The large stone church of St Clement's at Rodel is built on a rise within an expanse of irregular turf, pasture, and rock. Its medieval architects set the cruciform body on a relatively flat area, but the transepts are unaligned, and the square tower (its foundation is about 11 feet – 3.35 metres – above the church floor) rises some 56 feet (17 metres) from higher, rocky ground at the church's west end.

Distinctive though it is, the church's relationship to the landscape is organic – grey stone within a frame of sea and sky. It has been a landmark for travellers coming by land or by sea for centuries. When I first saw the church from the headland path I walked with El, approaching from the southwest, I had noted how it drew the eye and "grew" from the earth around it, without thinking it might hold meaning for me. El didn't especially like churches but he'd accompany me patiently when I would show interest in any on our travels. This time, I thought I was doing him a favour when he insisted on a visit when I only wanted to be outdoors. It was when coming up to St Clement's from the harbour, along the deeply cut roadway to confront its atmospheric bulk, that it occurred to me that it might be he who was doing a favour for me.

The early-sixteenth-century church built by Alasdair Crotach, the MacLeod of Harris chief who'd had an elaborate tomb constructed for himself within it, as I learned from Historic Scotland's scant information board on that first visit, was erected on the remains of a thirteenth-century church. With further inquiry I understood that it was on or very near the site of a c. twelfth-century Augustinian Priory which was founded "on the site of an ancient Culdee cell." The Culdee's cell itself was likely "founded on a pre-Christian Druid temple … dedicated to the worship of the sun." As late as the nineteenth century, a remembrance of these ancient beliefs was enacted when corpses were "carried three times sun-wise round St. Clement's Church." In the little available about the church's earliest incarnations, there is "a reference to some relics having been shipped [from St Clement's] to Rome in the ninth-century, for protection from the Norse invaders." It is another detail which makes it clear that what is visible now where St Clement's stands is one end of a very long story.

However, with scarcely any information to guide me initially, and only two other people who came and left while we were there, I had been able to absorb what I could, unhindered.

This was stone-bathing, the church stark and cool, its walls rough, bare, and beautiful in dim light reflected by time-polished flagstones. After wandering and lingering where I later learned that Mary MacLeod was interred, I had gone into the tower, climbed its stone steps, and then ascended the wooden ladders attached to the tower walls. These looked and felt unsafe and were utterly inviting. From the third-storey windows I had gazed over the countryside and seen no one.

From the churchyard, I had tried to identify the carved figures fixed about halfway up on each face of the tower. On the north face is a bull's head, the emblem that appears on the MacLeod crest, a reminder of the

tale of Malcolm, the third MacLeod chief, overcoming a wild bull on
his way back from a "clandestine" meeting in Glenelg in the fourteenth
century. Earlier on this journey we had taken the tiny turn-table ferry
between Glenelg on the mainland and Kylerhea on Skye, the waters patrolled by sea eagles, the countryside on both sides of the narrow strait
still breathtakingly untamed. An encounter with a wild bull on either
side of the passage would not have felt out of keeping.

On the tower's west face, in a canopied niche supported by another
bull's head above the tower door, is a bishop, likely the church's name-
sake, although no one is sure from which of several St Clements the
church takes its name. It could be the first pope, bishop of Rome, mar-
tyred c. 99 AD "by being cast into the sea with an anchor attached to
his body." If so, he is without his usual anchor and other signifiers. It
could be a bishop of Dunblane in the thirteenth century, a period con-
gruent with the church's first dedication. Or the name St Clement's is a
corruption of St Calman / Columbanus, from whom potential identities slide like cloaks of his saintly calling.

Two fishermen in a boat, possibly St Peter and St Andrew, who Jesus
said would be "fishers of men," confront the sea from the tower's east
side, presiding over Rodel fishermen landing their catch in the harbour
as well as those at the mercy of the Blue Men in the open waters.

On the south face is what is delicately referred to in certain St Clement's Church histories as "a female nude" or "a squatting female figure."
The figure is a Sheela na gig / Sìle nan Cìoch, "blatantly sexual with
pagan overtones," and quite rare to see in Scotland. Her legs are spread
to display her vulva. She holds a bundle that might be a child, nestling
between her hip and one raised knee. A similar figure can be found on
the south wall of the ruined nunnery on Iona. Other examples of Iona's
influence in St Clement's include the building stone itself, likely imported from the same quarry used for the Iona cathedral, and Iona pattern and detail in the tower and other windows.

Before Alastair MacLeod restored the church to house his tomb, Iona
was the MacLeod chiefs' burial place. After Alastair's break with tradition, St Clement's became the repository of a succession of MacLeod
chiefs. Interred indoors with them were the hereditary bearers of the
fairy flag – the famous, magical standard that only the bearers had the

right to unfurl. This was a heavy responsibility since the fairy flag's powers were limited to just three unfurlings. The bearers' sarcophagus was put under the floor of the chancel. As I had learned at Dunvegan, the standard-bearers, one after the other, were interred in the same stone coffin, the remains of each sifting through an iron grating to mingle with the others at the bottom, an expression of unity of purpose as well as practicality. The last such standard-bearer was interred this way in the early eighteenth century. Also honoured by the MacLeods were their hereditary pipers, the MacCrimmons, some of whom, it has been claimed, were laid to rest here, too.

Whatever may be in doubt, it is certain that the church at Rodel has been spiritually significant to the MacLeods for hundreds of years. It endured the Protestant Reformation, and its destruction of Catholic imagery, with its tombs and carvings intact and is one of a few surviving pre-Reformation churches in the Western Isles. Its iconography carries the memories and beliefs of its origins; its burials express clan structure and values through human exemplars, and preserve these things – literally, in the case of the flag-bearers – layer by layer. After the passing of laws outlawing Catholic practices in 1560, the church was "abandoned," although the churchyard remained the chosen site for MacLeod burials. Mary's sister was brought here and buried in the churchyard, as was Sir Norman MacLeod, even though by the year of his death, 1705, the church is reported to have been in a "ruinous" condition.

Mary's death occurred about two years later at Dunvegan or on Berneray. "Her remains were ferried across the Minch [or the Sound of Harris if from Berneray] in MacLeod's Birlinn to be interred at St. Clement's church." Before interment, her body would have been carried three times sunwise (*deiseil*) around the church, and then through the door and inside to be deposited beneath the south transept floor.

All of this – the church's history and its symbolism, its pivotal role in clan identity – is why I wanted to come back. I am hoping that being here again will help me make sense of Mary MacLeod's last request – the words for which she is known far more than for any lines of her poetry. On her deathbed (while praising whisky, or not) she asked that she "be placed face downward in the grave – '*beul nam breug a chur foidhpe*'" – words which her hearers found impossible to forget and which have echoed down the centuries, words which Gunn translates as "to put the mouth of lies under her."

88.

We drive along the sunken road towards St Clement's, the church filling the skyline, its tower pale against a splay of low dark cloud. Judging by the number of cars stopped nearby, we are not St Clement's only visitors. We park and I ask El to wait a minute. A little whitewashed hut with red doors nestles into a cutbank just beyond the church's stone perimeter fencing. Several sheep graze the verge. When I was first here, the toilet doors were locked; but today, not only is the ladies' open, but inside the small space is a table with a guest book and a vase of fresh cut flowers. When I leave, three English women enter the toilet cell together. More cars, several bicycles, and a few hikers have arrived in the interim, but it isn't until we are indoors within the pewter light of the church that I realize that more than the number of visitors to the church and its amenities has changed.

People congregate to read an extensive series of placards along the walls. The panels give highlights of the history of St Clement's, providing texts, photographs, drawings, and explanations. Two poets are mentioned. One is a religious poet, John Morrison / Iain Moireasdan (with dates given as 1796–1857 but more likely to be 1790–1852), whom I do not know, and the other is Mary with an unfamiliar death date, a novel location of burial, and said to be the leader of a group of women poets. A handful of female writers flourished between 1650 and 1750, but if they were a group with Mary as their leader, the scholars I have consulted do not say so.

I turn to walk once more through the church, but it is difficult to ignore its busyness and my own swirling thoughts. It isn't the people – there really aren't that many – but it doesn't help that when I pause in the south transept below the window, several find their way to my side. I head for the stairs to the tower for respite, but the stairs are blocked off from the landing upwards and the ladders that gave me access to the tower's height before have been removed from the walls.

El is already outdoors. I join him among the tombstones and enclo-sures.

89.

Sìleas na Ceapaich / Cicely MacDonald of Keppoch, c. 1665–c. 1729, and Mairghread nighean Lachlainn / Margaret MacLean from Mull, 1660–c. 1751, were poets who, like Mary, trespassed on men's territory by composing panegyric and political poetry. A few others of the period who similarly transgressed by "practising the literary conventions and codes of their male counterparts" included Catriona nighean Eòghain Mhic Lachainn / Catherine Maclean, 1650–fl. 1680, from Coll, and Diorb-hail Nic a' Bhriuthainn / Dorothy Brown, c. 1624–c. 1710, from Luing.

Each of these women broke taboos limiting what women could express in song. They achieved prominence within their societies but suffered questioning of their legitimacy. Ultimately, charges of "unac-ceptable sexual and 'unnatural' or magical powers" circulated around the legacy of their work.

All but one of these women was roughly thirty-five to forty-five years younger than Mary, women who, because of the prominence of the MacLeods and the interrelationships of the clans, most likely knew of her and her songs. A look at the map shows that when Mary was taken by sea from either Dunvegan or Berneray into exile on Scarba, she would have passed near the islands on which three of these four poets practised their craft. Catriona was on Coll, Mairghread on Mull, and Diorbhail on Luing. The exception in this group was Sileas, who was born not far from Skye, but on the Scottish mainland. Political events after Mary's death gave rise to Sileas's best-known poems. Catriona's surviving works (like the other women, she was a Royalist) also refer to events after Mary's death.

Mairghread is often directly linked to Mary even though she was born about forty-five years later and lived until 1751, about forty-four years following Mary's demise. She was reputed to have witch-like powers, and – like Mary – to have requested face-down burial. Mairgh-read was "buried face down … under a heap of stones at Kilninian in

Mull." In the vicinity of her grave there appears to have been a much earlier church than the present one, dedicated to the Celtic St Ninian. It "is believed to have once been known as 'The Chapel of the Nine Maidens,' or in Gaelic 'Cill Naoi Nighean,' although another possible name was 'The Church of the Holy Maidens' or 'Cill Naoimh Nighean.'" Like Mary on Scarba and like Mary interred face-down in St Clement's, there are roots in situ that connect these women poets to Celtic Christian and pre-Christian origins. The Nine Maidens or Nine Holy Virgins of the eighth century were the daughters of the Scottish St Donald / Domhnall, their memories preserved in the names of hills and wells. The Nine Maidens of the Celtic otherworld, whose foundations bled into the overlay of Christianity, were guardians of the arts and dispensers of inspiration whose breath inspired the brew of the Celtic cauldron of blessings, rebirth, and the arts. It is not an unthoughtful location for the grave of a female poet.

Diorbhail on Luing was closest to Mary in age. She was born about 1624 when Mary was likely still a girl. Her island was less than two miles (about three km) from where Mary was exiled on Scarba. (Luing is home to Shane Cadzow who grazes cattle on Scarba and who told me much about that island.) The little of Diorbhail's work which has been preserved makes clear that she was a Jacobite with strong anti-Campbell, pro-Royalist, and anti-Covenant views. A surviving song dated to 1645 praises a leader of the Royalist cause under Montrose. She died c. 1710 and was buried, probably at Kilchattan (twelfth century) in the old churchyard in Luing.

Mackenzie, in 1865, comments that "there must have been great pungency in her songs" and tells us that "long after her death, one Colin Campbell, a native of Luing, being at a funeral in the same burying-ground where she was laid, trampled on her grave, imprecating curses on her memory. Duncan Maclachlan, of Killbride, in Lorn, himself a poet, and of whom the translator of Ossian makes honourable mention as a preserver of Gaelic poetry, being present, pulled him off her grave, sent for a gallon of whisky, and had it drunk to her memory on the spot." It would seem that as much as Diorbhail's songs offended Colin Campbell's clan dignity, it was the memory of Diorbhail's very existence that licensed his anger.

Could these women have been an informal group with an older, more famous leader in Mary? I like the idea that as Mary voyaged south into banishment and passed their islands, whether she was on her way to Mull or Scarba or other region of exile, thoughts of their affinity, purpose, and talent might have given her courage. I spend a few minutes imagining the women as lights within the darkness of Mary's grief over her estrangement from her home, and hope that it is true.

90.

From in front of the house I can look beyond the trees to the shoreline encircling the waters of the Sooke Basin and the lights which sprinkle its rim. There is comfort in them, a relief from isolation. It's the same when we sail among the islands of Georgia Strait between Vancouver Island and the mainland. We ease along in the dark, peering for navigation markers to keep us from hazards, eyes drawn to circles of illumination along the clifftops or shining through the forests from scattered cabins. The fewer lights there are, the more we feel connection to any people who might look out from their dwellings and see us.

"This little light of mine," we sang in the Marigold Hall on Monday nights while Mr Speller waited for us outside in his van when I was a child, "I'm going to let it shine."

XVI

Time's Witness

I take away the cord
that holds the imprisoned hurt.
The hurt has come away.
It is as I say.

I bury the cord in the earth.
Earth, receive this cord,
make it earth of earth.
It is as I say.

– Robin Skelton, "To Banish Pain"

91.

The face-down burial Mary requested, or which was inflicted on her in the spirit of the Campbell who trampled on Diorbhail Nic a' Bhriut-hainn's / Dorothy Brown's grave, is said to be the "Norse method for burying a witch." If Mary herself, or others, meant it as punishment, it is a paradox preserved with Mary in her entombment, for no other place of burial illustrates acceptance by Mary's Gaelic world as does the interior of St Clement's. The year she died, her ally, John (Iain) Mac-Leod of Contullich, Sir Norman's son with whom she shared a long history and political views, was managing Dunvegan's affairs as its former factor and the current "tutor" of the infant MacLeod chief. Iain may have advocated for her to be honoured in St Clement's, although this raises the question of whether he could have arranged this without the agreement of other clan leaders. From a practical point of view, burial beneath the church floor would have prevented desecration of her remains if there were those who objected to her presence: then, too, this was 1707 when the church was in poor condition, not much in use, and what was done there might have been less of an issue than in an earlier period. Still, Mary's words encompass a knot of possibilities.

That a bard of Mary's spirit and accomplishment would have asked to be buried face-down "to put the mouth of lies under her" in repudiation of her life's work seems unlikely, but it is a widespread belief. Her words have been interpreted as deathbed repentance, acknowledgment that those who criticized her were right all along, an admission that she had overstepped the bounds by writing praise poetry, and because "As it was not always the truth that was portrayed in her poetry, but often vain and arrogant flattery, Mairi asked to be buried face downwards when she died, so that her lying tongue could not point to Heaven." This form of burial is also linked to Mary's "reputation" for composing obscene verses. Such verses may "offer an explanation for the tradition that Mary and at least one other woman bard in Scotland were buried face-down – along with the ambivalence toward their kind that it implies."

"The clear implication is that Mary's songs were somehow false."

Why would she have turned against what she had fought for her whole life, especially at the end of it when she would more likely be considering her legacy? It makes more sense that she would compose a song about whisky than that "'on her death-bed' she composed a song of praise for the chief who had banished her to Mull." (Mull is one of the islands other than Scarba to which Mary may have been transported.) This tradition appears to derive from George Henderson's 1896 book, *Dàin Iain Ghobha*, in which he discusses the background and work of the Harris poet John Morison (Iain Ghobha). Morison, who was born at Rodel in 1790 and died in 1852, is the other poet mentioned on the information boards inside St Clement's: he is buried in its churchyard. Henderson does not give the source of his report but is quoted as saying further that "[a]s punishment and penance, she [Mary] made a death-entreaty ... that she should be buried face downwards in token of the ignominy which would forever consume her conscience, although she slept in Rodel of her ancestors, the idyll of her heart."

And yet, I have returned to St Clement's where I began this journey, because having spent this time with Mary, I know that place and words and context matter in her story. And having come here again, I have found the lesson of St Clement's to be that Mary is exactly where she belongs.

92.

Henderson collected, edited, and published John Morison's poems in Scottish Gaelic, but he wrote the "Memoir," from which his words about Mary are taken, in English. I have encountered Henderson before but hadn't read everything he had to say about Mary. Assessing his words as excerpted and interpreted by others makes me uneasy, and so I return to the original. As I had remembered, Henderson is an admirer of Mary's work. He calls her Gaelic poems "unsurpassed poetic classics" and gives her her due as "poetess to Iain Breac Macleod," the chief who we know made Dunvegan "the hospitable haunt of the wandering bards, the musicians and the story-tellers."

When I come to the paragraphs in which Henderson discusses Mary's death-bed words, I have to reread them. Far from having written a song of praise for the chief who had banished her to Mull, Henderson says that "whatever her relation to him who ordered her banishment to Mull, on her deathbed *she was seized with qualms at having forgiven him* [my emphasis], and specially for having, on being released, composed a song in his praise." With the missing words restored, it is obvious that Mary regrets the compromises she made to be returned from exile. The false song of praise she wrote then is what bothers her. The lie in it was a betrayal of her integrity and responsibilities as a bard; and it is a lie that will endure forever within the song. That is the ignominy – the shame – which would forever consume her conscience.

Mary cannot undo what she has done, but the death-entreaty through which she exacts a promise to be positioned face-down in the grave is remediation. The style of burial – indicative of a Norse witch – is a statement of her identity and is intended to be remembered. Its "truth" is preserved with her. In the setting of her ancestors, in Rodel, "the idyll of her heart," Mary MacLeod becomes a symbol of the MacLeods' ancestral origins, beliefs, and virtues, all of which she promoted in her poetry. It is a clear assertion of her role and the practices she followed. Her words are no puzzle to those who thought as she did, and for everyone else, they are an unmistakable stimulus to enquiry.

But why should we believe Henderson when he does not cite his sources?

Henderson may not have said how he acquired the information he gives about Mary, but he does discuss the materials he drew on overall. These include manuscripts, letters, journals, and "trustworthy information" supplied to him by John Morison's / Iain Ghobha's eldest son and others of the poet's family and friends. Henderson's discussion of genealogy hints at a possible route of transmission stemming from John Morison's ancestor the Clàrsair Dall / Roderick Morison, the Blind Harper, who was a younger contemporary of Mary's at Dunvegan. John Morison himself was known for his "marvellously retentive memory."

The Clàrsair Dall / Roderick Morison was born in 1656 on the west side of Lewis at Bradhagair, which is fourteen miles or twenty-three kilometres from Stornoway, where before my return to Rodel I had investigated the story of John Bowering and *Swallow*. Morison studied in Ireland and was engaged as harper by the MacLeod chief Iain Breac MacLeod when Mary was, by many accounts, his poetess. The Blind Harper praised the chief in his verses, but the chief dismissed him from Dunvegan sometime between 1688 and the chief's death in 1693. This was likely because of the Clarsair Dall's strongly expressed Jacobite advocacy in contradiction of the chief's attempt to pursue a path of neutrality between the exiled Stuarts and King William of Orange. The Blind Harper's dismissal could indicate that Mary suffered a similar treatment at a similar time and for similar reasons, and that she was also exiled by this chief whom she loved. Both Mary and the Clarsair Dall subsequently criticized Iain Breac's successor Roderick / Ruairidh Òg who purged Dunvegan of Gaelic culture.

It wasn't until after Ruairidh Òg's death and the accession in 1699 of his brother Norman, an enthusiastic patron of bards and musicians, that Dunvegan's customs were restored and the Clarsair Dall and Mary were welcome there again. We do not know when the Blind Harper returned to Dunvegan, except that he was there c. 1713–14 when he died, and that Dunvegan is where he is buried. Whether he was present at Mary's death c. 1707 – at Dunvegan or on Berneray – isn't known, but if anyone were able to have knowledge of what occurred, and to pass the story on, it would be him.

93.

The poet Iain Ruadh Stiùbhart / John Roy Stewart (1700–1752) lived nearer to Mary's time than Henderson did. Iain, a young boy around the time that Mary died, became a military officer who served with the Scots Greys in the King's Service, then left it and went to France. There he joined other Jacobites who had enlisted with the French, and in May of 1745 fought with them in the Battle of Fontenoy in Flanders where they defeated an Anglo-Dutch-Hanoverian army under King George II's youngest son, the Duke of Cumberland. A few months later, Iain Ruadh returned to Scotland to fight in Prince Charles Edward's army in the 1745 Jacobite "rising" where he would face the duke again.

Iain Ruadh gave distinguished service at the Jacobite successes of the Battle of Prestonpans (21 September 1745), the Skirmish at Clifton (18 December 1745), and the victory (but indecisive follow-up) of the Battle of Falkirk (17 January 1746). It was after Government losses there that the Duke of Cumberland took charge of the Crown's forces. Iain Ruadh's last battle was the disastrous Culloden (16 April 1746). Before it, "he advised that the army should be withdrawn from Culloden to a stronger and more strategic position, where they might rest till the absent men had returned and they were reinforced by the Frasers and Macphersons, who were hastening to their support." Some thought that Colonel Roy Stewart (Iain Ruadh Stiùbhart), "the most capable and trusted officer in the army," should have been appointed commander of the prince's forces, but other opinions prevailed, and he was not.

After the defeat, Prince Charles Edward's army dissolved, and Iain Ruadh and hundreds of its officers and men were hunted throughout the Highlands by the Duke of Cumberland's soldiers. Although Iain Ruadh was well-known and considered by Cumberland to be a principal enemy, he managed to evade his pursuers and escape to France where eventually he died in exile. His bitter, grief-stricken poem "Culloden Day," written with the immediacy of the battle's aftermath, blames the leaders who brought about the catastrophe, and mourns the slaughtered men:

> The white bodies
> That lie out on the hillsides,
> Uncoffined, unshrouded,
> Not even buried in holes ...

The poem describes the murder, ruin, and famine inflicted on the Highlands by "Butcher Cumberland" and his policy of genocide, with the pursuers of the Highlanders

> Coming towards us with people and sword
> Like ravening grey-hounds on bodies
> Scouring the permafrost, graveyards, rocks, and hillsides ...

The same tactics are used in modern warfare in programs of obliteration of defeated soldiers, civilians, homes, villages, land, language, and culture. The idea, grown familiar in war after war, is to starve and demoralize a population and leave it broken, without redress. But it is the poet's job to witness:

> Woe is me! The land you've entered now,
> You have swept flat and bare,
> Without oats without crops standing,
> Without choice seed in desert or ground;
> You've taken the hens from the henroosts
> Even our spoons you have stolen,
> You are cursed destruction like a splitting tree,

Withered pine from top to bottom.
We are now outlaws
And must take to the glens and hills
Without diversion, without sport,
Without Happiness, without pleasure, without song;
With little food or fire
On the rocks where the cold mist lies,
Like to another Barn-Owl ...

Culloden was a turning point. With the advantage given by its military success, the British government enacted laws that restricted religious freedom and disabled clan relationships, affecting everything in
the Highlands from land to language and music and dress. The lords
and chiefs who had supported the Jacobites were stripped of their estates, and those estates cleared of the people who had lived and supported themselves there for countless generations. As Iain Ruadh said
of the soldiers he had fought with, those who survived were driven permanently from their lands into exile. The "Clearances" of the Highlands
and Islands continued for more than a hundred years with consequences lasting into the present. In what must have seemed to some
an ultimate assimilation, some Jacobite chiefs who afterwards raised
Highland regiments to fight with the British army had portions of their
estates returned to them.

Near the beginning of "Culloden Day," the poet writes lines that al-
lude to Mary MacLeod's request for face-down burial. Sharron Gunn
translates them as:

My ruin, beautiful Red-haired Charles,
To be doomed for King George of the beasts
That was the sentence of justice
The truth and her mouth under her (face down).

Gunn says, "It looks like Iain Ruadh considered himself unjustly sentenced for doing what was right, fighting for the rightful heir, who lost."
The ironically meant "justice" of "King George of the beasts" is to bury

the truth and those who would speak it. Gunn says, "Truth is a feminine noun and I think personified as a woman here; truth is treated badly and sentenced to lie face-down as was Màiri."

With these lines, Iain Ruadh summons Mary's memory and allies himself to her story. His connections to her are specific: he was a Highlander and, like Mary, he was a poet; also like her, he opposed English-based colonization by siding with the Royalists. As a result, he was, as she was, treated unjustly in the attempt to silence the truth embodied in a culture and its relationships to land and people. His means of keeping truth alive, like Mary's, was by composing songs with the potential to transmit that truth through time.

94.

There is a summoning of companionship in literature, an affinity of spirit with the achievements of others that can thread a work with encouragement. At its brightest, it is inspiration. "Culloden Day" is not "bright": it is weighted with anger and suffering; but it strikes a kinship with Mary MacLeod and energizes it with the force of her request to be buried face-down "to put the mouth of lies under her." Her words make us pay attention. Their strangeness has the power to evoke indignation at how she was treated. By aligning his words with Mary's earlier ones, Iain Ruadh directs us towards similar feelings about Culloden.

The bards' view was the long one of ancient established identity extending into a timeless future. Through the recitation of descent, the poets kept the dead joined and present to the clan's evolving character and its welfare. When, on Culloden Moor the morning of 16 April 1746, the poet Iain Ruadh Stiùbhart / John Roy Stewart faced the Government army, it was from within a force composed of families who knew each other, or who were related, or with whom they were familiar by repute: families with fathers, sons, cousins, brothers, and uncles standing together. "In the moments before battle was joined, they did something characteristic of a Celtic host. Together, they summoned the army of the dead. In what is known as *Sloinneadh*, the naming of the names, each man recited his genealogy, and many could go back twenty generations. Before they charged across the heather into the gunfire, the clansmen wanted to recall their ancestors and fight in their shadows."

In that time and on that battleground, the ancestors could not match the Government artillery, but the bards and pipers and others within the perspective of the Gaelic framework knew that the ancestors are not governed by time, but by remembrance. Each time a song was sung, or a pibroch played, or a genealogy and history recited, the ancestors were given – are given – continuance as a resource on which the living can draw.

95.

In the year 2020, in north-central British Columbia, women of the Wet'suwet'en nation rang bells and called on their ancestors in the face of the arrival of RCMP helicopters and the advance of heavily armed police tactical squads come to enforce a court order permitting the building of a gas pipeline through Wet'suwet'en traditional territory. The women wore regalia; around them in the snow, hanging from branches, red dresses symbolized hundreds of missing and murdered Indigenous women for whom there had been no accountability or justice. The dresses were a representation of the human cost of resource extraction and its man-camps on First Nations territory – human damage in accompaniment to the despoilment of the land itself. "We're trying to save the water, the land for all humankind. Not just us. And they won't listen … So that's why it had to come to this."

96.

Watson mistrusted what "Seekers after Celtic Mysticism" might find in Mary or "any other Gaelic poet," saying that Mary "is nothing if not concrete and clean-cut in her ideas and her expression." The Gaelic conceptual framework, though, "is a very different model from … the view that man is the nearest to God at the top of the pyramid of animals, and different from the Christian model of an inanimate earth on which a transcendent God creates animals and man, from which we are to proceed to a superior spiritual place called heaven." That model celebrated an economic, religious, and social hierarchy unfolding to God's plan. In Celtic mythology, "As far as we know, there is no myth of cosmogony of places beyond the earth ... If time is conceived of as circular, there is indeed no need for a beginning to the world or to time." The world is always now.

When Mary stood on the threshold neither indoors nor out and composed in defiance of the rules of the external world, she asserted her right to speak and to be heard in the moment. Bardic practice taught the technique of composing in the dark with a stone on the belly, a dreaming aided by sensory deprivation but "homed" by the stone's weight. When Mary was on the threshold, whatever creative dreaming there might be was "homed" by the board or stone or earth under her feet. When Mary was on the threshold, she enacted a metaphor for the Gaelic conceptual world in direct challenge to contemporary rule-setters.

97.

The other woman poet known to have been buried face-down, Mairghread nighean Lachlainn / Margaret MacLean, was, unlike Mary, married. She had many children and was also nurse to sixteen children of "the best families of Mull." All these children predeceased her. In her age, Mairghread "used to go very frequently to the grave of the last of [her own children] and sit there." When she composed her poems, it was always indoors. "Not with eyes covered, and a stone on the belly, as the *filidh* [high-level, formally trained bard] ... composed, but indoors, nonetheless – she simply could not compose out of doors. And at the proper moment, she *saw* her poems running along the green turves that formed the intersection of wall and roof. The phrase used by the *seanchaidh* [storyteller] who supplied ... this information was: *A' feitheamh na bàrdachd a' ruith air na glasfhadan* [Awaiting the poetry running atop the walls]."

In whichever manner the house was built – whether of turf walls and a thatch roof or with walls of stone or a sandwich of turf and stone with turf on top for insulation, there was a point where roof and walls met: it is there she focused her gaze. Possibly her lines appeared and vanished as they formed, or they seeped in from outside. More likely, the poems took visual form as the thoughts within her pushed into view, a feeling familiar to poets as a heaviness in the body behind the eyes and in the chest, which signals the readiness of a poem and is only relieved once the words are on paper or on screen. "Where one singer may remember songs through sounds, emotions, and moving images or sequential tableaux, another may actually visualize the words themselves, with letters."

Robin Skelton said he wrote poetry in a trance. Many others have described something similar; some poets find lines, even whole poems, in the untethered space between sleeping and waking. Many do their best work at night while others sleep, and they feel "unwatched"; or when they are walking and find that a poem emerges from the rhythm of movement. Poets say lines come to them, artists say the pen or brush has a mind of its own – a will-o'-the-wisp character in a time-gobbling negotiation with difficult study and practice. Such art might not be worth it, it might offend propriety or make others uneasy; it is unlikely to make money. It might – though – be important.

The Rev. Wm. Matheson "propounds the theory that Mairi was regarded with hostility because of participation in a certain kind of verse-making that did not properly belong to her sex. He writes: 'Mary MacLeod was herself buried in Rodil – face downwards, so it is said … It is to be noted that in Mull there is the same tradition about the poetess *Mairearad nighean Lachainn*, who is buried under a heap of stones in Kilninian Churchyard … The explanation of such a proceeding is probably to be found by looking for the common factor in these two cases. This appears to be an addiction to a certain type of composition which it may have been tabu for a woman to produce … There is even a suggestion that the offence in question was regarded as not being far removed from witchcraft; for in Norse times, it was the fate of a witch to be buried under a heap of stones.'"

XVII

Abetted by Cosmic Forces: Witchcraft

the milk of that cow down
the milk of that cow up
in my own dear coggie

rest dim shadows
in the field of the slut

Janet McNicol
somebody's daughter
who nobody wanted
made her way north
as a hare and a mouse

Janet McNicol
in somebody's house

– Tighnacraig

98.

Between the passing of the Witchcraft Act of 1563 and its repeal in Scotland in 1736, an estimated 3,837 people were tried as witches; 2,558 of them were executed and burned.

In the complex political and religious climate of post-Reformation Scotland, the war against witches was a war on Satan led by God's

chosen – powerful civic and clerical leaders who acted from a certainty
of divinely conferred authority. "No cost was too great because witch-
hunting served the greater good of Christendom … They believed that
witchcraft inverted society's key values, disturbed godly order, challenged the divine right of kings – the ancient doctrine that rulers derive
their right to rule from God – and diminished the majesty of God. It
was thought that witch-hunting saved souls and averted the wrath of
God by purging society of evil as the End Times loomed."

In Gaelic areas, by contrast, there was generally little sense of a witch
as "impelled by a natural malevolence encouraged and abetted by cos-
mic forces of evil." Sharron Gunn affirms that "[t]he devil and the demonic pact did not enter Gaelic folklore as it did English and Lowland
folklore." Instead, there was "a uniquely Gaelic attitude to the evil eye,
fairies and other nature spirits, and to the overall practice of magic as
a legitimate means of furthering one's own designs and thwarting enemies." Use of magic "incurred censure in proportion to the amount of
damage inflicted, and of deception and spite involved, but this was also
true of the employment of physical weapons. There seems to have been
little sense of witchcraft as an inherent force of evil in itself."

Scottish Gaels did not view themselves as victims of demonic forces
against which they were helpless, as others did; they participated in a
world of variable forces, some of which were threatening and feared.
And some of which were both magical and beneficial.

99.

In the middle of the forest clearing behind the cabin is the remains of
a bonfire. The charred wood in its centre rests in a deep bed of ash. I
walk past it several times as I explore the property we are thinking of
buying. We have asked my father to come and give his opinion about
what it would take to finish building, and – to tell the truth – if he'd be
willing to help with the construction and teach us what to do. The cabin
is a small cedar Pan-abode, a summer cabin, built with an outhouse at
the back. Recently the owners have added an indoor bathroom and
begun to frame-in an addition. Whatever their plan was, it is halted

now because of a failure of will or money or love, and maybe all three. We have been told they are splitting up.

There is no well, only a small holding tank and several rain-barrels for water. The road from Victoria is long and winding, considered dangerous by people who drive it, and the access road to the property is made of potholes and gravel; but there are wide views of the sea from the cabin and there is a rainforest of moss-hung red cedars in the ravine. I have already slid down a boulder-strewn slope through ferns taller than I am to get to the stream that divides the property on two sides from the deep woods. Near the house, the Douglas firs are eighty feet tall and growing; and there are rocky knolls to climb through bleached grass and moss, wildflowers, and wild strawberries. In front of the cabin is room for a herb garden; below it is terracing: first a deer meadow and then a dense screening of salal berry, salmon berry, Oregon grape, blackberry, redcurrant, and wild rose. We're not long back from living in Scotland and this is the first time we've seen anything that could be a home.

My father stands at the burnt-out bonfire gazing at the ashes. I join him and see what he sees – the bright white skull of a deer. Its presence underlines the feeling I have of this as shared land. However much we have been looking around and noticing that there are ravens calling from the treetops, and eagles circling overhead, we are being noticed too. Not only by the birds but by other inhabitants of this semi-wild territory where, as I will come to learn, there are rats and voles, and black bear, and cougar that follow the deer. At night, owls hoot from the woods and frighten the cats, and at dawn quail families scoot across the dirt driveway, all too aware of their vulnerability. The force of the wind and rain will at times be frightening and I'll cower downstairs in fear of trees falling on the roof. Once, that will happen. But I want this feeling of the company of other species more than I have wanted anything before, and I want to believe that I'll not be too much in their way.

In the mornings, with my small daughter in my arms, I open the curtains and we greet the deer in the clearing. In the evenings, we find them in the lower meadow and know from droppings and crushed grasses where they sleep higher up on rock ledges. They move through the seasons in small families in familiar patterns. At the cove, they cross the beach mudflats at low tide, stepping carefully around seaweed and through beds of clamshells. Later, when my daughter is older, she and I will find a doe under the front deck where it has come to die, and the two of us will ease it onto a sheet of cardboard and drag it to where there's a graveyard for all our animals under the trees. It is the place where my father and El and I buried the skull.

100.

A poem composed at Garbhath Mór, in the Highland region of Bade-noch, tells how a woman who had just given birth watched in horror as one of her young sons, in mimicry of his father's sacrifice of a lamb to ensure the safe delivery of his wife, prepared to behead his younger brother with an axe. She leapt from her bed to stop him, and in doing so the axe in the boy's hand deflected and struck and killed the infant in her arms. "When she saw what had occurred, her reason fled; she sprang to her feet and with lightning speed flew to the hills and joined the deer. There she grew as fleet of foot, as sharp of sight, as keen of scent and as wild of nature as the wild deer themselves." Seven years passed. On the day of her husband's pending remarriage, she "ap-peared in their midst and took her place beside her husband." She was dressed and sane and sensible, but "covered with fine fur or soft down ... like the cub of a grey seal of the ocean or the fawn of the red hind of the mountains."

The woman had crossed into the realm of another species. While there, she gave service to the deer, warning them of hunters and dogs, leading them to safety, away from human beings. It was an extra-ordinary relationship that benefited everyone except possibly her hus-band, who had been prepared to "move on," and her mother, who "was persistent in hounding the deer with the dogs and in driving them from the straths to the mountains." The woman's suffering had given her the ability to enter this alternate existence; and her ability to adjust and use her human abilities in alignment with the needs of another species enabled her restoration and return. It is a story which mirrors, for me, the discomfiture of those left behind by those who transit a threshold, but which requires no explanation since it has nothing to do with "belief." It is just what happened. It would be nice to know the perspective of the woman's surviving children; and of the deer; and of the women who followed the deer cult on the island of Jura, which Mary viewed from Scarba.

101.

Ideas of witchcraft as demonic took hold "in frontier zones of the Scottish Gàidhealtachd, where economic, political and religious links with the non-Celtic national mainstream culture were strongest." They also took hold through projects such as King James VI & I's attempt to civilize and de-Gaelicize the island of Lewis by bringing settlers into a plantation scheme, "a conduit by which mainstream Scottish culture could be introduced into the Hebrides."

James VI & I initially planned to murder all the native inhabitants of Lewis to facilitate settlement, but he was persuaded out of the envisioned "slauchter, mutilation, fyre-raising, or utheris inconvenieties if necessary" on the grounds of impracticability.

The King granted ownership of the island to a group of noblemen (the Gentlemen Adventurers from Fife) although the island had long been MacLeod territory. After the plantation scheme failed, in part because of MacLeod harassment and the murder of settlers, and in part because of the settlers' incompetence, the King permitted the MacKenzies, rivals of the MacLeods, to attack the island and expel any MacLeods found there in exchange for the land.

In 1631, when Mary was about sixteen years old, a group of Mackenzies was awarded a commission to try two sisters from Stornoway (Lewis's principal town) for witchcraft. The sisters were Marie McGillimichell, who may have survived, and Christian Riache, who was burned. A December 1630 letter linked to Christian's case suggests that she was "[p]erhaps part of the Mackenzies' 'grite trouble and chargis … in planting and civilising' of Lewis." In other words, that it was an execution motivated by personal grudge and venality more than the "detestable cryme of witchcraft sorcerie, inchantments and uthers devilish practises offensive to God, scandalous to the trew religioun and hurtfull to diverse our good subjects," of which she was accused.

Witch-hunting like this was not "Gaelic business as usual, for the Mackenzies had arrived in the island as part of [the] royal attempt to settle a plantation there." More typically, "[t]he deeper into purely Gaelic areas … the more the powers of the fairies in it seem to wax and those of witches to wane." In the end, Lewis proved not to be a lasting exception to this rule, for "when the attempt finally petered out, no more is heard of witchcraft accusations on Lewis."

In 1661, the most severe year of the Scottish witch hunt, the year in which Norman of Berneray was knighted by Charles II, six hundred and sixty-four witches were "named" in Scotland, but in the whole of the Gaelic-speaking north and west there were only eight witches cited. None were in the islands. The last accusation of witchcraft recorded in the entire Hebrides was on Skye in 1670; the last execution for witchcraft in Scotland as a whole occurred in 1727 on Scotland's east coast, about two decades after Mary's death. During her lifetime, the beliefs from which she drew strength and identity had – in the larger Scottish and English worlds – become increasingly related to treason and heresy.

Mary could not have been naive about the risks she ran as her conduct confronted changing political and religious realities. When women were prosecuted as witches, the punishments were extreme. Witches in Mary's time were strangled and burned and, in severest cases, burned alive. Their charred bones and ashes were dug in where they died. They were not buried face-up or face-down in marked graves. They were not given graves at all. To mark a place of burial is to memorialize it, even if only by a pile of stones. To heap stones on the site of a burial is to build a cairn, to indicate where others can come to remember. Mairearad had a cairn. Mary does not: instead, she has the flagstones of St Clement's in the church of her ancestors; instead she has her unforgettable words.

102.

Prone burials are not common: only about six hundred have been discovered around the world. Two hundred of these are in Britain with fewer than a dozen of them located in Scotland. All that can truly be said is that "to be laid in the grave prone is not an accepted burial position" and "that prone burial was an almost universal technique for differentiating or 'othering' the corpse." The othering is a mystery, its meaning altering until by the seventh and eighth centuries in Scotland these graves are located away from principal burying areas and associated with punishment and loss of hope for bodily resurrection together with true believers in Christ at the end of time.

A different type of prone burial was discovered in a rich archaeological site on the Barvas machair on the west side of Lewis, bounded by the sea, rivers, and the main road to Stornoway. The fragile sandy turf made of shell, sand, and peat changes constantly through erosion, storms, and climate. "Sites may appear and disappear within days or, in extreme conditions, hours." The wind is a near constant: a newly exposed structure may vanish and then, through wind-shift and sediment-lift, reappear. People have lived here, making homes and tending fields for crops and grazing, for thousands of years, from Neolithic times to the present, moving when they had to, but always in touch with the past and repurposing its resources. Discoveries in the machair range from the late Neolithic through the Bronze and Iron Ages, the period of Norse habitation, and into the sixteenth century. Even today, "walking the machair has something elemental about it. The soles of your feet, and therefore your body in touch with the soil."

The prone burial on the Barvas machair is Iron Age. Inside a long cist (a stone-built box) "capped by an eroded cairn of beach pebbles" was "an extended, prone, female inhumation accompanied by an iron ring, probably a bracelet." The "grave was particularly carefully constructed and lined with matched local stones. The bracelet was "beautifully worked ... with bronze embellishments, the only such find in Scotland ... She was a big strong woman – tall for her time at 5′ 6″, well-muscled and quite young. She was buried sometime between 212–387 AD at least 1,600 years ago, and her burial has been carefully made." Each of the pale beach pebbles that made up the cairn had been brought from up to a kilometre away at the shore. Whoever she was, she had been important to her community, and they cared how she was remembered.

We cannot know exactly what Mary intended by asking for prone burial, but writer, artist, academic, and contemporary witch Yvonne Owen proposes that Mary's stated preference to be buried face-down "may have to do with this mouth, with its powerful voice, being directed toward the heart of Earth, with benefices or blessings instead of anathemas or curses.

"Yes," Owen continues, "the bizarre characterizations of women poets as somehow transgressive never cease to surprise and dismay, from Sappho to Patti Smith. (Of course, there is some credibility to the claims describing the female Bard's magical power to curse or bless with their oration ...)"

103.

We're on the Pentland Road driving across Barvas Moor as the long summer twilight slowly darkens. The road is a single-track ribbon crossing the seemingly unending moor with nothing to mark it but a few bothies and a scattering of rock amidst grasses changing colour beneath an overturned bowl of sky, a cauldron of boiling cloud and light. The cloud formations are so stunning that, as we learn the next morning at our B&B from Guido, a professional cloud watcher, people come from all over the world to see them. We had left Stornoway late after a long day in the library, then writing up notes, and a quick fish-supper, to follow the backroads with no real destination in mind. We encounter no one, neither human nor animal, until we meet a car near a turn-off with a sign for the Callanish standing stones. Despite the advanced hour, we take the turn. The menhirs pin the skyline, and the site is open, the stones darkening against the sunset. We climb a little track and walk into a menhir circle with a monolith at its centre. Three young men, present when we arrive, leave soon. We stay as long as we can find our way, stumbling over grass and turf in and out of a formation that has been there for five thousand years.

We are nearer the coast than I had thought. I would like to drive right to the sea, but full darkness falls, and we are out of time. We head slowly back, rabbits sprinting across the road in front of the headlights, and car after car, a dizzying stream of them, travelling swiftly towards us, late to wherever it is they are going.

104.

The Norse descent that Mary and other MacLeod bards celebrated in their poetry began with Leod, son of Olaf the Black, King of Man and the Northern Isles, who lived in the thirteenth century. The Norse had raided from a base on the Shetland Islands, and by the end of the twelfth century were in control of the Hebrides. When the King of Norway gave up the Hebrides to the King of Scots, Leod took advantage of ensuring uncertainties to claim most of Skye and much of Lewis and Harris as well as a coastal section of the mainland. Whatever the extent and legitimacy of MacLeod claims to such territory – claims which King James VI & I had shown on Lewis that he could disregard – they were best muted when their promotion in songs, and their celebration in the poetry of Mary and other MacLeod bards, could be interpreted as disloyalty to the Crown. Regardless, Mary requested prone burial, which tradition says referenced Norse links and magical practices, both of which were outrages to Crown and Church.

In the Viking age, a woman who practised magic was known as a Völva. She practised *Seidr*, which in Old Norse means "to bind" – spellmaking to bring things together that are not normally tied. In poetry, this could be a description of metaphor, the poet's tool for exploring the nature of the world through language. "How far volur and other magical practitioners were poets we cannot say, but where first-hand records survive from later time, witches and particularly shamans are typically guardians of the imaginative world of poetic inspiration."

A Völva was usually unmarried. She had close ties with clan leaders but was set apart from wider society because of her role, making her both respected and feared. She was a wanderer, separated from the norms of society, especially those associated with being a woman, as she went from place to place, performing commissions in exchange for food and lodging. In her Norse form she was said to practise from within a liminal space between personal experience and the otherworld and to wear bright colours and a hat made of cat fur; but she was most clearly identified by the decorated staff or wand she carried. The grave of a Völva found in Denmark contained a metal wand, a blue and red dress with white sleeves, and a gold-plated silver brooch.

At the least, this description of a Norse witch is resonant with accounts of Mary as unmarried, close to clan leaders, and living outside the bounds of conventions for women. In her later years, Mary was described as a wanderer throughout the islands who wore a tartan cape fastened with a large silver brooch, and who carried a silver-headed cane. At the most, Mary lived consciously within the traditions of the Norse witch, and chose to carry its art, power, and memory towards the future. A name by which Mary was also known and praised was Màiri Seud or Mary the Jewel.

XVIII

Lying Men/Things

Not for me

the dark   indoors
I like to walk   rain

drinks me   up

all afternoon   I watch the deer
undo their skins

the skittish quail
that cross   my path

The sea comes in
a slippery mind   a salty

brain   No door   is shut

I get to   sleep
just where   I want

– *Threshold*

105.

It troubles me to leave Mary within the stones of St Clement's. I know it isn't rational, but it doesn't feel right that her personality, talent, purpose, and strength should be constrained even there. Like the poet Robert Bringhurst's definition of "the wild," she is "unmanaged and unmanageable, and in some sense unconfined by those who would manage [her]." Every strand of her mystery followed to its end, instead of concluding, joins a fractal complex of culture. What I am certain of, though, is that throughout her life and at the end of it, Mary believed she would be heard. She was never silenced: what she was and what she created were always there to be discovered. If I have listened a little differently from others, I am glad. She has reminded me that poetry is a community: its differences are minor compared to its affiliations. She has reminded me that vocation is a trust. Nothing that happened to her could prevent her from composing, nor could it break her reliance on her foundations as a bard and on the power of her traditions and knowledge of the role of women in them.

The pipers, some of whom are buried at St Clement's too, have their own beliefs about her. Piper friends have, as I have mentioned earlier, told me of rumours that a piper was Mary's lover. They have spoken of her friendship with the legendary Dunvegan piper Pàdraig Mòr Mac Cruimein (c. 1595–16??) and his son, Pàdraig Òg Mac Cruimein (1645–1723), who succeeded his father at Dunvegan in 1670. The famous and still-played pibroch "Lament for Mary MacLeod," composed by Pàdraig Òg after Mary's death, has unsettling qualities. It is dramatic, "spooky," and weird, with some pipers refusing to play it or allow it to be played in their presence because she was a "white witch." What counts for most, though, is that Mary stood up for Gaelic society in the face of its undermining from without and within. When such pipers play "The Lament," they play it for her. Others believe there may be a private message from the composer in the odd effects of parts of the pibroch – the work is as unusual as she was. "When she died," a piper wrote, "it must have seemed like the end of an era (as indeed it was) to many, including the piper who made this tune. It can be seen as a lament for a lost world."

When I listen to "The Lament," it taps at the grief I carry from loss of family members. Its message to me is that a heart has been torn from its stem. It makes me think of the anchored kelp of my west coast Pacific world when it is stripped from its roots in the kelp forest and the shelter and nourishment of the forest is diminished. Its mood is recognizable: it is sea-swept and wind-swept, caught at the impasse of struggle and acceptance of the shoreline.

106.

In the opening stanzas – the emotional ground – of "Crònan an Taibh" / "The Ocean Croon," a praise poem for Sir Norman likely written during one of Mary's exiles, Mary expresses feelings of emptiness and abandonment because of the change that has unravelled her life. The poem's date of composition is known only as some time after Norman's knighthood and his second marriage – that is, any time after about 1666. Mary begins: "At the ocean's sound my mood is forlorn – time was that such was not my wont to hear." Instead, she has been used to hearing "the great shrill-voiced pipe, all music surpassing / when Patrick's fingers stirred it." Patrick (Pàdraig Mòr Mac Cruimein) is a figure of metonymy, representing the life she is no longer part of. Both Patrick and the ocean are literal as well: he is a colleague and friend, and the ocean is a barrier that keeps Mary from where she wants to be; and it also represents boundless, near uncrossable distance. The word for "ocean" that Mary uses "refers specifically to the Atlantic, west of the Hebrides" – which helps locate her and underscores the extent of her isolation.

Mary tells us that there are three ways in which unexpected change occurs. It comes from trusting an unreliable world: "often / hath it changed its perilous step"; and through the created world's natural mutability: "More varied its course than the drops of dew on a morn- / ing in May's beginning" (May was when Mary habitually returned to Dunvegan each year); and by what she has observed for herself: "Never under the sun have I beheld him to whom it [the world] gave / not his day of trouble." Mary cannot expect to be an exception to these workings, but she asks that her verses be taken to Sir Norman's house where other kinsmen have found help in their distress and where the generosity practised there has formed "the theme of my melody" in the songs she has composed for her patron. It is "a wide / house liberal and welcoming" to which "poet-bands" and friends would travel – this is the company Mary wishes to rejoin. In the remainder of the poem, Mary praises Sir Norman's person, virtues, origins, accomplishments, and his wife, addressing her appeal to both of them.

Indications are that Mary might not have been far from the house on Berneray when she composed "The Ocean Croon." She tells us that it is "over yonder beneath / the slope," perhaps the small hill I climbed my first time on Berneray or on nearby Pabbay. Yet the poem is a map of dislocation, not of place, and "over yonder" can be both immediate and unreachable when it is the centre of all that matters.

In my very unofficial reading (the poet Erin Mouré calls a poetic response to a literal gloss "an e-translation," presumably after herself!) the sound of the ocean in the first lines of "The Ocean Croon" is layered with the absence of Mary's usual self: this self and Patrick's missing music are like ghosts. She lives (or does not live) in two locations at once, both of which have had love abstracted from them, leaving each incomplete. Mary's gift is to make us receive the poem through this duality of presence and absence, a like presence and absence to that which has characterized my journey with her.

107.

Adam Zagajewski's poem "She Wrote in Darkness" reveals the hidden layers of a woman poet's life. He pictures her writing in near-darkness and silence so as not to disturb her mother who is ill. In her isolation, despondency, and middle age, the poet becomes the means of expression of darkness itself. The only compassion shown to her is by the arrival of dawn. Even so, as she finally falls asleep, black birds begin their morning plaint. The realities of the poet's truth are that sorrow and song hold to earth, and cycle without reference to her watchfulness or her pain. But in the beginning of the poem Zagajewski aligns the weight of words that emerge from the poet's despair with the nature of a comet. Her existence, her poetry and awareness are alive with visible fire.

108.

It is dark and too cold for the good clothes and shoes I wear. There are no streetlights. I stumble along the gravel beside my grandmother. We had gone to the parish hall with our neighbour, Mrs Scott, in her small olive-green car with beige leather seats. It was cosy inside the hall, and I had liked the friendly unfamiliar ladies and learning to play bingo. We'd had to leave after the priest came to bless the tea and cookies. (I had never seen a priest before.) There was a misunderstanding between my grandmother and our neighbour. I look back the way we have come but can no longer see any lights. I glance at my grandmother, her profile pale above the collar of her navy coat. She looks straight ahead. Her forearm is crooked to hold her navy handbag against her body. I have never had to walk this far before. I start to cry but pebbles have collected inside my shoes. I stop crying and stoop to shake them out.

As my eyes grow used to the dark, I am less afraid. We walk and walk. There are a few houses far back from the road, some telephone poles, muddy ditches, and croaking frogs. After a while I discover stars between breaks in the clouds, and my grandmother becomes less strange. I feel the softened warmth of her body radiate towards me as she tells me a story of coming home in the dark with her sisters. Someone or something had been lost. They had been out on the commons so maybe it was they themselves who had been lost. People sometimes disappeared or died, but you didn't give up on them. They were always brought home or found their own way to where they belonged unless the sea took them. If so, you waited at the shore.

109.

My cousin waited at the dock with the Evinrude outboard engine he had bought with his own money, my grandfather out on the lake in the fourteen-foot runabout they had built together, the old man raising a bedsheet on a paddle for a sail, tacking, and then coming about, the bed-sheet flapping. Speedboats towed water-skiers past him and made lace wake-patterns on the water.

110.

"We knew an old man, called Alexander McRae a tailor, in Mellen of Gairloch, whom we have heard sing many of Mary's songs, not one of which has ever been printed. Some of these were excellent, and we had designed to take them down from his recitation, but were prevented by his sudden death, which happened in the year 1833. Among these was a rather extraordinary piece, resembling MacDonald's 'Birlinn,' composed upon occasion of John, son of Sir Norman, taking her out to get a sail in a new boat."

The joy Mary took in the trial of the new boat in the company of Sir Norman's son is shown by her creation of an "extraordinary" song about it. Her feelings are as plain to me as my grandfather's satisfaction with the "sea-test" of the pleasure-craft he had built with my cousin. Creation and completion come with exhilaration and blessing each time what is made is shared. Mary's song was remembered for well over a hundred years. A witness has left testimony not only to its exceptional nature but to where we might look for its traces. My cousin's boat was built to fulfill an adolescent's dream of speed and mastery. His feelings as a witness to that first sail without him were – as he has told me – complicated. Yet I do not think my grandfather went out in the boat again, whereas my cousin spent years of summers with it on the lake. I was one of many he taught to water-ski, towed behind it. The song of which Mackenzie tells us is not only a tally of a loss as gone and buried as its maker, of a story of the past, but a tale which carries the hope that although Mary may still be in the shadows, the essence of this work is alive, doing its work enfolded – as poetry has always travelled – within the body of another.

111.

It is only about four kilometres (2.5 miles) from Rodel to Leverburgh, the village from where we took the ferry to North Uist and Berneray at the end of my first trip to Harris. We drive through the town quickly; Sorrel Cottage where we had stayed is closed. Many of the shops that were open then are shut. It is late afternoon, but the town feels less closed for the day than empty. A mist softens the lines of its grey and beige buildings and what remains of early-twentieth-century structures built for the fishing and whaling schemes of Lord Leverhulme, who renamed the coastal village after himself from its original Gaelic, An t-Òb. About six hundred people live in the larger village environs. Leverhulme had envisioned a population of ten thousand.

We stop briefly where the tiny township of Nisisidh once stood within a swatch of arable land and encroaching machair. By the 1880s, Nisisidh, mentioned by one source as another possible birthplace for Mary MacLeod, consisted of just seven buildings, one of them roofless, plus three enclosures for sheep. Between 1828 and 1853 villages were cleared all along the west coast of Harris to make way for large sheep farms. "Even the stones were taken from the cleared blackhouses to build the endless walls of the new sheepfarms." All that is left to show where people once lived is an extensive pattern of lazybeds rippling the green slopes.

Not far past Sandview House where we had first stayed on Harris, we come to Clach Steineagaidh, the single remaining standing stone of an extensive circle, where we had paused before. Today, the waters of the Sound are a choppy blue, navy, turquoise, and grey in quick succession, and the panoramic view is clear enough to display the stone's connection to its neighbours – the standing stone on Taransay (Tarasaigh) to the north and the MacLeod Stone (Clach Mhic Leòid) on a headland

to the northeast. "All the stones in the landscape would have been located in relation to each other, as well as to their landscape setting."
Those relationships, meaningful to people who gathered here in Neolithic times, are hidden to us, as is what there is to learn from a mound
"which may be the remains of a Neolithic chambered burial cairn, or
possibly of a later circular monument ... which was built next to the
stone circle." There is more to be discovered and no doubt it will be,
given resources and cause to look here rather than elsewhere. In the
meantime, we have a running catalogue: the standing stone began as
part of a circle of thirteen or fourteen stones. In 1914 it stood with four
"prostrate pillar stones," each smaller than the 6 ft. 7 in. (186 × 97 × 17
cm) stone still upright. In 1969 there were three fallen pillar stones; in
1980, there were two. An optimistic note on the historic interpretation
sign asks that visitors not disturb any archaeological remains on the
ground. Generations have removed materials for building from sites
like this as time weathers the inviolable into the useful. Still, what remains may yet offer insight into Mary's story.

Màiri nighean Alastair Ruaidh's reported reason for requesting face-
down burial was "*beul nam breug a chur foidhpe*" – "to put the mouth
of lies under her." The words can be interpreted as a demand for punishment for having told untruths, shutting up her voice symbolically
even beyond death; or as their opposite – to ensure that her mouth "with
its powerful voice" be placed in direct communication with the "heart
of the earth" – female divinity, fertility, and power. Sharron Gunn, whose
knowledge has supported me throughout this journey, tells me that
"the *tursachan* (standing stones) were also called *fir nam breug* – lying
things/men," and Mary's words "could refer to non-Christian history,
folklore, etc. as well as outright lies." For those alert to the possibility
that a poet could choose to speak in metaphor, Mary's astonishing appeal preserves not only the injustice done to her but the role of the old
beliefs as her foundation. In this way, Mary continues in conversation
with the earth's creative springs and its resources of healing. It is a message to all of us.

112.

"You will never get to the bottom of the mystery of Mary MacLeod," the curator in the red pullover on Berneray told me on a day that remains as vivid to me now as it was then, even though his words have accompanied me through much of a decade. They remain true, but the mystery resides in the poetry and the poet's tale; and at every stage of poetry and path, it attempts to reveal itself. I may not find exactly why Mary's way crossed mine as it did – but the reach to understand has helped me bring a poet's story to those who have not heard of her, and it has uncovered, like a seam of gold in my own foundations, a grand-mother, and others whose gifts to me I had neglected; and it has restored my love of poetry.

With these riches in hand, I can turn from what may seem like the closing in of night on body and spirit and even, at times, on the story of human existence, and stand with the fallen, unfallen, and buried stones on the shore in the low west light one more time at least, as the late light meets the sea, fractures into colours, and transforms the waves.

END

Acknowledgments

The initial stage of research for *More Richly in Earth* received financial assistance from the Access Copyright Foundation and the Canada Council. Subsequently, both Ursula Vaira of Leaf Press and *Exile Magazine* published versions of my poetic conversations with Mary MacLeod under the title of *Threshold*. The selection of poems in *Exile* received the Gwendolyn MacEwen Poetry Prize (co-winner) while the Leaf Press publication became a co-authored book with the photographer, Xan Shian. The story of the journey itself began to take form in a talk commissioned by the Elephant Mountain Literary Festival; the essay generated by the talk was published in *Prairie Fire Magazine*.

So many have helped along the way. Sharron Gunn's expertise and enthusiasm have been fundamental to my ability to undertake and complete this work, as any reader will see. I am also indebted to the generosity, correspondence, and conversation of writers, academics, historians, pipers, acquaintances, and friends, including Meg Bateman, Shane Cadzow, Aonghas Phàdraig Caimbeul, Maoilios Caimbeul, Alex Dougall, Sam and Carolyn Finlayson, Rita Hunter, Richard Kennedy, Cathlin Macauley, Alasdair MacLeod, the late Aonghas MacNeacail, Dave Mercer, Gillian Munro, Yvonne Owen, Liz Rideal, Sean Virgo, Gordon Webb, and Mark Wringe. Each challenged, inspired, supported, and sometimes daunted me. The joy that I found through this quest was best heard in the voices of the Victoria Gaelic Choir, and uncovered in the company of Michael Elcock, whose love of the byways of his homeland has been the beginning of many adventures.

All errors, omissions, misunderstandings, and missteps are mine alone.

Mary MacLeod's work has been kept alive not only by her culture but by the dedication of scholars. Prof. Colm Ó Baoill's *Màiri nighean Alasdair Ruaidh, Song-maker of Skye and Berneray* (2014) is the product of extensive knowledge and long study of its subject. It has been with me while I have consulted J. Carmichael Watson's ground-breaking 1934 *Gaelic Songs of Mary MacLeod*. I am grateful for both books and for the commitment and life-long learning required to write them.

In the preface to *Gaelic Songs*,* Watson wrote, "It is my only wish that this booklet will be as a stone on the cairn of the woman poet of the Islands, and to keep Scottish Gaelic in good condition." I echo his wish imperfectly but have gained from his love of the language and from translators everywhere who share the world's inheritance of literature. I am not alone in being the richer for it.

*The full text of Watson's *Gaelic Songs of Mary MacLeod* is available from the National Library of Scotland at https://archive.org/details/gaelicsongsofmaroomacl/mode/2up.

Notes

EPIGRAPH

page v "A mystery ... of the spheres": George Mackay Brown, *For the Islands I Sing* (Edinburgh: Polygon Books, 2008), 168.

PREFACE

page ix "Much we long ... remember long": J. Carmichael Watson, "Marbh-rann" / "Dirge," *Gaelic Songs of Mary MacLeod* (London and Glasgow: Blackie & Son Ltd., 1934), 95.
page ix "O glory ... search thy volume": Dante, "Inferno," in *The Divine Comedy: Inferno; Purgatorio; Paradiso by Dante Alighieri*, translated by Allen Mandelbaum, 1. ll. 82–4 (Everyman's Library Classics Series, 1995).
page x "your heart ... among stones and ghosts": Marilyn Bowering, " (Simple)," from an unpublished manuscript (Tighnacraig: 1978).

I A TRAVELLER'S TALE

3.
page 7 "Mountains divide us ... to thy homeland": "From its first, anonymous appearance in *Blackwood's Magazine* for September, 1829, the 'Canadian Boat Song' has tantalized its admirers, for the question of its authorship has remained an unsolved puzzle," from Linda Dowler, "The Authorship of the 'Canadian Boat-Song': A Bibliographical Note,"

https://www.canadianpoetry.org/volumes/vol6/dowler.html (accessed 7 August 2023).

5.

page 9 "Don't any of you … the sea more than the land": Archilochus, "Anything May Happen," in *The Penguin Book of Greek Verse*, edited by Constantine A. Trypanis (Harmondsworth: Penguin Books, 1971), 130.

page 10 *an important modernist poetry lineage*: I encountered Margaret Avison by chance in a church, and Dorothy Livesay at a reading. Robin Skelton recommended P.K. Page as "one of the good ones." The poet Charles Lillard, with his vast bibliographic knowledge of BC literature, pointed me to pioneers such as Anne Marriott, Doris Ferne, and Floris McLaren whom I met or corresponded with. I found Hermia Harris Fraser in Vancouver and invited Marya Fiamengo and other women poets to read at the Open Space Gallery series in Victoria, which Susan Musgrave and I curated together.

page 11 *Little Loch Broom*: Marilyn Bowering, "Little Loch Broom," from an unpublished manuscript (Tighnacraig: 1978).

Little Loch Broom
under the moon
glinting and gleaming
running to sea

Trollers and navies
divers and sailors
seals, salmon and whalers
running to sea

But
under the night
and the mountains and pine trees
Little Loch Broom
comes back to me

8.

page 15 *growing up on South Harris*: Finlay J. Macdonald, *The Corncrake and the Lysander* (London: Macdonald & Co., 1985), 87.

II THE LANGUAGE OF BIRDS

page 19 "A red dog lays … strains towards moonrise": Marilyn Bowering, "Winter Birds," from an unpublished manuscript (Tighnacraig: 1978).

9.

page 19 *buried there at the age of 105*: John Mackenzie, *Sàr-Obair nam Bàrd Gaelach or The Beauties of Gaelic Poetry* (Glasgow: Macgregor, Polson and Co., 1841), 21.

page 20 *she lived 103 years from 1590 to 1693*: George Henderson, *The Poems of John Morison collected and edited with a Memoir by George Henderson*, vol. 1, 2nd ed. (Archibald Sinclair, 1896), xiii, https://digital.nls.uk/75880064.

page 20 "might be an equally good guess": *Màiri nighean Alasdair Ruaidh, Song-maker of Skye and Berneray*, edited by Colm Ó Baoill (Glasgow: The Scottish Gaelic Texts Society, vol. 22, 2014), 2.

page 20 *on the road south from Scarista*: Anne Loughran, *Gaelic Literature of the Isle of Skye, an Annotated Bibliography* (APJ Publications, 2016), http://www.skyelit.co.uk/; J. Carmichael Watson, *Gaelic Songs of Mary MacLeod* (London and Glasgow: Blackie & Son Ltd., 1934), xiv; Ó Baoill, *Màiri nighean Alasdair Ruaidh*, 7; John M. MacAulay, *Silent Tower: A History and Description of St. Clement's Church at Rodil* (Edinburgh, Cambridge, and Durham: The Pentland Press, 1993), 35.

page 20 *in Rodel, where I had lingered*: Watson, *Gaelic Songs*, xix.

page 20 *a collection begun in the 1930s*: These songs can be heard online through the sound archive *Tobar an Dualchais* (Kist o Riches), https://www.tobarandualchais.co.uk/?l=en (accessed 7 August 2023).

page 21 *imprisoned in Hungary's Stalinist concentration camp from 1950 to 1953*: George Faludy, "Learn by Heart This Poem of Mine," in *Learn by Heart This Poem of Mine: Sixty Poems and One Speech*, edited by John Robert Colombo (Toronto: Hounslow Press, 1983), 113.

10.

page 21 *and her dates as 1590 to 1693*: *The Gaelic Bards: from 1411 to 1517* [i.e. 1715], edited by Alexander Maclean Sinclair (Charlottetown: Haszard & Moore: 1890), 39, https://archive.org/details/gaelicbardsfrom100sinc.

page 21 *Gaelic manuscripts to Canada with him*: "Gaelic in Canada," Department of Celtic Studies, St Francis Xavier University, https://stfx.ca/depart ment/celtic-studies/gaelic-canada (accessed 7 August 2023).

page 22 *of its collector, Dr Hector Maclean*: Kenneth Nilsen, "Sinclair, Alexander MacLean," *Dictionary of Canadian Biography*, vol. 15 (Toronto and Quebec City: University of Toronto / Université Laval, 2003), http://www.biographi.ca/en/bio/sinclair_alexander_maclean_15E.html.

page 22 *was dedicated – that is, to Mary's lifetime*: MacLean Sinclair gives the provenance of Dr Maclean's work in "Dr. Maclean's Manuscript," in "Appendix" to *The Gaelic Bards*, edited by Alexander Maclean Sinclair, 208–9.

page 22 *"he met his … literary information"*: Nilsen, "Sinclair, Alexander MacLean."

page 22 *a Gaelic-speaking character there until the 1960s*: Kenneth E. Nilsen, "Scottish Gaelic," in *Celtic Culture, a Historical Encyclopedia*, vol. 1, edited by John T. Koch (ABC-CLIO, 2006), 380.

page 22 *who spoke either Scottish or Irish Gaelic*: "Gaelic in Canada," Department of Celtic Studies.

page 22 *"on which Maclean Sinclair worked assiduously"*: Nilsen, "Sinclair, Alexander MacLean."

page 23 *which are accepted as cultural norms*: Michael Kennedy, "Introduction," in John Shaw, *Gaelic in Prince Edward Island: A Cultural Remnant* (Gaelic Field Recording Project), 2002, https://islandstudies.com/files/2014/07/GAELIC-IN-PRINCE-EDWARD-ISLAND.pdf.

page 23 *aesthetically acceptable to his views and times*: Kennedy, "Introduction."

11.

page 25 *"the precise generality … only provisional"*: Patchen Markell, "Hannah Arendt & The Case of Poetry," Hannah Arendt Center for Politics and Humanities, Bard College, 2012, https://medium.com/quote-of-the-week/hannah-arendt-the-case-of-poetry-ae2def780670.

12.

page 26 "seekers ... other Gaelic poet": Watson, *Gaelic Songs*, xxvii.

page 00 *through her father*: Ó Baoill, *Màiri nighean Alasdair Ruaidh*, 2; Loughran, *Gaelic Literature of the Isle of Skye*; Watson, *Gaelic Songs*, xi, xii.

page 26 *we still take the ferry to Skye*: Ó Baoill, *Màiri nighean Alasdair Ruaidh*, 3.

page 26 *westernmost islands in the United Kingdom*: Watson, *Gaelic Songs*, xvii.

page 26 *where Mary's mother's family had land*: Alexander Carmichael, *Carmina Gadelica, Hymns and Incantations*, vol. 5, edited by Angus Matheson (Edinburgh and London: Oliver and Boyd, 1954), 341; Ó Baoill, *Màiri nighean Alasdair Ruaidh*, 3, ref. Matheson.

page 27 *but of high caste*: Ó Baoill, *Màiri nighean Alasdair Ruaidh*, 3, ref. John MacInnes.

page 27 "somewhat advanced in life," "of privilege ... preceding period": Watson, *Gaelic Songs*, xi.

page 27 *under the impact of anglicization*: Watson, *Gaelic Songs*, xv.

page 27 *one had sent her away*: Watson, *Gaelic Songs*, xvi–xvii.

page 27 "She directed ... 'beul nam breug a chur foidhpe'": Watson, *Gaelic Songs*, xix. Sharron Gunn's translation as "The mouth of lies to be put under her," private email.

page 27 *to repudiate her own work*: Ó Baoill, *Màiri nighean Alasdair Ruaidh*, 15–16, ref. Henderson.

page 27 "usually ... of witchcraft": "'Government Plans for Gaelic,' Sabhal Mòr Ostaig Lecture," St Cecilia's Hall, Edinburgh, 19 December 2007, http://www.foramnagaidhlig.net/foram/viewtopic.php?t=154.

13.

page 27 "the most original ... a smooth bed of polished granite": Mackenzie, *Sár-Obair nam Bárd Gaelach*, 21.

page 27 "Her Gaelic poems ... contemporary with Shakespeare and Milton": Henderson, *The Poems of John Morison*, xiii.

page 27 "much repetition ... occasional images of some vividness": Derick Thomson, *An Introduction to Gaelic Poetry* (London: Gollancz, 1974), 132–5. This poet, Aonghas "Dubh" MacNeacail remarked after Thomson's death, "transformed Gaelic poetry. He was the first Gaelic poet to work in free verse really, and that released people like myself into using the language in new ways, using new rhythms. That break from centuries of tradition … also opened Gaelic poetry to the influence of contemporary European poetry." Quoted in Marco Werman and Carol Zall, "Scottish Poet and Publisher Derrick Thomson 'Transformed' Gaelic Poetry," *The World*, 28 March 2012, https://www.pri.org/stories/2012-03-28/scottish-poet-and-publisher-derick-thomson-transformed-gaelic-poetry.

page 28 "narrow strait-jacket" *as* "meeting … audience": Sharron Gunn, private email. Gunn also notes that there were seven grades of professional poets. "The common ones were *ollamh* – top grade; *an roth* – the wheel, relationship with sun; *filidh*; and *bàrd* – low grade!"

page 28 "freshness … phrase," "a narrowness … significance": Sorley Mac-Lean, *Ris a' Bhruthaich: The Criticism and Prose Writings of Sorley MacLean*, edited by William Gillies (Stornoway, Isle of Lewis: Acair Ltd., 1985), 81.

page 28 "those great … of the MacLeods were": MacLean, *Ris a' Bhruthaich*, 81.

page 28 *can be a challenge*: one online listing of the MacLeod succession of chiefs can be found here: https://clanmacleod.org/genealogy/chiefly-descent/ (accessed 7 August 2023).

page 28 "were the movie … well-remembered in the Highlands": Sharron Gunn, private email.

page 29 *Mary's style can seem thin-blooded*: Two examples of Gaelic anonyms given by MacLean, *Ris a' Bhruthaich*, 79, are:

You killed my father and my husband,
I love you, Black Allan of Lochy;
You killed my three young brothers,
I love you, Black Allan of Lochy;
Allan, Allan, I rejoice that you are alive.

and

I was late last night with you in a dream
Over in Jura of the cold mountains,
Your kisses were like green water-cress,
But the dream is gone and the pain has stayed.

page 29 *with the transparency of confession*: Richie McCaffery, "'Committed and Confessional': Sorley MacLean's Poetry of World War Two," *eSharp* 20, New Horizons (2013): 1–21, https://www.gla.ac.uk/media/Media_279278_smxx.pdf.

page 29 *an aesthetic it did not seek to follow*: MacLean, *Ris a' Bhruthaich*, 76, 77, 80.

14.

page 29 "remember ... to the intellect": Watson, *Gaelic Songs*, xxvii.

16.

page 33 "What makes her ... Lowland education": Aonghas MacNeacail, private email correspondence.

page 33 "And there ... ourselves anew": Aonghas MacNeacail, "Monologue: 'I'm on a Train Again,'" in *Long Story Short* (7.84 Theatre Company, 1989).

III KENNINGS

page 35 "Since thou ... to rise": Watson, "Marbhrann do Fhear na Comraich" / "Dirge for the Lord of Applecross," *Gaelic Songs*, 15.

17.

page 36 *a pamphlet* ... "all fugitives ... persecution": D.A.D. MacLeod, *The Celtic Saint of the Sanctuary of Applecross* (Northampton: The Swan Press, W. Mark and Co. Ltd., c. 1933–44).

page 37 *trial in which he gave evidence*: Ian Mackenzie, "Applecross History," in *The Companion to Gaelic Scotland*, edited by Derick S. Thomson (Glasgow: Gairm Publications, 1994, 1996).

page 37 "Sleeping With Lambs": Marilyn Bowering, *Sleeping With Lambs* (Victoria and Toronto: Press Porcépic, 1980).

18.

page 38 "Dirge for the Lord of Applecross": Watson, *Gaelic Songs*, 15.

page 39 *John MacInnes ... Mary included*: This is my paraphrase. John MacInnes, "The Panegyric Code in Gaelic Poetry and Its Historical Background," in *Dùthchas nan gàidheal: Selected Essays of John MacInnes*, edited by Michael Newton (Edinburgh: Birlinn, 2006), 265–319.

page 40 "Since thou … with grief": Watson, *Gaelic Songs*, 15.

page 40 "the bones … a bereaved person": Sharron Gunn, private email.

page 40 *metaphor … mighty tree*: Sharron Gunn, private email.

page 40 *that comes … a kenning*: MacInnes, "Panegyric Code," 284–5.

page 41 "When the folk … their burden": Watson, *Gaelic Songs*, 21.

page 41 *if there … of a bee*: Carmichael, *Carmina*, vol. 2, 361; Hilda Ransome, *The Sacred Bee in Ancient Times and Folklore* (Mineola, NY: Dover Books on Anthropology and Folklore reprint, Courier Corporation, 2004), 161.

page 42 *John McInnes … "a code"*: MacInnes, "Panegyric Code."

19.

page 43 "loud shouting … swordblades": Watson, *Gaelic Songs*, 17.

page 43 "without strength to rise": Watson, *Gaelic Songs*, 17.

page 43 *However, youth … the ambiguity*: based on a private email from Sharron Gunn. Gunn notes, "There is a lament for Simon Fraser, a rebel of the 1745, who wasn't young when he was executed. The lament suggests he was youthful and vigorous."

20.

page 45 *crucial to immediate Royalist hopes*: Ronald Williams, *Montrose, Cavalier in Mourning* (London: Barrie & Jenkins Ltd., 1975).

page 45 "thy company" *gathered … "beneath thy shirt"*: Watson, *Gaelic Songs*, 19.

page 45 *the marriage may be figurative*: Watson, *Gaelic Songs*, 113.

page 46 *or other advantages with them*: Mary Dowd, "Family: Marriage Patterns and Family Life from 1500 to 1690," in *Encyclopedia of Irish History and Culture*, https://www.encyclopedia.com/international/encyclopedias-almanacs-transcripts-and-maps/family-marriage-patterns-and-family-life-1500-1690 (accessed 23 August 2023).

page 46 *Norman of Berneray's … familiar to them*: W.D.H. Sellar, "Marriage, Concubinage and Divorce in Gaelic Scotland," *Transactions of the Gaelic Society of Inverness*, vol. 51 (1978): 464–93, https://archive.org/details/tgsi-vol-li-1979-1980/page/485/mode/2up.

page 46 *Norman of Berneray … and his wife Margaret*: "MacLeod Genealogy Database, Sir Norman MacLeod, The Associated Clan MacLeod Societies," 2023, https://mgd.clanmacleod.org/genealogy-database/macleod-sir-norman/; Alexander Mackenzie, "The MacLeods of Bernera," *History of the MacLeods* (Inverness: A&W Mackenzie, 1889), 241–61, https://archive.org/details/historyofmacleod00mack; "Sir Norman Mac-Leod, 1st of Bernera," Clan MacFarlane and Associated Clans Genealogy https://www.clanmacfarlanegenealogy.info/genealogy/TNGWebsite/get person.php?personID=I21525&tree=CC (last modified 24 August 2015).

page 47 *a widower until 1666*: "Sir Norman MacLeod," Clan MacFarlane.

page 48 "O it is ... in the time of my need": Watson, *Gaelic Songs*, 19.

IV O'ERSWEPT BY A DELUGE

page 51 "Of eight ... west wind": Marilyn Bowering, "Of Eight Stones," from an unpublished manuscript (Sleat, Isle of Skye: 1977).

23.

page 52 *Aonghas's view* ... "of language": Aonghas MacNeacail in conversation with the author; see also "Some Reflections on the Poetry of Skye," 168–9, https://www.ssns.org.uk/wp-content/uploads/2019/10/10_MacNea cail_Barra_2006_pp_167-183.pdf (accessed 10 August 2023).

page 52 *poets with ... trained bàrds*: Vernacular poets are generally called either "poets" or "bards," but "bàrd" indicates a level of specific professional training.

page 53 "An Talla ..." / "Macleod's Wonted Hall": Watson, *Gaelic Songs*, 21–5, 113–14.

page 53 "strange ... anigh it": Watson, *Gaelic Songs*, 23. "Anigh" is interesting because of what I later learn about the location of Mary's own house.

page 53 "in the hall ... wont to be": Watson, *Gaelic Songs*, 21.

page 54 *being* "o'erswept" *by a* "deluge": Watson, *Gaelic Songs*, 21–3.

page 54 "is beautifully constrained, uses no abusive language, but it says a great deal between the lines": Aonghas MacNeacail in conversation with the author.

page 55 *The poet ... chief's negligence*: All quotations here are from Watson, *Gaelic Songs*, 21–5.

page 55 *The poet turns ... is Sir Norman*: All quotations here continue to be from Watson, *Gaelic Songs*, 21–5.

page 55 *Once ... origin stories*: e.g., King, Jeffrey, "Lebor Gabála Erenn," in

World History Encyclopedia, https://www.worldhistory.org/Lebor_Gabala_
Erenn/ (last modified 9 January 2019).

page 56 *Pabbay was ... its final abandonment*: "Hebrides: H2, Pabbay/
Pabaigh (Harris)," The Papar Project, 2005, http://www.paparproject.org.
uk/hebrides2.html; Bill Lawson, *Harris in History and Legend* (Edinburgh:
John Donald Publishers / Birlinn Ltd., 2002), 83–7.

page 56 "The bards ... aped the manners of the South": Alexander Nicolson,
History of Skye, 3rd ed., edited by Cailean Maclean (Isle of Lewis:
Islands Book Trust, 2012), 114.

24.

page 58 *or* "coming near": the phrase is the translation found in Ó Baoill,
Màiri nighean Alasdair Ruaidh, 43.

V A PICTURESQUE FIGURE

page 59 "Dressed in tartan ... conventions": George Henderson, "The Literature of the Highlands 1500–1745," in *Home Life of the Highlanders 1400–
1746* (Glasgow: Printed for the Highland Village Association by R.
Maclehose, 1911), https://www.electricscotland.com/history//home9.htm.

26.

page 63 "It is Joycean ... of language": The novel by Tormod Caimbeul is *An
Druim Bho Thuath*.

page 64 *Mary's poem ... I know best*: "Do Mhac Dhomhnaill" / "To Mac-
Donald," in Watson, *Gaelic Songs*, 76–81.

page 65 *At the court ... by outsiders*: Nicolson, *History*, 114.

page 65 "The pibroch ... now forgotten": A pibroch is an extended composition for the bagpipes with variations woven around a theme; in its serious-
ness and importance, in literary terms, it is analogous to the epic.

28.

page 68 "poets ... indigenous foundations": Robert Bringhurst, "Jumping
from the Train," in *Everywhere Being Is Dancing* (Kentville, NS: Gaspereau
Press, 2007), 332, 336–7.

page 69 "However ... milk": Sharron Gunn's translation of Gaelic text in

Angus Peter Campbell (Aonghas Phàdraig Caimbeul), *An t-Eilean / Taking a Line for a Walk through the Island of Skye* (Isle of Lewis: The Islands Book Trust, 2012), 7, 14.

29.

page 69 *Mary's poem ... of Sleat*: "Do Mhac Dhomhnaill" / "To MacDonald," in Watson, *Gaelic Songs*, 76–81.

page 70 *His estates ... Dun Flò*: Nicolson, *History*, 115–18; Angus Peter Campbell, *An t-Eilean*, 76.

page 70 *The MacDonalds ... clan hospitality*: Carmichael, *Carmina*, vol. 4, 344–5.

The Lullaby of the Snow:

Cold, cold this night is my bed,
Cold, cold this night is my child,
Lasting, lasting this night thy sleep,
I in my shroud and thou in mine arm ...

page 70 *We cannot know ... at Dunvegan*: Angus & Archibald Macdonald, *The Clan Donald*, vol. 3 (Inverness: Northern Counties Publishing Company Ltd., 1904), https://archive.org/details/clandonald03macduoft/page/n9/mode/2up.

page 70 *Another sister ... at Dunvegan*: "John (c. 1637–1693) Eighteenth Chief, Chiefly descent, The Associated Clan MacLeod Societies," 2023, https://clanmacleod.org/genealogy/chiefly-descent/.

page 71 *he was succeeded ... "English establishment"*: Nicolson, *History*, 114. This is the Roderick mentioned with the song "Macleod's Wonted Hall" as being the likely cause of Mary's despair as her culture is "o'er swept."

page 71 *"dismissed Blind ... in debt"*: Sharron Gunn, private email; I.F. Grant, *The MacLeods: The History of a Clan, 1200–1956* (Edinburgh: Spurbooks, Holmes McDougall Ltd, 1981), 330.

page 71 *That this new ... as his factor*: The factor was responsible for managing MacLeod's properties and estates; it was a position dependent on loyalty and trust. Ó Baoill, *Màiri nighean Alasdair Ruaidh*, 222.

page 72 *In 1700 ... rising of 1715*: Donald J. Macdonald of Castleton, *Clan Donald* (Gretna, LA: Pelican Publishing Co., 2008), 422–4; Angus & Archibald, *The Clan Donald*; Nicolson, *History*, 151.

page 72 "the estates ... peerage in 1716": "MacLeod, Norman (1706–72), of Dunvegan, Skye" (The History of Parliament Trust, 1964–2020), https://www.historyofparliamentonline.org/volume/1715-1754/member/macleod-norman-1706-72; Ó Baoill, *Màiri nighean Alasdair Ruaidh*, 222–5.

30.

page 73 "I have a treasure ... for gold": All excerpts from "To MacDonald" are taken from Watson, *Gaelic Songs*, 76–81, unless specifically indicated as from the translation of "To MacDonald" in Ó Baoill, *Màiri nighean Alasdair Ruaidh*, 161–7.

page 73 "my shapely ... was told": Ó Baoill, *Màiri nighean Alasdair Ruaidh*, 161.

page 73 "the fosterling ... me with": Ó Baoill, *Màiri nighean Alasdair Ruaidh*, 167.

page 74 *James VII & II died ... plots flourished*: The succession problem was "settled" a few years later, around the time Mary died, by the 1707 Act of Union of the Crowns in which the English Parliament made the Act of Settlement part of Scottish Law.

page 74 *Watson says ... is* "unusual": Watson, *Gaelic Songs*, 143.

page 74 "Your court where ... in exile": Ó Baoill, *Màiri nighean Alasdair Ruaidh*, 163.

page 75 "woe betide ... when *those nobles* [*my emphasis*] were pursing them": Ó Baoill, *Màiri nighean Alasdair Ruaidh*, 165.

page 75 *The convention ... cement loyalties*: MacInnes, "Panegyric Code," 276.

page 75 "some of them ... us believe": Watson, *Gaelic Songs*, 133.

page 75 "Some of the clans ... rebellion in 1689": Sharron Gunn, private email.

page 75 "But this is precisely ... realities": MacInnes, "Panegyric Code," 276.

page 75 *But everyone knew ... for the Stuarts*: Iain Breac's predecessor had lived a life of great extravagance in the south, after finding that Charles II, whose Restoration he had supported, demonstrated no concrete gratitude for the MacLeods' services during the English Civil Wars. This chief (Roderick, "the Witty") vowed never to "raise a finger on behalf of the

Stuarts again," a policy that Iain Breac discreetly followed. Nicolson, *History*, 108–10.

page 76 "She was allowed ... the envelope": Sharron Gunn, private email.

page 76 "a woman ... on our ankles": Adrienne Rich, "Translations," *Diving into the Wreck* (New York: W.W. Norton & Company, 1973), 40.

VI THE PLACE LONGED FOR

page 77 "down the path ... and fat": "Little Pig" from an unpublished manuscript (Tighnacraig: 1977).

33.

page 79 *The song ... to access*: Watson, *Gaelic Songs*, 117. There are two other islands where tradition places Mary in banishment. Watson says Mull, one of these islands, is unlikely to be the place referred to (it was well-populated and resource-rich). He does not bring up Pabbay in this context, although he discusses it elsewhere in connection with another song written in exile. Several oral accounts, as well as Pabbay songs, place Mary on Pabbay after being sent there as punishment. One informant says it was because she was pregnant with the child of the chief's son. "Màiri nighean Alasdair Ruaidh, Donald MacDonald" (Harris: *Tobar an Dual-chais*, July 1968), https://www.tobarandualchais.co.uk/track/45603?l=en.

page 79 "I have been ... [Where I spent my youth] ...": Unless otherwise specified, all excerpts of "Tuireadh" / "A Plaint" are from Sharron Gunn's translation. Sharron Gunn, private email.

page 80 *spoken of ... was* "joyful": The word "joyful" is from the version in Watson, *Gaelic Songs*, 35.

page 80 *It is just that ... where we are*: "Chi Mi na Mòrbheanna" / "I See the Great Mountains," by Iain Camshron (John Cameron):

Chorus (after each verse):
Oh I see, I see the great mountains
Oh I see, I see the lofty mountains
Oh I see, I see the corries
I see the peaks under the mist

I see right away the place of my birth
I will be welcomed in a language which I understand
I will receive hospitality and love when I reach there
That I would not trade for tons of gold

I see woods there, I see thickets
I see fair, fertile lands there
I see the deer on the ground of the corries
Shrouded in a garment of mist

High mountains with lovely slopes
Folk abiding there who are customarily kind
Light is my step when I go bounding to see them
And I will remain there awhile willingly

page 81 "I will go home ... with resonance": Sharron Gunn, private email.
page 81 "Crònan an Taibh" / "The Ocean Croon": Watson, *Gaelic Songs*,
   44–9.
page 81 *Mary's childhood ... grass and shelter*: excerpts from of "Tuireadh" /
   "A Plaint" in the remainder of this section are from Watson's translation.
   Watson, *Gaelic Songs*, 32–5.
page 81 *The Gaelic words ... or flagstones*: Sharron Gunn notes that *làr*
   means floor, usually earthen; but *urlar* (the word used here in the Gaelic)
   means literally "new floor" of planks or flagstones.

34.

page 82 *view westwards ... Durinish peninsula*: Alastair Crotach, the chief
   who built Dunvegan's "Fairy Tower" in the early sixteenth century, once
   gave an elaborate feast on the "tables" to show to a Lowland earl who considered the chief uncultivated that "[i]n our country we could show you a
   roof that is even more impressive [than in the King's palace in Edinburgh],
   a table greater and grander than this by far, and candelabra that are more
   wonderful than those that support the lights of our chamber to-night."
   Nicolson, *History*, 39.
page 82 *Ullinish Point and ... for* "corne and gerssing": Peter Hume Brown,
   Scotland before 1700: From Contemporary Documents (Edinburgh: David

Douglas, 1893), 257, https://archive.org/details/scotlandbefor1700brow/page/n5/mode/2up.

page 83 "Sharp is the wind ... warriors of Norway": Bill Lawson, *Harris in History and Legend* (Edinburgh: John Donald Publishers [Birlinn Ltd], 2002), 28. The lines quoted in Lawson are from Magnus MacLean, *The Literature of the Celts* (London: Blackie and Son Ltd, 1916), 105, https://archive.org/details/literatureofceltoomacl/page/n5/mode/2up.

page 83 "reared // On ... women": "Tuireadh" / "A Plaint," in Watson, *Gaelic Songs*, 33, 32–5.

page 83 "Through fosterage ... parents of the child": Steve Murdock, "Chapter One," in *Network North: Scottish Kin, Commercial and Cover Associations in Northern Europe, 1603–1746*, vol. 18 of *The Northern World and the Baltic c. 400–100 AD*, edited by Crawford et al. (Leiden and Boston: Brill, 2006), 34–6, https://books.google.ca/books?id=8hg_LcAusLQC.

page 83 "*Comhdhaltas* ... to twenty": Sharron Gunn, private email.

page 83 *In most cases ... seven years*: Alexander O. Curle, "Notice of four Contracts or Bonds of Fosterage; with Notes on the Former Prevalence of the Custom of Fosterage in the Scottish Highlands," *Proceedings of the Society of Antiquaries of Scotland*, vol. 30 (Dec. 9 1895), https://archaeologydataservice.ac.uk/archiveDS/archiveDownload?t=arch-352-1/dissemination/pdf/vol_030/30_010_022.pdf (accessed 17 August 2023).

page 83 "for the purpose ... or bred": "History of the Scottish Highlands, Highland Clans and Scottish Regiments," in *General History of the Highlands: Scoto-Irish Kings (1830–1870)*, edited by John S. Keltie, https://www.electricscotland.com/history/genhist/hist20.html.

37.

page 87 "Mantled with cotoneaster ... to the sea-gate": W. Douglas Simpson, *Dunvegan Castle, Official Guide* (Aberdeen: The University Press, 1947), 8.

page 88 *the famous fairy flag ... twice before*: Simpson, *Dunvegan Castle*, 13–15.

page 88 "This tomb ... mingled in one coffin'": Simpson, *Dunvegan Castle*, 15.

page 89 "the custom ... chief's household": Grant, *The MacLeods*, 373.

page 89 *although* "the fact ... son of Sir Roderick Mòr": Watson, *Gaelic Songs*, xiv–xv.

page 89 "it banished the pang": "Fuigheall" / "A Fragment," in Watson,
Gaelic Songs, 73, 73–5.

38.

page 90 *the small village … to be from*: Watson, *Gaelic Songs*, xiii.

page 90 *The travellers, indigenous … in the 1950s*: Timothy Neat, *The
Summer Walkers* (Edinburgh: Canongate, 1996), vii, 73, 192, 191.

page 90 *Without a shared …* "proudly born[e] addiction": Neat, *Summer
Walkers*, vii–viii. "These Scottish nomads are not Gypsies. They are indigenous, Gaelic speaking Scots who, to this day, remain heirs of a vital and
ancient culture of great historical and artistic importance to Scotland and
the world beyond … they live in family groups, many carry the great clan
names – Stewart, MacDonald, Cameron … As an Aberdeenshire Traveller
said … to differentiate himself from an eccentric Irish tramp … "[He's]
not one of us. [He] just lives frae day to day – but we … live entirely in
the past."

39.

page 92 *One day, much later … clairvoyants alone*: A tape containing much
of this information is part of the Jurgen Hesse collection T4230:0001 in the
British Columbia Archives, https://www.memorybc.ca/jurgen-hesse-fonds.
It was recorded in 1961 and aired 5 July 1965 on the CBC radio program
Soundings. Hesse died 30 July 2008. See also John Powell, *Encyclopedia
of North American Immigration* (New York: Facts on File Inc., 2005), 115,
https://books.google.ca/books?id=VNCX6UsdZYkC&lpg=PA115&pg=PA11
5#v=onepage&q&f=false; and Evan Heimlich, "Immigration to America,
Gypsy Immigration," "Countries and Their Cultures Forum" (World Cul-
ture Encyclopedia, 2023), https://www.everyculture.com/multi/Du-Ha/
Gypsy-Americans.html.

page 92 "our business … get out to get!": Neat, *The Summer Walkers*, 54.

VII A GATHERING

page 95 "For many … would fare": "Crònan An Taibh" / "The Ocean
Croon," in Watson, *Gaelic Songs*, 47.

42.

page 96 "believed to be … life and death": Florian Mussgnug and Liz Rideal, *Feu Follet* (London: Slade Press: 2018), unpaged.

page 96 "Tracing … the universe": Rideal, *Feu Follet*; Mario Barenghi, ed., *Italo Calvino, Saggi*, vol. 1 (Milano: Mondadori, 1995), 2979.

page 97 *Gillian Munro*: Gillian Munro: now the principal of Sabhal Mòr Ostaig.

page 97 "The picture … at Berneray": Anne Frater, "Màiri nighean Alasdair Ruaidh" (Paper presented at Crossing the Minch, Isle of Skye, 2007), https://pureadmin.uhi.ac.uk/ws/portalfiles/portal/1935026/MNARfinal.pdf.

page 97 "The best … visited there": Frater, "Màiri nighean Alasdair Ruaidh," 2. Frater says, "It appears that she was fostered for a time in Uilinnis in Skye as a young girl, and that one of Ruairidh Mòr's milkmaids was her foster-mother, or muime."

page 98 "Màiri got in trouble … had to say": Roderick Morison, a younger contemporary of Mary's, was harper and bard of Dunvegan under Iain Breac at the same time Mary is said to have been "the poetess of Iain Breac." Henderson, *The Poems of John Morison*, 188.

page 100 "poets such as Margaret / Mairearad Lachainn": This is Mairearad Nighean Lachainn (1660–1751) from Mull. Her burial place is unknown.

43.

page 102 *In the T'Sou-ke … of years*: Sandra Laurie, Darlene George, and Francine George, *Legends of T'Sou-ke and West Coast Bands* (Sooke Region Historical Society and Sooke [T'Sou-ke] Band, 1978), 38.

VIII METAPHORS FOR POETRY

page 107 "The pagan Celtic … regeneration": Bateman, "The Landscape," 150.

page 107 "Taken on a sledge … to a friend": Marilyn Bowering, "Is There a Friend," from an unpublished manuscript (Tighnacraig: 1977).

48.

page 109 *Watson's analysis … role of repetition*: Watson, *Gaelic Songs*, 142–4.

page 109 *for the Free Church*: The Free Church is an Evangelical and Presbyterian denomination widespread in the Hebrides.

page 109 *Maoilios attended ... Sandy Bell's pub*: Maoilios attended university in Edinburgh. Of his relationships with other poets in former days, Maoilios wrote, "I drank with Hamish Henderson but not with Smith and Garioch in Edinburgh. I did meet Robert Garioch once or twice but not in Sandy Bells. I met ICS [Iain Crichton Smith] later when I worked in Mull and he was in Oban. We visited each other a couple of times." Maoilios Caimbeul / Myles Campbell, private email.

page 110 *They have written ... a Christian one*: Myles Campbell / Maoilios Caimbeul and Margaret Campbell, *Island Conversion* (Isle of Lewis: The Islands Book Trust, 2011).

page 110 *Many poets ... engaged closely*: Most poets don't discuss their "hauntings" publicly, but Kate Braid has been open about the creative empathy involved in her writing in *A Well Mannered Storm: The Glen Gould Poems* (Vancouver: Caitlin Press, 2008). A well-known example is given by W.B. Yeats in *A Vision* (New York: Collier Books, 1966 ed.), 8. A few days after his marriage in October 1917, Yeats's wife, Georgie, attempted automatic writing. What came, in disjointed fashion, so excited Yeats that he asked her to give time each day "to the unknown writer." Through his wife, he conveyed to the intelligence that he was prepared to devote the rest of his life to exploring what the fragments had to offer. But "No," came the reply. Instead, the purpose of the messages was to give Yeats "metaphors for poetry."

page 110 "all ages are contemporaneous": Ezra Pound, *The Spirit of Romance* (London: J.M. Dent, 1910), vi. The line was important to W.S. Merwin when he was finding a direction for his poetry. See Merwin's account of meeting Pound in "Chapter One," in *The Mays of Ventadorn* (Washington, DC: National Geographic Society, 2002).

page 111 *Traditionally bards ... for inspiration*: Martin Martin, *A Description of the Western Islands of Scotland ca 1695* (Edinburgh: Birlinn, 2018), 86.

page 111 *Meg Bateman ... are the donors*: Bateman, "The Landscape," 146. During the later fifteenth and throughout the sixteenth and into the seventeenth centuries, conversation and familiarity with fairies, as well as other folk beliefs, were conflated with witchcraft and demonic powers. See Lizanne Henderson, "'Detestable Slaves of the Devil': Changing Ideas about Witchcraft in Sixteenth-Century Scotland," in *A History of Everyday Life in Medieval Scotland, 1000 to 1600*, vol. 1, edited by E.J. Cowan and L. Henderson (Edinburgh: Edinburgh University Press, 2011), 226–53.

page 111 *Some cultures ... mental process*: Shari Ann Cohn, "Scottish Tradition of Second Sight and Other Psychic Experiences in Families" (Edinburgh: Edinburgh Research Archive, 1996), https://era.ed.ac.uk/handle/1842/9674.

page 111 "the unknowable ... to be or not": Myles Campbell / Maoilios Caimbeul, "Lifestory" (personal blog, 2016), https://maoilioscaimbeul.wordpress.com/.

49.

page 112 "a great ... came upon thee": "Marbhrann do Iain Garbh" / "Dirge for Iain Garbh," in Watson, *Gaelic Songs*, 26–31; 29, 31.

51.

page 115 *It is about ... much time*: "Sir Norman's house, part of which is still standing, was near the sea on the north-east side of Bernera ... At a short distance from this spot was the house which Sir Norman gave to Mary MacLeod in a place called Tobhta nan Craobh, and close beside a great well used by Sir Norman and called Tobar mòr Mhic Leòid, which is still in use. The remains of the house are still to be seen, though covered with turf." Watson, *Gaelic Songs*, xiv–xv.

page 115 *Tobhta nan Craobh (Ruins of the Trees)*: "*Tobhta nan Craobh* = toft of trees; the toft was the top of the walls where men could stand to re-thatch the roofs as the roofs were recessed; also means ruins." Sharron Gunn, private email.

page 116 *By 1000 AD ... Mediterranean*: Dr Kate MacDonald quoted by Susan Irvine, "North Uist, Outer Hebrides: Adventures in Outer Space," *The Telegraph*, 12 February 2011, http://www.telegraph.co.uk/travel/destinations/europe/uk/scotland/8318204/North-Uist-Outer-Hebrides-adventures-in-outer-space.html. Sharron Gunn comments, "According to Koch & Cunliffe, the editors and authors of the series *Celtic from the West*, the links with these lands were established as early as 2500 BC."

IX CAULDRON

page 118 "I reached ... alive": Marilyn Bowering and Xan Shian, "Cauldron (of Vocation)," in *Threshold* (Lantzville, BC: Leaf Press, 2015), 11.

52.

page 119 "I see her" ... *first book*: Marilyn Bowering, "The Fisherman's Dream," in *The Liberation of Newfoundland* (Fredericton: Fiddlehead Poetry Books, 1973), 3.

page 119 "'I love you, Mother ... to bring ...'": by Mary A. Cragin who wrote under the pen name Joy Allison.

53.

page 122 "Sitting here ... armed host": "Luinneag Mhic Leoid" / "MacLeod's Lilt," in Watson, *Gaelic Songs*, 36–43. These lines p. 37.

page 122 *In Ó Baoill's ... his death*: Ó Baoill, *Màiri nighean Alasdair Ruaidh*, 63, 60–7.

page 123 "sundered" *instead of* "parted": Watson, *Gaelic Songs*, 39.

page 123 "fair of form ... of fashioning": Watson, *Gaelic Songs*, 41. All quotations of the poem in the rest of the discussion, unless otherwise noted, are from Watson's translation, 40–3.

page 123 *notes that* "To judge" ... *are in the way*: Ó Baoill, *Màiri nighean Alasdair Ruaidh*, 71.

54.

page 124 *sucked down ... for several kilometres*: Rod Macdonald, "Into the Corryvreckan Whirlpool," in *The Darkness Below* (Dunbeath, Caithness: Whittles Publishing, 2013), 62–8, https://www.whittlespublishing.com/userfiles/shop/122/The%20Darkness%20Below.pdf.

page 124 "[t]he sea ... a loud report": Martin Martin, *A Description*, 159.

page 124 *the noise ... away*: W.H. Murray, *West Highlands of Scotland* (Glasgow: Collins, 1968), 127–8.

page 124 *Locally, the ... Corryvreckan vortex*: Bateman, "The Landscape," 144.

page 125 "Oh! Then ... Choir!": I am told that the choir was started by a group of Gaels in Vancouver. Mabel's role is unconfirmed.

55.

page 127 *There is also ... Mary's sojourn*: "Scarba, – One Mountain and a Tidal Race" ("Southern Hebrides of Scotland," 2015), https://www.southernhebrides.com/isle-of-scarba/; Patrick H. Gillies, "Chapter VII – Scarba: Gulf of Coirebhreacain," *Netherlorn and Its Neighbourhood* (London:

Virtue & Co., 1909), https://archive.org/details/netherlornargylloogilluoft/
page/n7/mode/2up.

page 127 *One of Scarba's* … "all her days": Martin Martin, *A Description*, 158.

page 128 *I had encountered…* "old stone bench": B.N. Peach, "Memoirs of
the Geological Survey of Scotland: The Geology of the seaboard of mid Ar-
gyll including the islands of Luing, Scarba, The Gravellachs, and the Lesser
Isles, together with the northern Part of Jura and a small portion of Mull
(Explanation of sheet 36)" (Printed for H.M. Stationery Off., Glasgow:
James Hedderwick & Sons, 1909).

56.

page 132 *Blàr Nan Sith* (Plain of the Fairies): "Scotland's Places, OS1/2/66/
49," Ordnance Survey Name Books 1868–1878, Argyll volume 55,"
https://scotlandsplaces.gov.uk/digital-volumes/ordnance-survey-name-
books/argyll-os-name-books-1868-1878/argyll-volume-66/49.

page 132 "The Natives … with pigmies": Martin Martin, *A Description*, 167.

page 132 "myths abound … of ghosts and faeries": https://paulmclem.
weebly.com/scarba.html.

page 134 *Irish monks … Scarba's west side*: K. Ralls-MacLeod, *The Quest for
the Celtic Key* (Edinburgh: Luath Press Ltd, 2013); Gillies, *Netherlorn*.

page 134 *The Paps … deer-goddess cult*: Mairi Hedderwick, *An Eye on the
Hebrides* (Edinburgh: Canongate Publishing Ltd, 1989), 32; McKay, "The
Deer-Cult and the Deer-Goddess Cult of the Ancient Caledonians" ("Folk-
lore," vol. 43: 1932), 161–2; J.F. Campbell, "Tale 46," in *Popular Tales of the
West Highlands*, vol. II (Paisley: Alexander Gardner, 1890).

57.

page 136 "Jack Frost," *he says*: Marilyn Bowering, "Jack Glass," from an
unpublished manuscript (Tighnacraig: 1977):

He comes to the gate
and he opens it up
and there isn't a fence
that can keep him out
and he comes to the door
that is tightly shut

but there isn't a house
that can keep him out

and he climbs the stairs
to the top of the house
and there isn't a room
that can keep him out

and he makes ice-blossoms
on the sheets
and he empties ice dreams
into your sleep

and because it is cold
and the stars are bright
you follow his steps
to the end of the night.

X A WEAKNESS FOR WHISKY

page 137 "and her behaviour ... and snuff": Watson, *Gaelic Songs*, xviii.

58.

page 138 "Welcome to ... manuring": Gaelic original from Watson, *Gaelic Songs*, xviii. Translation by Sharron Gunn. Gunn supplies an additional version:

Mary MacLeod:
Welcome to yourself, Mary Smith,
Although you are growing brown and grizzled.
Mary Smith:
You are as sallow as a dun-coloured duck,
Although you are under a manure heap of years.

page 138 *John Mackenzie ...* "we like a drink]": Mackenzie, *Sár-Obair nam Bárd Gaelach*, 288, https://archive.org/details/sarobairnambardg07mack /page/288/mode/2up.

page 138 "was much given ... whisky and snuff ": Watson, *Gaelic Songs*, xviii. Watson also gives the title of Mary's song, "Hò rò gur toigh leinn drama," and its text in Gaelic as found in William Ross's poem, "Moladh an Uisge-bheatha" / "The Praise of Whisky," in *Orain Ghae'lach le Uilleam Ros*, edited by John Mackenzie (Inverness: R. Carruthers, 1830), 51, https://archive. org/details/orainghaelachleu00ross/page/50/mode/2up.

page 138 "O how we like ... your praises": Translation by Sharron Gunn, private email.

page 140 "It's no surprise ... your corpse to the grave" : Fr Allan Macdonald, *Gaelic Words and Expressions from South Uist and Eriskay, 1958* (Oxford: Oxford University Press, 2nd ed. 1972), as cited by Ó Baoill, *Màiri nighean Alasdair Ruaidh*, 6. Translation by Sharron Gunn, private email.

59.

page 142 "Freedom an' whisky ... your dram": Robert Burns, "The Author's Earnest Cry and Prayer," 1786, https://www.robertburns.org/works/87. shtml.

60.

page 143 *John Mackenzie ... to gossip*: Mackenzie, *Sár-Obair nam Bárd Gae-lach*, 21; Sharron Gunn comments that it sounds like Mary wore a version of what Highland woman wore – a woman's plaid or *earrasaid* – and that "[i]f she had a silver brooch, she wasn't poor."

page 143 *Nothing ... Mary's mouth*: Iain Mac Ghrigair, *Orain Ghaelach* (Edinburgh: MacNeill, 1801), 196, https://archive.org/details/orainghlachoo macg/page/n199/mode/2up?ref=ol&view=theater; Sharron Gunn translates Mac Ghrigair's verse as: "The boasting of Iain Lom (Bare/Scathing John), and the polish / elegance of Broad Mary / Shining from your language, and each verse a measure of music / As you'd read from your youth each speech and story / Life or death would not lock your mouth."

page 143 *Whether or not ... of custom*: "*Tobar an Dualchais* – Kist o Riches, 'Màiri nighean Alasdair Ruaidh [MacLeod, Mary],'" Donald Alex Mac-Donald recording: Harris, July 1968, Original Track ID SA1968.133, https://www.tobarandualchais.co.uk/track/45603?l=en. Sharron Gunn comments that "Gaelic had nine types of marriage or 'couplings'; a child which would be considered illegitimate in English society was not so con-sidered among Gaels. As long as the father recognised the child, it was

legitimate whether or not the parents were married in church. I think
the contributor's tradition was influenced by 19th century beliefs about
illegitimacy."

page 143 *As well as praise* … "raised boils with a song": Thomas McKean,
"A Gaelic Songmaker's Response to an English-speaking Nation" ("Oral
Tradition," 7/1: 1992), 5, 11.

page 144 "Gaelic society … and the abuse of power": Colm Ó Baoill, "Sìleas
na Ceapaich," in *The Edinburgh History of Scottish Literature*, edited by
Thomas Owen Clancy and Murray Pittock, vol. 1 (Edinburgh: Edinburgh
University Press, 2007), 313; Michael Newton, *Warriors of the Word* (Edinburgh: Birlinn Books, 2009), 158. Note that the definition of "bigger songs"
is by Sharron Gunn, private email.

page 144 *In this tradition* … *by her exile*: John MacInnes, "Gaelic Songs of
Mary MacLeod," in "Scottish Gaelic Studies," vol. XI, Part I, edited by
Derick S. Thomson (Aberdeen: University of Aberdeen, 1966), 7–10,
https://www.academia.edu/4737802/Gaelic_Songs_of_Mary_MacLeod.

page 144 "A legacy of frequent … at best liminal status": John Shaw, "What
Alexander Carmichael Did Not Print: The 'Cliar Sheanchain', 'Clanranald's
Fool' and Related Traditions." *Béaloideas* 70 (2002): 99–126, https://doi.
org/10.2307/20520795 (accessed 19 August 2023).

61.

page 145 "if we have … the world": Marilyn Bowering, "At Shian's Moor," in
The Alchemy of Happiness (Vancouver: Beach Holme Publishing, 2003), 85.

62.

page 145 "banished the pang": "Fuigheall" / "A Fragment," in Watson, *Gaelic
Songs*, 73, 72–5.

page 145 "I will sing" … at the beginning of May": Ó Baoill, *Màiri nighean
Alasdair Ruaidh*, 148–51.

63.

page 146 *I came to write* … *to hang in Canada*: Marilyn Bowering, *What It
Takes to Be Human* (Toronto: Penguin Group, 2006).

XI PLOVERS AND CHICKS

page 147 "You are my ... where I would sit": Mary MacLeod, "Hilliù-An, Hilleò-An," translated by Kate MacDonald (Edinburgh: *Tocher* 27, 1977–78), 150–1; Ó Baoill, *Màiri nighean Alasdair Ruaidh*, 282–3.

66.

page 150 "Siuthadaibh siuthadaibh ... *a rowing song*: from notes recorded in the School of Scottish Studies Archives library; see also "Oran Luaidh" ("Siuthadaibh, siuthadaibh, a mhnathan"), in Ó Baoill, *Màiri nighean Alasdair Ruaidh*, 279–82.

page 150 "In the first section ... Iain in Dunvegan'": "*Tobar an Dualchais* – Kist o Riches, 'Gu Dè Nist a Nì Mise,'" Kate Nicolson recording: 1963, Track ID 85699, https://www.tobarandualchais.co.uk/track/85699?l=en.

page 151 "That was where ... she made that little song": Kate MacDonald "Tocher"; "*Tobar an Dualchais* – Kist o Riches, 'Hilliu-An, Hilleo-An,'" Kate MacDonald recording: c. July 1964, https://www.tobarandualchais.co.uk/track/86294?l=en.

page 151 "to make no more ... that is, a hum, or 'croon'": Mackenzie, *Sàr-Obair nam Bàrd Gaelach*, 20–1, https://play.google.com/books/reader?id=KQIGAAAAQAAJ&pg=GBS.PA20&hl=en.

page 151 "There was a time ... on top of it / Hò my love, Fionaghala": Mary MacLeod, "Hilliu-An, Hilleo-An," translated by Kate MacDonald, "Tocher"; Ó Baoill, *Màiri nighean Alasdair Ruaidh*, 282–3. If the song had a connection to the chief's own children, as some think, it would have further offended him.

page 152 "the second most famous ... nor in the public sphere": Domhnall Uilleam Stiùbhart, "Highland Rogues and the Roots of Highland Romanticism," in *Crossing the Highland Line: Cross-Currents in Eighteenth-Century Scottish Writing*, vol. 14, edited by C. MacLachlan (Glasgow: Association for Scottish Literary Studies, 2009), 161, 161–93, https://pureadmin.uhi.ac.uk/ws/portalfiles/portal/15400519/Highland_Rogues_Crossing_the_Highland_Line_pp161_193_2009.pdf.

page 152 "Màiri nighean Alasdair Ruaidh's position ... to come": Domhnall Uilleam Stiùbhart, "Highland Rogues," 161.

page 153 "There is also an ... given up to the fairies": Michael MacMullin, "Tàladh Sìthe (Fairy Lullaby) (Story and Song)," CB Tape 2 Track 3 (St. John's: Memorial University of Newfoundland Folklore and Language Archive (MUNFLA), Memorial University of Newfoundland, 2022), https://mmap.mun.ca/folk-songs-of-atlantic-canada/performances/495.

page 153 "also refers ... creatures seen": Domhnall Uilleam Stiùbhart, "Highland Rogues," 61.

68.

page 154 *He has written* ... "between two worlds": Peter Narváez, "Newfoundland Berry Pickers," in *The Good People, New Fairylore Essays*, edited by Peter Narváez (New York: Garland Publishing Inc., 1991), 337ff.

page 154 "the fairy world ... no people": Sean Virgo, telephone conversation, 2002.

page 154 "Little People" *accounts* ... *Indigenous cultures*: Alan Safarik, conversation (Estevan, Saskatchewan: 2002); Lawrence Barkwell, "Metis Folklore: Little People, Ma-ma-kwa-se-sak or Memeguayiwahk" (Metis Heritage and History Research, Louis Riel Institute), https://www.metismuseum.ca/media/document.php/14521.Little%20People%20Metis%20Folklore.pdf (accessed 19 August 2023). Indigenous cultures with little people stories include the Sioux, Cherokee, Iroquois, Maliseet, Plains, Cree, Eskasoni, Shoshone, Choctaw, and Crow nations.

70.

page 155 "Last night ... my years": Marilyn Bowering, from an unpublished poetry draft (undated).

XII WHEN WE SPEAK OF ETERNITY

page 157 "we think ... for always": "When We Speak of Eternity," Bowering, *Threshold*, 58.

71.

page 157 Sir Norman ... the age of ninety-six: Ó Baoill, *Màiri nighean Alasdair Ruaidh*, 193–4.

page 158 *But Norman ... declined them*: "MacLeod Genealogy, Sir Norman";
Watson, *Gaelic Songs*, xiii, 138–40.

page 158 *Two of these songs ... website*: These songs are a 1967 recording of
"Marbhrann do Shir Tormod MacLeòid" / "Dirge for Sir Norman Mac-
Leod of Berneray," https://www.tobarandualchais.co.uk/track/108844?l=en,
and a 1955 one of "Mo Chràdhghal Bochd" / "Lament for Sir Norman Mac-
Leod," https://www.tobarandualchais.co.uk/track/20660?l=eno. Text in
Watson, *Gaelic Songs*, 88, 96.

page 159 "A great heaviness ... remember long": "Marbhrann" / "Dirge," in
Watson, *Gaelic Songs*, 88–95.

page 159 "I will long ... received of it": Ó Baoill, *Màiri nighean Alasdair
Ruaidh*, 191.

page 160 "With no will ... has tortured my body": "Cumha do Shir Tormod
MacLeòid" / "Lament for Sir Norman MacLeod," in Ó Baoill, *Màiri nighean Alasdair Ruaidh*, 203.

page 160 "[T]hy nobility ... my support": Watson, *Gaelic Songs*, 99.

72.

page 160 *Sometime after ... to be buried at Rodel, Harris*: Citing the papers of
William Matheson, Ó Baoill, *Màiri nighean Alasdair Ruaidh*, 3–5.

page 160 "a professional ... like to break her heart": The anecdote and Gaelic verses are found in Alexander Carmichael: "Threnody," in *Carmina*, vol.
5, 341.

page 160 "But, O King ... what was thy surname": Carmichael, *Carmina*,
vol. 5, 341. Alternative translations by Sharron Gunn.

page 161 *By listing ... or dead*: These are Kilmuir graveyard at Dunvegan;
Eynort, Skye with its processions to the MacLeod burial chapel of St
Maelrubha; and St Clement's at Rodel on Harris, to which the procession
is going.

page 161 "the social ... the individual": Bateman, "The Landscape," 150–1.

XII MIRROR

page 166 "What is the name ... the water's   edge": Marilyn Bowering and
Xan Shian, "Listen," *Threshold* (Lantzville, BC: Leaf Press, 2015), 44.

77.

page 168 "We crave ... denies us a reality": Florian Mussgnug and Liz Rideal, *Feu Follet* (UCL London: Slade Press, 2018), unpaged.

page 168 "Much we long ... and our / boast": "Marbhrann do Shir Tormod Mac Leoid" / "Dirge for Sir Norman MacLeod," in Watson, *Gaelic Songs*, 88–95.

78.

page 169 *composed one more ... the gift of a snuff mull*: "Luinneag do Iain mac Shir Tormoid Mhic Leòid" / "Song to Iain, son of Sir Norman," in Watson, *Gaelic Songs*, 82–7; Colm Ó Baoill, *Màiri nighean Alasdair Ruaidh*, 222–9.

page 169 *The "Snuff Mull" poem ... as factor*: "Song to Iain," in Watson, *Gaelic Songs*, 82–7.

page 169 *In recognition ... Jacobite peerage*: "MacLeod Genealogy, Sir Norman"; "MacLeod, Norman (1706–72), of Dunvegan, Skye," The History of Parliament Trust 1964–2020, https://www.historyofparliamentonline.org/volume/1715-1754/member/macleod-norman-1706-72.

79.

page 170 *Snuff boxes, carried ...* "medallions, fans and snuff boxes": Dennis Gallagher, "Snuff Is Enough: Tobacco Consumption in Eighteenth-Century Scotland," *Journal of the Académie Internationale de la Pipe* 8 (2015): 109, https://www.academia.edu/31241091/Gallagher_D_2015_Snuff_is_enough_tobacco_consumption_in_eighteenth_century_Scotland_JOURNAL_OF_THE_ACADEMIE_INTERNATIONALE_DE_LA_PIPE_8_109_114.

page 170 *It is made ... a Jacobite rose*: "Snuff Mull" (Aberdeen: University Collections, University of Aberdeen), https://exhibitions.abdn.ac.uk/university-collections/document/19283 (accessed 19 August 2023).

page 170 "hopefully suggests ... their owner's enemy": Jennifer L. Novotny, "Sedition at the Supper Table: The Material Culture of the Jacobite Wars, 1688–1760," PhD thesis (Glasgow: University of Glasgow, 2013), 117, https://theses.gla.ac.uk/4659/1/2013NovotnyPhD.pdf.

page 170 *In the University ... loss of 1745*: "Snuff Mull Snuff Box" (Aberdeen: University Collections, University of Aberdeen), https://exhibitions.abdn.ac.uk/university-collections/document/18168%20collections/document/18168; "Rob n.," Dictionary of the Scots Language (Edinburgh: Scottish

Language Dictionaries Ltd, 2004), https://www.dsl.ac.uk/entry/snd/rob_n;
Rev. Robert Forbes, *The Lyon in Mourning (1746–1775)*, edited by Henry
Paton (Edinburgh: The University Press for the Scottish Historical Society,
vol. I, 1895), 81, https://digital.nls.uk/print/transcriptions/lyon/vol1/pages/
081.pdf.

80.

page 171 *The water that drives ...* "that I borrow it": All quotations from
"Luinneag do Iain mac Shir Tormoid Mhic Leoid" / "Song to Iain, son of Sir
Norman," unless otherwise indicated, are from Watson, *Gaelic Songs*, 82–7.

page 171 *Iain as factor ... around the year 1700*: "Notes," Ó Baoill, *Màiri
nighean Alasdair Ruaidh*, 222–9.

page 171 *love for this* "mason ... to poet bands": this section is Ó Baoill's
translation. Ó Baoill, *Màiri nighean Alasdair Ruaidh*, 217, 218, 216–21.

page 172 *set a course for the future*: Sharron Gunn notes that in one of Iain's
own poems, he uses mill and quern language figuratively. Grant, *The
MacLeods*, 390.

XIV A DROWNING WAVE

page 173 "you chewed ... gleamed": "A Drowning," Bowering, *Threshold*, 40.

81.

page 174 *a view of the water*: "MacLeod Genealogy, Sir Norman."

page 174 *It looks easy ... themselves capsized*: Donald A. Mackenzie, "Chapter
IV, Blue Men of the Minch," in *Scottish Folk-lore and Folk Life: Studies in
Race, Culture and Tradition* (London, Glasgow, and Bombay: Blackie and
Son, Ltd, 1935 ed.; Obscure Press, Kindle Edition, 2013).

page 174 "Marbhrann do Iain Garbh" / "Dirge for Iain Garbh": Watson,
Gaelic Songs, 26–31.

page 174 "married a ... of Dunvegan (1573–1626)": Sharron Gunn (as Sheila
Currie), 2022, https://sheilacurrie.com/blog/2021/02/21/witchcraft-in-the-
scottish-highlands-good-or-bad/.

page 174 "Son of Mary ... shalt not be found": Watson, *Gaelic Songs*, 27.

page 175 *The fault ... spells for money*: John Gregorson Campbell, *Witchcraft
& Second Sight in the Highlands & Islands of Scotland* (Glasgow: James
MacLehose and Sons, 1902), 14–15.

page 175 *Another record … approach of bad weather*: Ó Baoill, *Màiri nighean Alasdair Ruaidh*, 275; Grant, *The MacLeods*, 336–8.

page 175 *Additional traditions … monster's head*: Frances Tolmie, *One Hundred and Five Songs of Occupation from the Western Isles of Scotland*, 1911 (Burnham-On-Sea, Somerset: Llanerch Publishers reprint, 1997), 271.

page 175 *Sharron Gunn's account … "men of the crew lost"*: Sharron Gunn (as Sheila Currie), "Witchcraft."

page 175 *These stories portray … kindness, and humility*: "The Seven Catholic Virtues" (The Spiritual Life, 2010), https://slife.org/the-seven-catholic-virtues/.

page 175 *There was enough … beliefs were tolerated*: Mirrsha Ganthan, "The Birth and Evolution of Witchcraft in Seventeenth Century New England," 2020, https://you.stonybrook.edu/crisisandcatharsis/2020/08/21/the-birth-and-evolution-of-witchcraft-in-seventeenth-century-new-england-with-mirrsha-ganthan/; Mark David L. Gibbard, "The Legality of the Supernatural: Fairy Belief in the Scottish Witch Trials," 2015, https://www.aca demia.edu/30187387/The_Legality_of_the_Supernatural_Fairy_Belief_in _the_Scottish_Witch_Trials.

page 176 *After the reformation … were accustomed*: Sharron Gunn comments, "After the Reformation (1560) there was a shortage of acceptable ministers in the Highlands. Only the lands of the earl of Argyll had sufficient ministers of the new religion. The Catholic incumbents in the Highlands remained in place until their deaths and were not replaced. By the early decades of the 17th century, Highlanders were considered heathens. But they kept their Christianity alive with the support of Irish friars from Bonamargy in Ireland as well as strong traditions of Christian custom."

page 176 *The Secret Commonwealth*: Kirk was supposed to have been kidnapped from Doon hill near Aberfoyle by fairies angered at his having published their secrets. When I climbed the hill with my family, I found messages to the fairies written on strips of rags tied to the branches of the pine tree at the top: "Dear Fairys [*sic*], I wish for my cousin to come alive again. From Alexander"; "Dear Fairies, I ask the angels in heaven to care for Breaker. He was a great dog"; "Dear Fairy Dandelion, I wish for a book"; "Dear Fairies, I wish my family would all be happy."

page 176 *These ferocious … features of the Hebridean world*: Ronald Hutton, "Witch-Hunting in Celtic Societies," *Past & Present* 212 (2011): 43–71

(Oxford: Oxford University Press on behalf of The Past and Present Society, 2011), 6, 12, 14, https://www.jstor.org/stable/23014785.

page 176 *to* "a drowning wave ... might upon them": Watson, *Gaelic Songs*, 31, 29.

82.

page 177 *But it was wartime ... serving at Gallipoli*: "The Royal Canadian Navy and the First World War," Government of Canada, https://www. canada.ca/en/navy/services/history/naval-service-1910-2010/first-ww.html (last modified 4 December 2020); "Newfoundlanders," Canadian War Museum, 20 June 2008, https://www.warmuseum.ca/firstworldwar/his tory/people/in-uniform/newfoundlanders; Nil Köksal, "Canadians at Gallipoli: Royal Newfoundland Regiment Honoured," CBC News, 24 April 2015, https://www.cbc.ca/news/canada/canadians-at-gallipoli-royal-new foundland-regiment-honoured-1.3046197.

page 177 *There was hope ... irretrievably lost*: Robert C. Parsons, "The Swallow Is Overdue," in *Collision at Dawn* (St. John's: Creative Publishers, 2008), 127–30.

page 177 *And then ... signed, "John Bowering"*: Larry Dohey, "Labrador Schooner with her crew, caught in the great storm" (Bay Roberts, NL: Archival Moments, Archives Bay Roberts, 2015), http://archivalmoments. ca/tag/bay-roberts/; Robert Parsons, private email.

page 177 *the privately printed poem ... "Captain John Bowering"*: Capt. John Bowering, *Trip of the Ill-Fated "Swallow"*, c. 1916 (St John's: Print Three reprint, 2021).

83.

page 178 *John Bowering's Tale*: Poetry quotations throughout this section are from Capt. John Bowering, *Swallow*, 5–13, 20. All other quotations can be found in Parsons, "The Swallow Is Overdue," 127–30.

XV RODEL OF THE HEART

page 188 "Sad the ... poets' phrases": "Marbhrainn sior Tormóid Mic Leoid" / "Elegy of Sir Norman MacLeod," in Watson, *Gaelic Songs*, 102–7. Watson notes (102–3) that this anonymous work is included "as a specimen of classic poetry for comparison with the style of Mary MacLeod's composition on the same theme." It was "edited and translated by Professor Watson … from a manuscript in the National Library of Scotland."

87.

page 188 *The large … west end*: Mary Miers, "Western Seaboard: An Illustrated Architectural Guide" (Edinburgh: Rutland Press, 2008), http://can more.org.uk/event/567069.

page 189 "on the site … Culdee cell": Culdees – Céli Dé, Companions of God. This Christian sect flourished in Scotland in the twelfth century but had mostly disappeared by the end of the thirteenth. Some sources link Culdee Scottish origins to St Columba in the sixth century and to much earlier Irish origins. The subject is many-faceted and controversial.

page 189 "founded … of the sun": MacAulay, *Silent Tower*, 5; Philip Graham, *Treasured Places, Royal Commission on the Ancient and Historical Monuments of Scotland* (RCAHMS [PJG], June 2007), https://canmore.org.uk/event/553847.

page 189 "a reference to … Norse invaders": MacAulay, *Silent Tower*, xiv.

page 189 *On the north … felt out of place*: Grant, *The MacLeods*, 72.

page 190 *It could be the … first dedication*: Miers, "Western Seaboard."

page 190 *Or the name … St Calman – Columbanus*: Grant, *The MacLeods*, 156.

page 190 *On the south … in Scotland*: "St. Clement's Church / Tur Chliamainn" (Undiscovered Scotland, 2000–22), https://www.undiscovered scotland.co.uk/harris/stclements/index.html.

page 190 *Other examples … and other windows*: "Field Visit, St Clement's Church, Rodil, 29 July 1923 – 31 July 1923," Outer Hebrides, Skye and the Small Isles (RCAHMS, 1928), https://canmore.org.uk/event/1103029; "St. Clement's Church, Rodil, Statement of Significance" (Historic Environment Scotland, 2018), https://www.historicenvironment.scot/archives-and-research/publications/publication/?publicationId=c6345fd2-40b8-4cfc-b09 4-a7b700d6b6ce.

page 191 *The last such … early eighteeth century*: Simpson, "Dunvegan Castle," 15–16; Grant, *The MacLeods*, 70–1.

page 191 *Also honoured … to rest here, too*: MacAulay, *Silent Tower*, 16.

page 191 *It endured … a "ruinous" condition*: "St. Clement's Church / Tur Chliamainn"; Miers, "Western Seaboard."

page 191 "Her remains" ... *south transept floor*: MacAulay, *Silent Tower*, 5, 16.
page 191 *On her deathbed* ... "lies under her": Watson, *Gaelic Songs*, xix;
Sharron Gunn, private email.

89.

page 193 *Sileas na Ceapaich* ... *Luing*: Anne C. Frater, "Women of the Gàidhealtachd and Their Songs to 1750," in *Women in Scotland c. 1100–1750*,
edited by Elizabeth Ewan and Maureen M. Meikle (East Linton, Scotland:
Tuckwell Press, 1999), 67–79, https://www.academia.edu/78841719/060_
Women_of_the_G%C3%Aoidhealtachd_and_their_Songs_to_1750.
page 193 *Dorothy* ... *from Luing*: Ewan, Innes, and Reynolds, *The Biographical Dictionary of Scottish Women: From the Earliest Times to 2004* (Edinburgh: Edinburgh University Press, 2006), 96.
page 193 *Each of* ... *their work*: Colm Ó Baoill, "Neither Out nor In, Scottish
Gaelic Women Poets 1650–1750," in *Woman and the Feminine in Medieval
and Early Modern Scottish Writing*, edited by S.M. Dunnigan, C.M. Harker,
and E.S. Newlyn (London: Palgrave Macmillan, 2004), 136, 149–50, https://
doi.org/10.1057/9780230502208_10.
page 193 "buried face down ... in Mull": Ó Baoill, "Neither Out nor In," 148;
Ó Baoill, *Màiri nighean Alasdair Ruaidh*, 16.
page 194 *It* "is believed ... or 'Cill Naoimh Nighean'": H.M. Peel, *A History
of Kilmore Church* (Isle of Mull: Brown & Whittaker, 2004), as found
at "Kilninian Church" (Mull Historical and Archaeological Society),
http://www.mull-historical-society.co.uk/churches/churches-2/kilninian/.
page 194 *The Nine Maidens* ... *and wells*: David Hugh Farmer, *The Oxford
Dictionary of Saints*, 2nd ed. (Oxford: Oxford University Press, 1990), 120.
page 194 *of the Celtic* ... *female poet*: Caitlin and John Matthews, *Encyclopedia of Celtic Wisdom* (Shaftsbury, Dorset: Element Books Ltd, 1994), 234–5.
page 194 *The little* ... *in Luing*: Ewan, *Biographical Dictionary*, 96; Anne C.
Frater, "Scottish Gaelic Women's Poetry up to 1750," vol. 1. PhD thesis
(Glasgow: University of Glasgow, 1994), https://theses.gla.ac.uk/701/1994
fraterphd.pdf; Zoe D. Fleming, "Archaeology Notes," 2007, https://can
more.org.uk/event/674689.
page 194 "there must have ... the spot": Mackenzie, *Sár-Obair nam Bárd
Gaelach*, 56.

XVI TIME'S WITNESS

page 196 "I take away ... as I say": Robin Skelton, from "To Banish Pain," in *The Practice of Witchcraft Today* (New York: Citadel Press, 1995), 170–1.

91.

page 196 "Norse method ... a witch": Anne Frater and Michel Byrne, "Gaelic Poetry and Song," in *The Edinburgh Companion to Scottish Women's Writing*, edited by Glenda Norquay (Edinburgh: Edinburgh University Press, 2012), 26, http://www.jstor.org/stable/10.3366/j.ctt1g0b5jr.7.

page 197 "As it was not ... not point to Heaven": MacAulay, *Silent Tower*, 16.

page 197 "Such verses ... that it implies": Shaw, "Did Not Print," 114.

page 197 The clear implication ... somehow false": Ó Baoill, *Màiri nighean Alasdair Ruaidh*, 16.

page 197 "'on her death-bed' she ... banished her to Mull": Ó Baoill, *Màiri nighean Alasdair Ruaidh*, 15. Ó Baoill is quoting Henderson, *The Poems of John Morison*, xiv.

page 197 "[a]s punishment ... the idyll of her heart": Ó Baoill, *Màiri nighean Alasdair Ruaidh*, 15. Ó Baoill is quoting Henderson, *The Poems of John Morison*, xiv.

92.

page 198 *Henderson collected ... are taken, in English*: Henderson, *The Poems of John Morison*, xiii–xiv.

page 198 *As I had remembered ...* "and the story-tellers": Nicolson, *History*, 110.

page 199 *These include ...* "marvellously retentive memory": Henderson, *The Poems of John Morison*, xxiv.

page 200 *The Clàrsair Dall ... it would be him*: William Matheson, *The Blind Harper (An Clàrsair Dall), The Songs of Roderick Morison and His Music* (Edinburgh: The Scottish Gaelic Texts Society, 1970), xl–lxxii, 150–1.

93.

page 200 *The poet Iain Ruadh ... prevailed*: Rev. W. Forsyth, "Chapter xx: John Roy Stewart," in *The Shadows of Cairngorm* (Inverness: The Northern Counties Publishing Company Ltd, 1900), https://www.electricscotland.com/history/cairngorm/index.htm.

page 201 *His bitter ...* "Culloden Day": J.L. Campbell, *Highland Songs of the Forty-Five* (Edinburgh: Scottish Academic Press, 1933, 1984), 165–77, http://tartanplace.com/tartanhistory/culoden.html.

page 202 *The Clearances ... to them*: Jessica Brain, "Butcher Cumberland" (Historic UK Ltd, 2017), https://www.historic-uk.com/HistoryUK/History ofBritain/Butcher-Cumberland/; Alison Campsie, "The Seized Jacobite Money and Land That Helped Build Scotland," *The Scotsman*, 8 January 2020, https://www.scotsman.com/heritage-and-retro/heritage/the-seized-jacobite-money-and-land-that-helped-build-scotland-1397974.

page 202 *Near the beginning ...* "as was Màiri": Sharron Gunn, private email.

94.

page 203 "In the moments ... in their shadows": Alastair Moffat, *The Hidden Ways* (Edinburgh: Canongate, 2017), 35.

95.

page 204 "We're trying ... come to this": Freda Huson quoted in Amanda Follet Hosgood, "RCMP Arrive at Unist'ot'en Camp in Helicopters; Leave without Arrests," *The Tyee*, 8 February 2020, https://thetyee.ca/News/2020/02/08/RCMP-Arrive-Unistoten/.

96.

page 204 "Seekers ... her expression": Watson, *Gaelic Songs*, xxvii.

page 204 "is a very different ... *The world is always now*: Bateman, "The Landscape," 145; David Abram, *The Spell of the Sensuous* (New York: Vintage Books, 2017), 8.

97.

page 205 *Mairghread* "used ... and sit there": Frater, "Scottish Gaelic," 29.

page 205 "Not with eyes ... the walls]": John MacInnes, "The Oral Tradition in Scottish Gaelic Poetry," *Scottish Studies*, vol. 12, part 1 (1968): 41; Thomas A. McKean, *The Flowering Thorn* (Logan, UT: Utah State University Press: 2003), 4, https://digitalcommons.usu.edu/usupress_pubs/68.

page 206 "Where one singer ... with letters": McKean, *The Flowering Thorn*, 4.

page 206 *The Rev. Wm. Matheson* "propounds ... of stones'": John MacInnes, "Gaelic Songs of Mary MacLeod," in *Scottish Gaelic Studies*, vol. 11, part 1, edited by Derick S. Thomson (Aberdeen: University of Aberdeen, 1966), 9, https://www.academia.edu/4737802/Gaelic_Songs_of_Mary_MacLeod.

XVII ABETTED BY COSMIC FORCES: WITCHCRAFT

page 207 "the milk of … somebody's house": Marilyn Bowering, "Janet McNicol," from an unpublished manuscript (Tighnacraig: 1978).

98.

page 207 "Between the … and burned": Caroline Davies, "Women Executed 300 Years Ago as Witches in Scotland Set to Receive Pardons," *The Guardian*, 19 December 2021, https://www.theguardian.com/uk-news/2021/dec/19/executed-witches-scotland-pardons-witchcraft-act. See also Julian Goodare, Lauren Martin, Joyce Miller, and Louise Yeoman, "The Survey of Scottish Witchcraft" (Edinburgh: University of Edinburgh, January 2003), http://witches.hca.ed.ac.uk/; "Places of Residence for Accused Witches" (Edinburgh: Interactive Witchcraft Map, Edinburgh University, 2023), https://witches.is.ed.ac.uk/; and generally, Larner, Lee, and McLachlan, *A Source Book of Scottish Witchcraft*; Sara Sheridan, *Where Are the Women*; Lily Seafield, *Scottish Witches*.

page 208 "No cost … as the End Times loomed": Sandra Miesel, "Who Burned the Witches?" https://www.catholicworldreport.com/2022/10/30/who-burned-the-witches-part-1/; https://www.catholicworldreport.com/2022/11/01/who-burned-the-witches-part-2/.

page 208 "impelled by … forces of evil": Ronald Hutton, "Witch-Hunting in Celtic Societies," *Past & Present*, no. 212 (August 2011): 58, 65, https://www.jstor.org/stable/23014785.

page 208 "The devil … Lowland folklore": Sharron Gunn (as Sheila Currie), "Witchcraft in the Scottish Highlands: Good or Bad?" https://sheilacurrie.com/blog/2021/02/21/witchcraft-in-the-scottish-highlands-good-or-bad/ (accessed 14 August 2023).

page 208 "incurred censure … in itself": Hutton, "Witch Hunting," 58.

page 208 *as victims … and feared*: Miesel, "Witches," Catholic World Report, Part 1 and 2.

100.

page 210 *A poem composed* ... "of the mountains": Carmichael, *Carmina*, vol. 4, 338–9.

101.

page 211 "in frontier zones ... national mainstream culture were strongest": Hutton, "Witch-Hunting," 70; "'Places of residence,' Interactive Witchcraft Map."

page 211 "a conduit ... the Hebrides": Hutton, "Witch-Hunting," 49.

page 211 *James VI & I ... impracticability*: "Gentleman Adventurers of Fife," Wikipedia, 8 April 2022, https://en.wikipedia.org/w/index.php?title= Gentleman_Adventurers_of_Fife&oldid=1081590046, citing Hamish Haswell-Smith, *The Scottish Islands* (Edinburgh: Canongate, 1996), 240–1.

page 211 *a group of Mackenzies ... was accused*: "Miscellany of the Scottish History Society XIII, Publications of the Scottish History Society," 5th ser., v. 14 (Lothian Print, 2004), 241–2; https://digital.nls.uk/scottish-history-society-publications/browse/archive/127316601#?c=0&m=0&s=0&cv=255& xywh=-426%2C-151%2C2490%2C3016.

page 212 "Gaelic business ... to wane": Hutton, "Witch-Hunting," 65.

page 212 "when the attempt ... accusations on Lewis": Hutton, "Witch-Hunting," 48–9.

page 212 *In 1661, the most ... were in the islands*: "'Places of residence,' Interactive Witchcraft Map"; Hutton, "Witch-Hunting," 49.

102.

page 213 *Prone burials ...* "accepted burial position": Caroline Arcini, "Prone Burials: Buried Face Down," *Current Archaeology* 231, vol. xx, no. 3 (June 2009): 31–4.

page 213 "that prone burial ... 'othering' the corpse": Thea Tomaini, *Dealing with the Dead: Morality and Community in Medieval and Early Modern Europe* (Leiden and Boston: Brill, 2018), 118.

page 213 *these graves are located ... at the end of time*: Adrián D. Maldonado-Ramírez, "Christianity and Burial in Late Iron Age Scotland, AD 400–650," PhD thesis (Glasgow: University of Glasgow, 2011), 118–19, http://theses. gla.ac.uk/2700.

page 213 "Sites may ... *and into the sixteenth century*: Sean Lisle, "Always Visible – How Lewis Archaeology Shows Enduring Love of the Land" (UHI Archaeology Institute, 10 February 2017), https://archaeologyorkney.com/2017/02/10/always-visible-how-lewis-archaeology-shows-enduring-love-of-the-land/; T. Cowie and M. MacLeod Rivett, "Machair Bharabhais: A Landscape through Time," *Journal of the North Atlantic* 9 (sp9): 99–107 (1 August 2015), 100, https://doi.org/10.3721/037.002.sp906.

page 213 "walking the machair ... in touch with the soil": Angus Peter Campbell and Cailean MacLean, *Suas gu Deas, Two Hebrideans Walking from the Butt to Barra Head* (Isle of Lewis: The Islands Book Trust, 2009), 4, 6.

page 213 *Inside a long cist* ... probably a bracelet": Cowie and MacLeod Rivett, "Through Time," 104.

page 213 *The* "grave ... has been carefully made": Lisle, "Always Visible"; Mary MacLeod, "Machair Bharabhais, A Landscape through Time" (University of the Highlands and Islands, 2010), https://www.slideshare.net/uhi/mary-macleod-machair-bharabhais-a-landscape-through-time?qid=72d4e79f-cad9-429c-b270-538fc525f153&v=qf1&b=&from_search=2.

page 214 "may have to do ... with their oration ...)": Yvonne Owen, private email.

104.

page 215 *The Norse descent* ... *disloyalty to the Crown*: Grant, *The MacLeods*, 25; Watson, *Gaelic Songs*, 125, 128; "Scottish History of the MacLeod Family," 2016, https://clan.com/family/macleod.

page 215 *In the Viking age* ... of poetic inspiration": Clive Tolley, "The Subversive Intent of Norse Myth and Magic," *ARV Nordic Yearbook of Folklore*, vol. 70 (Uppsala: The Royal Gustavus Adolphus Academy, 2015), 32, 15–37.

page 215 *A Völva was usually* ... *both respected and feared*: Daniel McCoy, "Seidr," 2012–19, https://norse-mythology.org/concepts/seidr/; Skjalden, "Völva the Viking Witch or Seeress," 11 March 2018, https://skjalden.com/volva-the-viking-witch-or-seeress/; Tolly, "Subversive Intent," 26.

page 216 *In her later* ... *a silver-headed cane*: Mackenzie, *Sár-Obair nam Bárd Gaelach*, 21.

page 216 *Màiri Seud or Mary the Jewel*: Watson, *Gaelic Songs*, xviii.

XVIII LYING MEN/THINGS

page 217 "Not for me ... where   I want": "Not for me," Bowering, *Thresh-old*, 42.

105.

page 218 *Like the poet ...* would manage [her]": Robert Bringhurst, *Wild Language* (Nanaimo, BC: Institute for Coastal Research, 2006), 11.

page 218 *The pipers ... at St Clement's too*: MacAulay, *Silent Tower*, 16.

page 218 "When she died ... a lament for a lost world": Bob Dunsire, "Bag-pipe Forums," https://forums.bobdunsire.com/forum/great-highland-bag pipe/piobaireachd/48730-#post662347; "Stories of the Tunes – Lament for Mary MacLeod," *Bagpipe News*, 1 August 2020, https://bagpipe.news/2020/ 08/01/stories-of-the-tunes-lament-for-mary-macleod/. The writer of "Stories" asserts that at Dunvegan, Mary was part "of a small group of musicians and bards that were dubbed later as the 'Talisker Circle' ... that included Roderick Morison (the Blind Harper) and Patrick Òg MacCrimmon (MacLeod's piper)."

106.

page 219 *In the opening ... one of Mary's exiles*: "Crònan an Taibh" / "The Ocean Croon," in Watson, *Gaelic Songs*, 44–9.

page 219 *The poem's date ... after about 1666*: Ó Baoill, *Màiri nighean Alasdair Ruaidh*, 97.

page 219 "the great shrill-voiced ... fingers stirred it": Watson, *Gaelic Songs*, 45.

page 219 *The word ... west of the Hebrides*": Ó Baoill, *Màiri nighean Alasdair Ruaidh*, 99.

page 219 *May was ... Dunvegan each year*: Ó Baoill, *Màiri nighean Alasdair Ruaidh*, 151.

page 219 "Never under ... his day of trouble": Watson, *Gaelic Songs*, 45.

page 220 *Sir Norman's house where ... wishes to rejoin*: Watson, *Gaelic Songs*, 45, 47.

107.

page 220 "She Wrote in Darkness": Adam Zagajewski, *Without End: New and Selected Poems*, translated by Claire Cavanagh (New York: Farrar, Straus and Giroux, 2003), 255.

110.

page 222 "out to get a sail in a new boat": Mackenzie, *Sár-Obair nam Bárd Gaelach*, 22.

page 223 *within the body of another*: Mark Wringe says, "Mackenzie's reference to 'MacDonald's Birlinn' is to Birlinn Chlann Raghnaill, (Clan Ranald's Galley) by Alasdair Mac Mhaighstir Alasdair (Alexander MacDonald). It's also sometimes called 'Sgiobaireachd Chlann Raghnaill,' particularly in South Uist ... It's a long and complex poem with some short prose passages, and the poet describes in detail the crew, their specialist skills, and every aspect of the ship and its rigging ... It runs to nearly 600 lines, and must have been composed between 1751 and the poet's death in 1770 ... If Mary had a song in a similar vein, we can only take Mackenzie's word for that." Whatever Mackenzie heard, he clearly believed he could hear Mary's song within MacDonald's later one.

111.

page 223 "Even the stones ... of the new sheepfarms": from the Sgarastadh Mhòr: Hebrides Archaeological Interpretation Programme information board, on site; "'Nisishee, Harris,' Canmore, National Record of the Historic Environment (Historic Environment Scotland)," https://canmore.org.uk/site/123223/harris-nisishee; "Archaeology Notes" (RCAHMS [SAH] 27, February 1997), http://canmore.org.uk/event/772996.

page 224 "all the ... stone circle": Mary MacLeod Rivett, "Clach Steineagaidh stone circle, Borgh," *The Outer Hebrides: A Historical Guide* (Edinburgh: Birlinn, 2021), 40–1.

page 224 *The standing stone ... there were two*: "'Archaeology Notes,' Harris, Borvemore, Standing Stone, Canmore, National Record of the Historic Environment" (Historic Environment Scotland), http://canmore.org.uk/site/10546 (accessed 23 August 2023).

page 224 "*beul nam breug a chur foidhpe*": Watson, *Gaelic Songs*, xix.

page 224 "to put the mouth of lies under her": Sharron Gunn translation, private email.

page 224 *to ensure … divinity, fertility, and power*: Yvonne Owen, private email.

page 224 "the *tursachan* … as well as outright lies": Sharron Gunn, private email.

ACKNOWLEDGMENTS

page 228 "It is my only wish … in good condition": Sharron Gunn's translation of "Is e m'aon mhiann gum bi an leabhran so mar chloich air chàrn ban-bhàird nan Eilean, agus a chum maith Gàidhlig na h-Albann," Watson, *Gaelic Songs*, viii.